DATE DUE

When Do I Start?

A MEMOIR

Karl Malden

WITH CARLA MALDEN

Simon & Schuster

Simon & Schuster
Rockefeller Center
1230 Avenue of the Americas
New York, NY 10020

Simon & Schuster and colophon are registered trademarks
of Simon & Schuster Inc.

Designed by Jeanette Olender
Insert design by Leslie Phillips
Manufactured in the United States of America

1   3   5   7   9   10   8   6   4   2

Library of Congress Cataloging-in-Publication Data
Malden, Karl.
When do I start?: a memoir/Karl Malden with Carla Malden.
p. cm.
Includes index.
1. Malden, Karl.   2. Actors—United States—Biography.
I. Malden, Carla.   II. Title.
PN2287.M25A3   1997
792'.028'092—dc21   [B]   97-18104   CIP
ISBN 0-684-84309-9

Foreword

I weighed five pounds three ounces when I was born, and, I am told, promptly lost the three ounces and a few more. They kept me in the hospital to fatten me up for a few extra days after my mother had gone home. My father always told me that when the big day came for me to be released, I was still so tiny that he carried me home in his overcoat pocket. I conjured up a strange and wonderful image of myself as an infant, somehow bolt upright, though newborn, in my father's deep, warm pocket, hands cupped over its rim, peeking out at the world.

I was embarrassingly old by the time it occurred to me that this story had to be apocryphal. Among other things, I was born in July and it was highly unlikely that even my father, constantly mocked within the family for wearing ridiculously unseasonable attire, would have on a topcoat in the middle of a New York summer. I suppose I had clung to the image years beyond reason because that pocket seemed like the safest place on earth from which to be introduced to the world.

The two years I spent writing this book with my father were a lot like crawling back into that pocket. As he led me on a journey through his life, I heard countless stories—some I had heard all my life, some I had never heard before, and still others we dusted off together, he and I, to uncover their truth under years of embroidery. We laughed a lot and we cried, too, often simultaneously.

As I learned more and more about my father's struggles, I began to realize that his is an American dream story. Hard work, perseverance, commitment—those are the qualities, along with his talent, that helped him to achieve. As exhilarating as it was to relive this success story step by step, it was also not inconsiderably disheartening. I began to wonder if those qualities that turned the American dream into a reality for my father were worth much today, or if they have been replaced with hopelessness, despair, and nihilism. I began to wonder if the American dream still exists at all. I can only hope that stories like my father's might help to revive that dream.

As anyone who reads this book will agree, my father would be loathe to be regarded as an archetype or a symbol of anything, yet there is something about him—an Everyman quality, a simple authority—that commands respect. I cannot begin to count the number of people who have said to me, over the course of my life, that my father reminds me of their fathers. It makes no difference whether these are people who know him personally or just through his work on screen. There is something fundamentally paternal about him. He can be stern, his temper can erupt, but somehow we know that here is a man who weeps while watching families being reunited on cheap TV game shows.

Writing this book has been one of the great pleasures of my life. I'd like to thank my mother for inspiring this book just as she inspires our entire family. I'd like to thank my sister, Mila, for being the keeper of so many family stories. I'd like to thank my husband, Laurence, for assuring me from the very start that my father's dinner-table anecdotes could grow up to be a book and for making sure it became the best book it could be. And I'd like to dedicate this book to my nieces, Alison and Emily, and most especially to my daughter, Cami . . . because this story belongs to them, too.

Finally, I'd like to thank my father for inviting me back into his coat pocket.

Carla Malden
April 1997

To my wife, Mona, who taught me how to live.

Prologue

≈

March 26, 1990. I stand alone in the wings at the Dorothy Chandler Pavilion. Alone with my thoughts. Alone in the darkness. Backstage mayhem swirls around me. Stage managers and crew are hauling cable, wrangling talent, scrambling. Usually, these people are dressed in jeans and T-shirts. Tonight they are wearing tuxedoes as they desperately try to get a show on the air. A show that will be seen by hundreds of millions of people around the world. The Oscars.

I remember how I used to watch newsreels of the Academy Awards in the days before the show was televised. The glamour and the excitement enthralled me like everyone else on earth. But they had nothing to do with my life as a young actor trying to make a living, to get a part, to make a couple of lines memorable if I did get the part. Even when I was fortunate enough to win an Oscar myself, the event was more like a company party. It was the spring of 1952. Still no television cameras. It certainly did not carry the weight that "Oscar night" does now.

Even as I sat in my seat in the Pantages Theater, waiting to hear if they would call my name, I did not have the same kind of butterflies I do on this night.

I knew—all too well—the butterflies you have when you're waiting an eternity to see the man in the inner office about a job. I knew the feeling of the butterflies you get when you're opening out of town and hope you stand a chance of making it to New York. I knew Broadway opening-night butterflies. I knew the butterflies you get the first day you show up on a movie set and find yourself face to face with an actor you have idolized. But the butterflies I'm having right now, the butterflies I feel in the pit of my stomach as I stand in the darkness backstage, are almost overwhelming.

Gradually, the buzz begins to calm, though a white hot tension still fills the air. The stage manager's flashlight leads the way. "Let me take you to your mark for your entrance." I stand there in the darkness for an endless two minutes.

Finally, I hear the announcer open the show. "Ladies and gentlemen, the president of the Academy of Motion Picture Arts and Sciences." It takes me a long moment to remember. That's me. It is the last thing on earth I ever dreamt I would hear myself being called.

I see the set part. The elaborate glittering flats in front of me slide off into the wings. As they do, the stage manager points at me and whispers: "Go!"

I take a deep breath and walk from upstage center down to the footlights. It's a short distance, no more than forty feet, but it's a very long walk. I scan this full house—some three thousand people—and try not to think about the millions more sitting in front of their television sets.

Faces gradually come into focus. There is Gregory Peck. He smiles at me. I smile at him, thinking, "He was president once.

He had to do this. I can do it, too." I spot other familiar friendly faces as well as the tense faces of this year's nominees—smiles plastered on gallantly—all clustered in the first few rows: Tom Cruise, Daniel Day-Lewis, Robin Williams, Michelle Pfeiffer. And the particular thrill of seeing Jessica Tandy (who would win that night) with whom I had played in *A Streetcar Named Desire* over forty years before. I spot my family several rows back and I take another deep breath. It's not going to be so bad after all. Even so, thank God for the teleprompter.

"I'm here tonight to tell you that Oscar is beside himself. I mean, this is one of those nights when 'One World' is more than a philosophical dream. It's a reality."

My mouth keeps drying up. Cotton mouth, they call it. In the back of my mind, a monologue keeps running: "My God, after all these years, my mouth is still getting dry. This is pathetic." But I make it through the speech describing the global thrust of this year's show, complete with its international satellite hookups.

"How can you have a closed society when the skies are open from Moscow to Beijing to . . . to you name it, Gary, Indiana."

I heave a sigh of relief. As I walk off, one thought overtakes all the rest—how incredibly far the stage of the Dorothy Chandler Pavilion is from Gary, Indiana.

facing page:

**My dad sent this photograph home
to his family in the old country. I'm standing,
age 7, so proud of my new high-top shoes.**

Chapter 1

Gary was a company town, one hour's drive along Lake Michigan from Chicago where I was born. My father moved us there when I was five years old. He was following the money, so he left behind a job shellacking doors and window frames in a lumber yard to work in the higher paying Gary steel mills.

Gary was a town of about sixty-five thousand. Immigrants with no trade or education were flocking there to work in the new mills. The town was a checkerboard of nationalities. East, west, north, south. Where you lived meant who you were. Irish, Scottish, Polish, Hungarian, Bulgarian, Greek, Serb. That was us. The Serbs. Living at 457 Connecticut Street in Gary, Indiana, U.S.A. But it may as well have been Yugoslavia.

A new young colony of Serbs was growing up around the steel industry and my father, Petar Sekulovich, fit right in. Having barely ventured out of the Serbian enclave in Chicago, he could now be an even bigger fish in the Serbian pond of Gary.

My father would keep the old world with him for the rest of his life. By the time we moved from Chicago, Pa had lived in this country for ten years, nearly half his life to that point. Yet he was still very much the immigrant. He could barely speak English, let alone read it.

It fell to me, the first child, to bring the new world into our home. As I grew up, I was constantly amazed at how unwelcome that world turned out to be. How often my struggle to be an ordinary all-American kid left me feeling the outsider, caught between my Serbian home and the entire rest of the world. Every son must battle his father on his way to becoming a man. But as I was growing up, I often felt like I was battling the entire old world.

You could make no mistake about it. Loyalty to Serbian heritage would always be held as the highest value in my father's home. His heritage positively defined my father. He was a funny, charming, well-loved man. He could captivate a room when he told a story. But more importantly, especially to him, he was a respected leader in the Serbian community. His community. His people. He was a Serb, obsessed with being a good Serb and with helping the people around him to be good Serbs. He clung to his old world heritage, almost for dear life. And he insisted that his home remain a cornerstone of Serbian culture in the isolated, insular Serbian ghetto he rarely ventured from.

I was born into this home—with the help of a midwife and my mother's mother—in the spring of 1912. March 22 to be exact, my mother's birthday. Mladen George Sekulovich. Saint George, the dragon slayer, was the patron saint of the Sekulovich clan. It was a mouthful of a name for a first generation American. The "ml" sound does not even exist in the English language. (On many first days of school, the teacher would be reading the roll and there would suddenly be a long pause. After a while, I new what that pause meant and I would interrupt the silence. "That's me.")

I only have snatches of memory of the home in Chicago where I was born. A fevered vision of a single lightbulb hanging over a kitchen table and chairs, the bulb draped in newspaper so the glare wouldn't bother my eyes. I must have been sick with measles or chicken pox because I remember my skin feeling itchy and tight under the crust of drying Calamine lotion.

I remember a small, two-bit costume house two doors away. The old couple who ran it would let me play with the hats and costumes, the swords and the guns. The tiny shop was filled with color—magnificent military uniforms of all descriptions with elegant braid and grand plumes. Within those four walls there existed a different world from the drab, bare-bones one that waited for me at home. It was the world of the imagination.

Every day I would put on some strange combination of items from the shop and become a different character. Of course, as a small child, I swam in most of the costumes. But I could make the hats fit, and I tried on every hat in the place. With each hat came a new character. The wild theater of make-believe allowed me to escape from the world around me. In my games, it didn't matter whether I spoke Serbo-Croatian or English.

I remember the taste of Serbian food, which my mother, a Czech, had learned to cook expertly. Breakfast was always dessert left over from the night before. Strudels, butter cookies, coffee cakes, little stuffed sweet rolls called "kolachi." My mother's strong arms were always rolling some wonderful yeast dough on the kitchen table.

It was like some marvelous ritual. She would lay a tablecloth over the whole kitchen table, sprinkle it with flour, and throw a ball of dough in the middle. She would roll it out with a rolling pin as far as she could; then, when it couldn't stretch any more, she would wiggle her wrist under the dough and start to work it out further, little by little, as she walked around the table. Finally, when it seemed the dough would stretch no further, she would nudge her elbows under the dough and stretch it out some more until it was so thin you could see through it. Today you can buy filo dough in the market, but it will never taste like that. When Ma turned it into strudel or spinach-filled "zalanitsa" or meat-stuffed "bourek," it was heaven on earth.

More than anything, I remember the music. Always music. Serbian music. The sound of the "tambouriza," a Serbian band, played on a tabletop Victrola, or an a capella choir (as is used in the Serbian Orthodox church), to this day conjures up the strongest memories of my childhood.

I was brought up to feel as though I myself had actually come from the tiny village of Bileca, though I had never set foot there and I wouldn't until I was a grown man. In truth, it was my father, Petar Sekulovich, who set sail from Bileca, Hercegovina for Ellis Island. He was a frightened sixteen-year-old hoping to fulfill the same dream that sustained everyone on every boat headed for that harbor. America. The promise of work (as well as escape from obligatory service in the Austro-Hungarian army) motivated Petar and two of his friends to come to this alien world. It also made it affordable. Passage was cheaper for able-bodied young men who could help form a work force in the new American mines and mills.

When Pa landed at Ellis Island, he was headed for San Francisco. One of his buddies had a brother already working there as a waiter. But fate, "sudbina," had something else in store for him. He set foot on American soil, wearing a tag on his lapel that declared his destination, on the day of the great San Francisco earthquake: April 18, 1906. The immigration officials explained to him that he could not be sent to San Francisco; that city lay in the wake of a disaster. He would have to go somewhere else.

The three boys panicked. They thought they had a life waiting for them in San Francisco. That was all that had kept them going during the miserable two week passage in steerage. Suddenly, they were without a plan. What to do? Where to go? They noticed that many of the other Balkanites were heading for Chicago. In an instant they decided that they, too, would go to Chicago. Anything, any place, instead of being sent back.

In New York they were put on a train headed for Chicago. Once in Chicago, they boarded a streetcar. The conductor told the boys to get off at the intersection of Clybourn and Fullerton Streets. They did as they were told though they had no idea why . . . until they looked around. Here they were in the middle of a foreign land, but the names on the signs in this neighborhood looked remarkably familiar. A store, a coffee house, a tavern. They all bore Serbian names. Simic, Nicolich, Tarilo, Philipovich. They were smack in the heart of Little Serbia. And, at least metaphorically, my father stayed there for the next seventy-five years.

It was a tough neighborhood. The Serbs kept to themselves, helping each other find work and inventing their own social life. Petar was at the forefront; he helped organize the first Serbian choir in America, the Branko Radicevich Choir, as well as a Serbian gymnastic club that gave exhibitions and threw dances. It was at one of their dances, called a "Sokol," that Petar met my mother, Minnie Sebera.

My mother was originally from the area of Bohemia, which would later become Czechoslovakia, though she had spent her early teenaged years working as a nanny for a wealthy family in Vienna. The Sebera family immigrated to this country in three waves: first, my mother's father with his eldest daughter; then her mother with three more children (including my own mother); and then the grandmother with the rest of the nine children. Arriving here at the age of sixteen, my mother (unlike my father) desperately wanted to fit in. She abandoned her given name, Sophie, with its Bohemian overtones, for something she thought had a more American ring: Minnie.

Minnie got a job at a pickle factory sticking labels onto the jars her mother filled with pickles. But Minnie and her sister, Annie, soon switched to a higher paying factory where they sewed canvas together for tents. That is how she was making a living when she met Petar at the dance.

Two years later, they were married. It was 1910. Petar and Minnie made a strangely handsome, if a bit comical couple, at their wedding. Still today, a blow-up of their wedding photo greets me every morning when I climb the stairs to my little study above the garage. There's Ma, a big woman—sturdy, robust, and standing as tall as my dad at five foot ten. And Pa: slight, but ramrod straight, wearing a fern that spreads across the entire lapel of his skimpily fitting suit with one tired carnation pinned to it. My mother's face stares at me like a deer caught in headlights. And there's my father beside her, stern and sober, ready to take his rightful place as the head of the household and the father of good Serbian sons.

My mother got more than she bargained for when she married my dad. She had to do things Petar's way. Sink or swim. She abandoned her Catholicism for Pa's Eastern Orthodoxy (even though the two religions are really just first cousins). She learned Serbo-Croatian and basically never spoke her native Czech again. (Pa spoke a little German, which Ma knew quite well, so in the beginning they communicated with a combination of German and a hybrid of Czech-Serb Slavic, but never in English.) She took her proper place in his patriarchal household and most importantly, she gave Pa three sons, starting with me. I was the first Sekulovich born in America.

Throughout my early childhood in Gary, the city had quite a "small town" feeling. In most cases, where you were from meant what you did. The Greeks repaired shoes and ran ice cream parlors; the Irish sold real estate; the Jews owned clothing and jewelry stores; the Poles ran the grocery stores. That may not be the American dream, but it was the American way for many people on their way to that dream.

During World War I, however, we were all of us saving tin foil, which we rolled into balls. That foil ball was the only school project I remember my father helping me with in my entire school career. He would bring home the foil cigarette wrappers discarded by the smokers at the mills. I was bursting with pride when I walked into kindergarten with my enormous foil ball. It was a time when contributing to your country, even with a ball of tin foil, could make a small child feel very worthwhile. I think that silly ball of foil meant something particularly special to me; it meant I really was an American after all.

I remember the night the mill whistles startled me from my

sleep at midnight. Anyone who has ever lived in a steel town knows that certain blasts from the mill mean danger. We lived only four blocks from the mill when we heard the emergency sirens wailing. My parents assumed this meant a fire had broken out at the mills, so we threw on our clothes over the underwear we slept in (we did not own pajamas or robes), and hurried into the street, joining all the other families in their nightclothes. Bracing ourselves against the cold November night, we all headed for the center of town, Broadway and Fifth, expecting to see smoke spewing from the mills. There wasn't any. Instead, a party filled the streets throughout the city. Armistice had been declared. To top it all off—no school the next day!

I think I spent that holiday, like all the rest, playing in the sand dunes that surrounded our house, which was the only structure on that side of the street. Across the street and a little way down lived the Nicoliches who ran a small hotel, a rooming house really, for steel workers. The Nicolich children, Bobby and Olga, were my playmates and the dunes were an open invitation to the three of us to dig caves and make believe. Occasionally, for a real treat, we would visit the horses behind our house. Slick's Laundry owned a stable there to board their delivery horses.

As much as Gary was still undeveloped at that time, the mills had already become the heart of the city. At night, the flames from the blast furnace lit up the sky for blocks. The mills rained a fine, gray dust over the city. But no one cared. The dust meant work. Even so, the dust coated everything and, in a way, smothered the dreams of most everyone who lived under it, who breathed it in, like a coating of grimy reality.

If my father had any dreams, he certainly managed to squelch them. I wonder if actually coming to America was the best he could imagine for himself. Anything beyond that was too much, too hard, too daunting, maybe even too greedy to hope for.

I picked up a little English playing with the neighborhood children, but my father did not seem to pick up much at his job in the mill. He was working as a millwright, one of a four man crew who temporarily fixed things that broke down just so that the slab mill could keep running until the broken parts could be fixed properly. It was a dangerous job that my dad detested, though he spent twelve long years working with the heavy equipment, often in the mouth of the furnace where the heat would be so intense you could hardly catch your breath.

There was little relief. No salt pills. No water coolers, only big buckets of water. They had to sprinkle oatmeal on top to absorb the flu dust so that the men would have to scrape the scum away in order to dip down for a drink.

Ultimately, Pa was injured on the job. He was positioning a two-foot-long, twenty pound chisel and his partner was wielding a thirty pound sledgehammer when the partner missed and smashed my dad's knuckles. Pa was in the hospital for a few days and he never returned to the mills again.

He remained out of work for about four months. Finally, he was offered a job at the Serbian-owned Cloverleaf Dairy. The previous milk wagon driver—another Serb, of course—had been driving the home stretch of his route one day when the horse, eager to be heading back, picked up speed. The wagon hit the curb and tipped over, falling on the driver. They needed someone to take over the route immediately. Needless to say, they turned to a fellow Serb.

At first, Pa was reluctant to take the job. It required dealing with the public and he was embarrassed by his English (though never quite embarrassed enough to try to do something about it). But my mother insisted, and Pa wound up delivering milk on that same route for thirty-eight years.

I suppose this job matched both his disposition and his ambition (or lack of it). He loved working outdoors, although he had a tough route compared to the routes on the wealthier north side. There, across town, one big apartment house could constitute half your route. But Pa was always dropping off a quart here, two quarts there, covering twenty miles with horse and wagon from Fifteenth to Twenty-fifth Street, Broadway to Virginia, then across Broadway to the Calumet River and back on Broadway to Grant. He delivered to the black and "hunky" areas—the Poles, the Slavs, the poorer sections of town, but in all his thirty-eight years on that route, he was never held up, never mugged, never had any problems.

Every once in a while, during summer vacation, I would go with my father on his route. There were no refrigerated trucks in those days. Actually, there were no delivery trucks at all, only horse and wagon. From June through September, he had to work from midnight until eight in the morning so the cool night air would keep the milk fresh on its way to customers' iceboxes. It was a great feeling to be out there all alone in the pre-dawn. The lilac bushes—white, lavender, deep purple—would be in full bloom; every other house had them, and the delightful smell wafted through the fresh early morning air. I can remember that smell to this day.

The sound of the horse's clip-clopping would punctuate the silence. Years later I would ask Pa which he preferred: the horse and wagon, the electric truck or the gas-powered truck. Without hesitation he said, "I take horse any day."

"Why?" I asked.

"'Cause horse, he knows route like I do. Truck, don't know route."

We didn't do much talking on those peaceful early morning rides. When Pa would let me have a turn carrying the order to the customer's door, he would whisper to me to walk quietly, not to make too much noise climbing the steps.

But it never failed that at some point during that eight hours, my father would begin to sing. He would sing for a good hour or so. He would sing the songs of his childhood—Serbian songs—quietly, to himself. And I would listen. I would never sing along. I didn't want to break the spell.

My father loved his music. He also loved the theater, especially the Serbian theater. Though there had been no theater in his tiny village, he had developed his love of the theater by doing recitations in school. In America, his stage was the Serbian church hall. He was not a deeply religious man, but he loved the music and pageantry of the church. He would say, "One who is born into a Serbian home who doesn't care to be a good Serb will not also be a good American."

Most of the Serbian community forced their children to attend Serbian School at the church once a week (much like Jewish children attend Hebrew School to learn the language and tradition). They went begrudgingly. They were there because they had to be there. But oddly enough, my father never made me or my brothers go. He believed that the best way for us to learn was by singing Serbian songs and putting on plays. He saw to it that in every play the church put on, there would be at least a few parts played by children even if they didn't specifically call for children.

My dad became the local authority on Serbian theater. I remember a constant parade of people through the house asking his opinion on what play to put on next. Pa's brother back in Yugoslavia would occasionally send him a play, so he had assembled a small library, just enough to make him a local authority. He would study it and come up with a selection. And several times a year, I would end up on that church stage, a skinny kid playing a menacing Turk wearing a thick black mustache. (These plays invariably dealt with some evil Turk taking advantage of the Serbs.) I would raise my sword and shout, "Napred!" ("Forward!") and the vast army—usually two or three other skinny kids like me—would march off earnestly. Such was the beginning of my theatrical career. But the audience loved it because it was their history. It was something that belonged to them.

While I was receiving my cultural education on the church stage, I struggled at school. Emerson School was a citified version of the one room schoolhouse. You started in kindergarten and stayed there until graduation form the twelfth grade; all the teachers knew you.

When I arrived there at the age of five, I spoke pitifully little English. Many other children found themselves in the same situation, but it didn't help any. The teacher would say something and I had no idea what she was talking about or what I was supposed to do. I remember that if you missed more than two words on the weekly spelling test you had to stay after school. I was always there, week after week, going over those words I had missed, too embarrassed to admit that not only could I not spell them, I didn't even know what they meant. I felt completely lost, utterly inferior. Throughout school, I always felt three or four grades behind, like I was playing catch-up . . . and secretly have all my life.

Though my folks were well-meaning, they did not value education. They themselves were not educated. They never read to me or took me to the public library. The first book I can recall reading was Jack London's *Call of the Wild*. I must have been about twelve years old by then and had been assigned the book for a book report. Academic achievement simply had not figured in my parents' lives and they saw no reason for my life to be any different from their own. No one they knew went beyond high school and few had gotten that far. They figured I would graduate, get a job in the mills, and have a life.

My father earned a living to feed his family. That was all they wanted for me. But as I grew older, a nagging sense of "Is that all there is?" would begin to haunt me. It was the same story that was being played out in millions of immigrant households.

The problem was that I was not an immigrant. I was an American. It fell to me, the first child, to bring the new world into our home, but somehow my life kept me caught between the two cultures. My natural temperament didn't help matters. I was (and always have been) a loner. It's hard to know which came first, not wanting to enter in or not knowing how. I suppose it really doesn't matter. The fact is, for most of my school life, I never felt like a part of anything. I was not a joiner then and I have never managed to become one.

When I reached high school, I finally found a way to become a part of things. Actually, I found two ways: athletics and drama. I developed these two passions simultaneously only to find myself constantly torn between them. Basketball and track versus what they called "auditorium," or music and plays.

For a time, I joined the ranks of all good Hoosier boys and basketball became my consuming passion. I spent many afternoons practicing basketball when I should have been in class. A couple of us juniors or seniors would ditch school after lunch and head for the gym at the Masonic Temple, since the local YMCA had been notified to be on the alert for us. We would sneak into the lodge through a back door, head up to the second floor, and jimmy the lock into the gym. It never failed that we would come upon the same younger boy there, day after day, shooting baskets all by himself.

We tried to act like big men, asking, "How did you get in here?"

"Same way you guys did."

We'd admonish him, "You ought to be in school."

"What about you guys?"

We had no answer for that.

If we needed a fourth to play a little two on two, we would ask him to join us. He was a nice kid and a good basketball player. He would grow up to be a great football player and ultimately a famous sports announcer. Gary's own Tom Harmon.

I broke my nose twice playing basketball. I must admit I had a good Slavic nose to being with, but breaking it twice certainly gave it a little extra "character." I guess I should be grateful (and so should Johnny Carson's joke writers). The first time I broke it I was a sophomore. I jumped for a rebound. As I was going up, another fellow came down, crashing his elbow onto my nose. I saw stars, but my nose didn't bleed so the coach kept me playing. The game came first.

Meanwhile, the "auditorium" classes had begun to lure me as well. My freshman year the auditorium group was putting on Gilbert and Sullivan's *The Mikado*. I thought, "What the heck? I'll try out with everyone else." After all, by that time I had been in more plays than I could remember in the church. Much to my surprise, they gave me a part. Pooh Ba, The Lord High Everything Else. I was surprised by how much I loved it—even the long rehearsals.

My sophomore year my sports schedule did not permit me to be in the play. But the following year I was amazed when one of the drama teachers asked me to play the part of the Gypsy King in the operetta, *The Bohemian Girl*. I rehearsed in the afternoons and made it to basketball practice in the evening.

Wouldn't you know it? The dress rehearsal fell on the same day as an important practice for the basketball sectional tournament. I remember sitting in classes that whole day, preoccupied with my dilemma, torturing myself about what to do. Like a fool, I kept the problem to myself. I figured that there would be other basketball practices so I ended up going to rehearsal.

The next day I was called in to see the coach.

"Where the hell were you?"

"I had to go to the dress rehearsal."

"You want to be in the play? Turn in your suit."

After a full season, here I was at sectional time, kicked off the team.

I fretted over my decision all night, but I should have known that sooner or later some other teacher would have talked to the coach on my behalf. That was the beauty of a school like Emerson. It was like a family and there was always someone there to run interference for you. This time, it was Hazel Harrison, the head of the auditorium department, and the next day I was back on the team. Besides, I'm proud to say the coach didn't want to go to the finals without me.

We went to the tournament and the next day, the newspaper read, "A one-arm heave by Sikulivich, Emerson guard, just as the timekeeper cocked his gun, found the net..." They butchered the spelling of my name, but it was great to get credit for winning a game I had almost been forbidden to play.

The coach came to me and said, "I guess I ought to kick you off the team more often, Sukie." (By then, Sekulovich had been shortened to the nickname, "Sukie," which stuck with me up through my early days in New York.)

I only wished my dad had been there to see my triumph. At least my younger brother, Milo, was. It cost fifty cents to get into the game—fifty cents that we didn't have—so I would give Milo my gym bag to carry in for me. I'd say, "He's with the team," and he'd march on in like a big man even though he was only in the third grade when I was a sophomore.

My parents were not thrilled with my participation in sports, to put it mildly. They were always looking ahead to how I was going to earn a buck. What can you do with basketball when you get out of school? Only kids play ball, my father believed. And by the time I reached high school, I was already too old to be a kid and should have been thinking about the future.

At that point, they would have died if they'd known that my future would lie in acting. I guess the odds of making a living as an actor are pretty frightening, even in comparison to a ballplayer, but I have never understood why my father looked down on the profession so much. It still makes no sense to me since he loved the theater so deeply.

I remember when I was about thirteen, my dad took me to see Maude Adams and Otis Skinner in *The Merchant of Venice* in Chicago one Sunday afternoon. Just the two of us. It was a big deal. I was all dressed up in my suit and good cap. In those days you were a "sport" if you wore a cap. I couldn't believe I was actually going to see a professional production as we rode along the South Shore Line. By the time we arrived at the Blackstone Theater on Michigan Avenue, my heart was pounding.

Of course, it never would have occurred to Pa to buy tickets in advance, so when we stepped up to the box office I was terrified that they might be sold out.

Pa said, "I want tickets. For me and my boy."

The woman behind the window asked, "Where do you want them?"

"How much?"

"Well," she explained, pointing to the seating chart, "we have three dollar seats here and a dollar seventy-five up here in the balcony."

Pa handed her his money. "Give me balcony. Two."

Balcony, orchestra, I didn't care. I just wanted to get inside the theater.

The Blackstone was a whole different world from the school auditorium and the Croatian Hall, the two theaters where I had seen all the other plays I had ever been to.

We started climbing the stairs to the balcony. Suddenly, Pa whipped the cap off my head. He said, in Serbian, "Do you wear your cap in church?"

"No."

"Well, this is like a church."

I knew my father loved the theater, but I had no idea how much until that moment. Oddly enough, however, that feeling did not spill over onto actors. The theater was like a church, but for some reason, acting was not a respectable profession. This contradiction is still a mystery to me.

It certainly didn't hold true for me. On that day, when I was thirteen, and the heavy velvet curtain went up, I was more enthralled with Otis Skinner's performance than anything else. Not the magnificent set, not the music of Shakespeare's poetry. It was his performance that hooked me. Looking back on it, he was a little hammy, but he sure made an impression on one wide-eyed kid. I will never forget the courtroom scene. I may not have understood every word, but I definitely felt, along with Shylock, the indignation of being trapped and double-crossed.

Pa and I just sat there in our balcony seats during intermission. I don't think we said a word to each other.

It wasn't until we were on the train home that Pa said to me, "You like it?"

"Yes. I liked it very much."

"Did you understand it?"

"They talk differently, but I understood what was going on."

31

Pa nodded. Looking back, I wonder if he was trying to get me to explain it to him. We were in the same boat really, father and son. We both struggled with the play from the language stand-point, but understood the drama loud and clear.

I don't remember my dad going to the movies. We kids did sometimes, when we could scrape together the twenty-five cents. The Palace Theater was the place to go. Typical of its time, it had a grand mural and twinkling lights on the ceiling to mimic the night sky—the works.

I spent my share of time in there watching Al Jolson, Lon Chaney, Clara Bow, Tom Mix, Charlie Chaplin. A kid could have himself a great afternoon, especially since Walgreen's Drug Store was right next door. That meant for twenty cents more I could get a malted, served with two cookies. (If you had a friend behind the counter, you'd get an even better deal—maybe two glasses' worth. What could be more fun?)

A double thick malt and a double feature; that was about as close to heaven as you could get in Gary. If you had a couple of buddies to share them with, so much the better.

My friends didn't think much about their futures. If they did, they sure didn't talk about it. I looked at the ushers and thought, "Wouldn't that be a swell job?" After all, they got to see all the movies for free. But I was never one of those kids who dreamt of being in the movies. It never occurred to me that some day my face might be up on that screen.

Even so, I plugged away in the drama department, managing to outrage the drama teacher as well as I had the basketball coach. I was playing the part of the Gypsy King in *The Bohemian Girl*. In one scene, I was sitting on a small platform, supposedly asleep, while the female lead sang her big number, the deadly dull and grandiose "I Dreamt I Dwelt in Marble Halls." She got to the eight bars between choruses and then she was standing

there. Just standing, as the orchestra played. Nothing was happening on stage. It was more than I could bear. I could hear the
teacher whispering to the other kids in the wings.

"If he moves, I'll kill him."

She might as well have rolled out a red carpet. I couldn't resist. "Asleep" on my platform, suddenly I stretched, made a big
show of leaning on the other side of the platform, got my laugh,
and "fell asleep" facing the other way.

The curtain came down and I knew what was in store for me.
As I headed into the wings, the teacher cornered me.

"What are you trying to do? Ruin the play?"

"No," I answered. "I'm trying to help it."

She turned on her heels and walked away.

Of course, my parents weren't there to witness this. They
never came to any of the plays I was in. In four years of my
playing high school basketball, they only came to one game. I
understand now that they were just trying to keep going. My
dad was always too busy; my mom was too tired. But at the
time, it felt as if they didn't care.

I was also in "Spice and Variety," the annual talent show at
Emerson, every year. One year I served as the master of ceremonies for the comic portion of the evening. Another, I organized a funny quartet called the Harmony Family. I must have
gravitated toward doing something musical in hopes that my father would appreciate that, that it would draw him to see me on
the stage. But he never came. Like every son, I guess I wanted his
approval. No doubt more than I knew. All I got was disappoint-
ment. But I never admitted it to myself while I was growing up.
That was just the way things were; my dad never showed up.

Even though my father was never interested in what I was doing in school, every night at the dinner table, he would ask one
question.

"What you do today?"

Like every kid, half the time, I'd say, "Nothing."

My dad would say, "Well, you never get that day back."

He instilled in me a fierce work ethic that has stuck with me all my life. The prevailing philosophy was: Wasting time is the greatest sin. To this day, when I am out of work (a frequent state for an actor), I have to create a project for myself. I don't care if it's replanting my vegetable garden or painting the back fence. I have to have something to do. You never get that day back. I learned that lesson well.

When I was twelve, my father insisted that I become an altar boy. This was not a topic open to debate. So an altar boy I became. The priest was a friend of my father's (of course), so Pa would know every move I made. I served with a buddy of mine from down the block, Johnny Colovich. Johnny and I used to count the congregation every Sunday, then slice up the bread for communion, always saving nice, big hunks for ourselves to eat on the walk home.

Though I would never admit it to Pa, I actually didn't hate being an altar boy as much as I expected. It was a new experience and while the religious aspect meant little to me, the ritual of the altar boy's chores appealed to me. Being up there in front of the congregation making sure all the little duties were executed just so was not unlike performing. The fact that I began to think of the parishioners as an audience may not have demonstrated the proper devoutness, but I suppose it offered a clue as to where my interest really lay.

I even had my share of stage fright in church. I panicked when I was selected to participate in the traditional Easter reading of the "Apostle." It was a three-part presentation: one in English, one in Serbian, and one in Staroslovinski, which is old Slavonic.

As luck would have it, I got stuck with the Staroslovinski. I was mortified. I had never even heard this language before. But it was the one time my father really pitched in and helped me and, on Serbian Easter morning (our holidays are celebrated according to the Greek Orthodox calendar), I managed to muddle through.

Traditions were as important as our religion. On the morning of January 7 (our Christmas), we didn't have to go to school. My father would wake me at dawn and I would have to get dressed and go across the street to the Rokniches' house. I was their "polaznick," or man of good cheer. Tradition held that you had to serve as host to someone first thing on Christmas in order to have good luck throughout the coming year. The Rokniches would give me a dollar for ringing their bell and having breakfast with them. I guess they thought they could buy their good luck.

Pa worked hard to keep these traditions alive, both in and out of the church. But after two years, I had had enough of being an altar boy. By now we were living on Virginia Street, the top floor of a duplex. It was closer to the dairy and closer to Emerson School. When I entered high school, I started spending more and more time at school. Before long I refused to continue as an altar boy. A battle ensued, and for the first time in my life, I won. I suddenly found myself with a will as strong as Pa's, and I think I surprised myself as much as him.

Pa was hurt, but I now believe that more than that, he was afraid. He desperately needed to keep his hold on me to feel like he was holding on to the entire younger generation. When I chose school activities over the church, that threatened the very foundation of his life. More than that, he could no longer ignore the possibility that I might take a path different from his own.

Even so, he was not defeated. He just tried even harder to keep me in the fold.

The church choir consisted of twenty-five to thirty men. At that time, in the 1920s, they were mostly fellas in their thirties, forties, and fifties who were working in the mills. The choir rehearsals offered a break in their work-a-day week. My dad was the president of this choir for ten years. (He was later to become a founder and the first president of the Serbian Singing Society of America and Canada, uniting the scattered choirs across North America into one organization.) One day when I was fourteen, my dad took me to choir practice. I was sitting in the back, ready to listen, when one of the tenors said, "I'm not going to sing. Only thirteen of us are here tonight and I've had a terrible day. That's all I need is to sing with an unlucky number." There was only one way everyone could think of to remedy the situation. Pull Mladen up on stage.

And that is how I became a member of the Serbian Karageorge Choir (named after a famous Serbian warrior). To this day, I do not know whether or not my dad masterminded the whole episode so that I would join the choir. I certainly wouldn't put it past him. Regardless, I became the youngest "man" to join the choir, and my dad was ecstatic.

These "choir boys" were the heaviest smokers and the hardest drinkers, always knocking back a few shots before going on stage to sing. And yet, if I reached for a cigarette, they slapped my hand away. If I wanted to act like a big man and have a beer with them, they'd pour me a soda pop. Even after five years, when I was nineteen and out of high school, they kept me "the kid." To this day I do not smoke or drink. I will always be indebted to the Karageorge singers for that.

And, more important, for helping me stand up to my dad. When I made the basketball team in high school, I had to get my dad to sign a permission slip. He refused. When the choir heard about this, they assured me not to worry. A lot of these fellas who had come from Europe remained unmarried even at forty and fifty. They had no home life so they were accustomed to hanging around together and going to sporting events. Unlike my dad, they were sports fans and understood what playing meant to me. They stepped in and talked to Pa.

He said, "What's Mladen going to do with ball when he finishes school?"

They reminded him, "It's a big deal, Pete. He made the team. Let him play."

Finally, one afternoon I arrived home to find Pa staring at the permission card on the dining room table. He looked at me, signed it, and handed it to me.

"You want play ball? Go play ball."

I couldn't thank the "choir boys" enough.

A lot of my growing up was in the company of the Karageorge Choir. One Sunday we were scheduled to perform a concert in East Chicago, Indiana. Twenty of us made the trip. (The full choir was never all together because about a third of the men were always working at the mill at any given time.) It got to be seven o'clock and no choir director. Seven-thirty, still no director.

Finally, my dad came to me. "The professor is not here. You must find notes on piano. Start us off."

Okay. I could do that. A few more minutes went by.

"You will direct."

"Are you kidding? I'll hit the notes."

"You will direct." This time it was an order.

I practiced the three notes softly, over and over as the members of the choir went out back to throw back some more shots of Slivovitz before they could face me. I hit the first note for the tenors, the second for the second tenors, and the third for the basses and baritones. They were all grinning at me as they hummed their opening notes. Like a bunch of big brothers, they loved putting me on the spot.

You never saw a baton shake so much as I led this group of grown men.

When we finished, they all told me they were sure they had never sounded better. I chalked it up to the Slivovitz. But it was good to feel they loved me, even if they liked to see me squirm.

My father instinctively knew enough psychology not to ask me himself when a lead role became available in one of the operettas the church group was putting on. Periodically, my father's brother would send him operettas from Europe and the group would be thrilled to have something new. In this particular play, the lead role was a young man and no one in the choir was young enough to play him.

Glisho, the codirector, approached my dad. "How about Mladen playing the lead?"

"You ask him," Pa said. "If I ask him, he'll say no."

At this time, I had been out of high school for about a year and was looking for a job. The last thing I wanted to do was waste my time with another ridiculous church play.

I told Glisho, "Listen, I don't have time for this. I've got to get a job. It's winter and I don't have an overcoat."

Glisho promised, "You do it and I will get you a coat."

I agreed to play the part. And on the first day of rehearsal, Glisho showed up with a coat. I have no idea where he got it but he kept his promise. I must say, the Serbs looked after their own. And it was the first time I was ever paid for acting, even if it was with a double-breasted, gray cloth coat.

The operetta was *Sudjaja* (*Destiny*). What's meant to be will be and there's nothing you can do to change that. It was the usual amateur production. We rehearsed maybe twice a week for a long, drawn-out period, three months or so just walking through the scenes. No one put much thought into the set or the lighting at the Croatian Hall. At the last minute they set up the folding chairs for the audience and that was that.

By now, I had had a taste of how things were done in the big time: Emerson School. I corralled some of my buddies into helping me. We took what they had at the hall and brought in some of our own stuff to make some scenery. We borrowed some lights from school and set them up. I was determined that if I was going to have a real part, then it was going to be in an honest-to-goodness play.

My dad played a wandering, storytelling Turk. What else? The climactic scene involved a scuffle between my character and Pa's that ended with my drawing a dagger and stabbing him. That was all that my dad cared about from the moment he learned we were doing this play: the dagger. What kind of dagger was I going to use? I suggested a retractable blade, one of those trick knives where you press a button in the handle, but that didn't make it with Pa. "You forget press handle and you really stab me."

He insisted on a rubber blade, but I protested. "I refuse to stab you with that floppy thing waving in the breeze. That will look ridiculous."

Out of desperation I decided to make the dagger myself. But now Dad insisted that it not be made of wood; he was still worried that I might get a little overenthusiastic in the heat of the moment. So I made a dagger out of beaver board and painted it as realistically as I could.

The problem was the Serbs never had dress rehearsals. The costumes were always brought in from a Chicago costume house at the last possible minute since they couldn't afford to rent them for any longer than absolutely necessary. That meant we had costumes for the night of the performance only. That made for some pretty wild get-ups as the actors tried to patch together a costume out of pieces that fit them. Gradually the people at the costume house began to know this motley crew. "Oh, Sekulovich is playing that part? This'll fit him," and so on. Even so, there was no time for rehearsing in the costumes or with the props.

So there we were the night of the performance. I came at Pa with the knife and stabbed him so hard the damn thing broke. There I stood, in the middle of the stage, holding a handle with no blade. I tossed it away and carried on with the play. But as my dad, the Turk, lay dying, he stared up at me with a fierce look of "I told you so."

The audience loved it anyway. It was their story.

The ways of the old country died hard. The entire time I lived at home, we never owned a car. We never even had a telephone. I rarely went on dates and never had a steady girlfriend. I can't recall ever inviting friends to my house. I never got an allowance.

If I needed a little pocket money, I'd spend Saturdays working at the clothing store owned by a friend of the family. A Serb of course. From nine in the morning until nine at night I washed the glass showcases, swept floors, dusted shoeboxes, and straightened ties for a whopping dollar and twenty-five cents. Sometimes he'd give me an extra twenty-five cents, especially in the summertime when I would man the straw hat stand out front. For that two bits, I would walk a couple of doors down and buy a hot dog, a glass of milk, and a piece of pie. A little money could go a long way, but it never occurred to me to ask my parents for any spending money, even if I needed something in particular. It never occurred to me to ask them for anything.

When I was still in high school, I was informed that, as president of the senior class, I had to attend the prom. I panicked. I had no transportation, no date, and nothing to wear. I had reached my full height and was delighted that I could no longer share my father's $22.50 suits and $4.00 Thom McCann shoes as I had in junior high. But I had nothing to replace them. Somehow I managed to get my hands on a half-way decent looking suit.

But that was only half the problem. I still had no transportation and no date. Hazel Harrison, the head of the auditorium department, nudged me into inviting Winona Gustavson, the class vice president. I breathed a sigh of relief when she accepted. When a buddy of mine suggested we double-date in his father's Hudson, I thought I was home free . . . until he suggested we take our dates somewhere after the dance. You had to do that to be cool. But that would cost money.

I scrambled to do odd jobs all over town for about three weeks. I must have swept up half of Gary in order to be able to drive into Chicago in that boat of a car and have Chinese food at the Oriental Gardens. I gave Winona the usual high school kiss at her door and when the night was over, I'd had a swell time and managed to fulfill my obligations as class president to boot.

I had been shocked to have been elected in the first place. Like the presidency of the Academy of Motion Picture Arts and Sciences nearly sixty years later, the senior class presidency was nothing I ever really went after, nothing I campaigned for.

The election was held one afternoon at the beginning of the school year. Football season. The senior class congregated in the auditorium to vote and, much to my surprise, I was nominated. The final ballot came down to me and Mr. Popularity, a member of the "A" crowd's prestigious "High Y Club." It was a tie. Then another tie.

Suddenly, someone realized that the entire football team was not present and ran out to poll them on the field where they were practicing. I may not have been a member of a fancy club, but I was an athlete, already captain of the basketball team. There were twelve seniors out on the field at that moment. All twelve votes went to me. And that is how I became president of the senior class—in the fluky sort of way that has characterized every election I have won ever since.

My success in the high school drama department was equally quirky. After my Emerson School debut in *The Mikado*, one of the drama teachers asked me to be in a play called *Seventeen*. The catch was that this offer came one week before the play was to open. The boy who had originally won the part became ineligible because he was flunking too many classes. My first reaction was that I would never be able to memorize all those lines in so little time, but this was my chance to really find a niche in the drama department. I came up with a plan.

I was to play the part of the father who sat in an easy chair through much of the play. I decided he would be reading a newspaper. I would paste the script on the inside of the paper to help me get through the play. That was just fine with the teacher; anything to get a warm body at the eleventh hour.

I may have saved the day for one teacher but I loused things up with the department big shot, Miss Sandles. I have never been any good at camouflaging my feelings about people, particularly when I find them to be phony. Miss Sandles was the kind of self-important character given to illusions of grandeur who all too often populate school drama departments. Mostly, she had nothing to teach us. Since I made no effort to hide the fact that I couldn't abide her, she had it in for me.

With Miss Sandles putting the kibosh on me by excluding me from the drama club, I made it my business to do something really good in spite of her, or maybe, more truthfully, to spite her. I went out and found a one-act about World War I written by a boy at Notre Dame. I organized the production, directed it, built the scenery, the whole shot. Then I went to another—a lesser—drama teacher, Miss Fuller, and told her we wanted to present this production. She okayed it and when the play was well received, that did me in with Miss Sandles for good.

With great amusement I recently discovered her inscription in my high school yearbook. In flowery script covering an entire page, she wrote: "TO 'HIM' OF THE TEMPERAMENTAL TEMPERAMENT, WHICH IS UNDERSTANDABLE IF SOMEDAY I FIND MYSELF IN THE MOST EXPENSIVE SEAT IN THE MOST EXPENSIVE THEATER SAYING, 'TEACHER.' BEATRICE ELAINE SANDLES." Presumptuous to the end. That woman never taught anyone anything worthwhile.

I'm sure Miss Fuller was really putting herself on the line for me when she invited me to play the lead during my senior year. The play was George Bernard Shaw's *Arms and the Man*. Fortunately, this time the play didn't conflict with my basketball schedule. By now, I was comfortable on stage and had a deeper love of the theater than I even realized at the time. Regardless of all the craziness that went along with the Serbian church plays, when music and the theater are in your home throughout your childhood, I believe they are in you for life. But it still had not dawned on me that I might be able to make a living in the theater. It was just something you did to occupy your time. My father had taught me, by example, that making a living and having fun were two very different things.

I saw what had happened to the boys who had graduated before me, that vast majority who didn't go to college. They got jobs in the mills, got married, started paying off their cars and making the mortgage. Their lives stretched out before them like so much quicksand. I knew that wasn't for me. But what could I do about it?

A few months after I graduated from high school in 1931, I approached my basketball coach. One of the wonderful things about Emerson was that the kids there were used to going to their teachers for help and advice. I asked the coach if he could think of any way I could go to college.

He said he thought he could get me a scholarship at a small Presbyterian college in Batesville, Arkansas where he had some connections.

"You can go down there and play ball," he told me. Wonderful.

It was the depths of the Depression and there was very little work to be had. There was nothing to do but stand on the corners, like the song said, and watch the girls go by. I had been doing piddly little jobs whenever I could, anything to make a buck. I had saved a total of four dollars when I went to my dad and told him I wanted to go to college. (There was no including my parents, enlisting their help in devising a plan; any plan had to be fully worked out before I presented it to Pa.) I know he thought it was a foolish idea, but I had no steady job and there were no prospects. He said, "All right, give it a try," and handed me five dollars.

I set out with one little suitcase, my gym bag, and the nine dollars in my pocket. I studied the map, marked the most direct route to Batesville, and hit the highway with my thumb out. Hitchhiking was becoming one of the mainstays of transportation at that time. It was the only means an awful lot of people could afford. Needless to say, I was one of them.

Truckdrivers would always pull over and ask where you were headed. In two rides, I made it all the way to Indianapolis. I spent the night in the bus station there, then stuck out my thumb the next morning and made it to Little Rock by that night. Another night in a bus station and I made it to Batesville, Arkansas in a couple of rides and many long hours later the next day.

I showed up at the college athletic department from out of the blue. Like the ignorant kid I was, I appeared without ever writing a letter or accepting their offer in any way.

The coach looked me over. "You're a pretty big fella. Why don't you go out for football?"

"I'm a basketball player. I'll go out for track, but football's not my game."

"Give it a try," he ordered.

Clearly, this was not negotiable. The next day I suited up. I tried it for two days—end, center—I tried it all. And I got clobbered. I hated it. My nose had already been broken once by then. I saw no reason to put the rest of my body in jeopardy. I told the coach I couldn't continue with football. Policies were very different then. Athletics were not the high-ticket item at colleges they are today. Kids didn't have the luxury of specializing, especially at such a small school.

"Well, we can't give you a scholarship for just one sport."

I packed up and stuck out my thumb again. My total traveling time to and from Arkansas was just about as long as my college career there. When I returned home, my father said nothing. I would rather he had told me, "I told you so," than that miserable silence. But I was telling myself off enough for both of us. I had set out all ready for my future to begin, eager for something to happen, and nothing had happened. One step forward and ten steps back.

I returned to the street corners, hanging around doing nothing with a couple of the guys. Sometimes we would play basketball for various organizations or businesses. The first was Peacock Cleaners. Then, when some local yokel ran for mayor, he had jerseys made up for us to wear so we advertised CLAYTON FOR MAYOR as we played.

During this period of playing pick-up and sponsor games, I broke my nose for the second time. I was guarding someone when, once again, I took an elbow to the nose. This time, another player taped it up, but that didn't help. A whopper shiner appeared the next day, just like the first time, but this time I didn't manage to hide it from Pa.

He looked at my mother. "See. This is what sports brings him. A broken nose."

I had a hard time breathing for a week or so, but who cared about a nose if you were strong and could work in the mills? After all, wasn't that what I was headed for?

At night I would listen to the radio. My folks had given me a Silvertone from Sears-Roebuck for graduation, the first and last real present I ever remember receiving from them. But it ended up in the living room so we were always bickering about what to listen to. I always wanted to listen to W.L.S. Barndance, a predecessor to Grand Ol' Opry, which was about as hip as anything we could pick up.

But playing pick-up basketball and listening to the radio was not exactly an auspicious beginning to a life. I had to get a job. When you had to get a job in Gary, you went to one place—the steel mills. It was finally time for me to face the inevitable.

F.D.R.'s National Recovery Act was in full swing. The usual two shifts at the mills were turned into three eight-hour shifts. With the mills running twenty-four hours a day, more men were put to work. In a scene that would foreshadow the dock scenes in *On the Waterfront*, men would gather at the football field every morning waiting to be hired by the mill supervisors. But at the mills, they were waiting to be selected for steady jobs, not day labor. I stood there for one long day. Then for a second day. Nothing. I was too young. All the old-timers were being chosen. Men with families to support were always given top priority and there were plenty of them.

After the second day I came home and told my dad, "They won't even look at me."

The next morning my dad said, "I go with you."

He stood there on Gleason Field beside me. Finally, someone called, "Pete!"

My dad stepped forward, proud to be singled out by name.

"Pete, you want a job?"

Pa said, "Mr. White, I have a job. My boy, he finished high school. Now he needs job."

"I'll hire you, but I can't hire him."

Where else to turn? Pa sent me to the one authority higher than himself in the Serbian community, the priest. With no hesitation Father Shukletovich said, "Come with me." Together we walked directly to the mills, right to the head of personnel.

The man hired me on the spot. In Gary, you didn't mess around with a request from a priest.

So, like every good Gary son, I did my time in the steel mills. I worked the wheel mill where we manufactured train and streetcar wheels. A round slab of metal would be inserted into a tremendous press that stamped out a "rough." A crane lifted out the hot circles and stacked them to cool for a few days. Then they would be rolled like hoops—all eight hundred pounds of them—to the machine shop where they would be trimmed and smoothed out. My job was to assist the machinist loading the lathe that shaped the wheels and cleaning out the chips left behind in the machine. It was dangerous work, especially operating the small forklift. You had to make sure the prongs were securely snapped around the wheel and that the wheel was properly balanced on the lift. If the wheel dropped, it could be a disaster.

After a while I learned that you could make more money in the open hearth, five dollars a day. I got myself reassigned there and wound up spending a year in the number two open hearth where I lined the massive fifty ton ladles with 2,500 bricks each. The hot iron ore would pour out of the oven into the ladle. A crane would hoist the ladle and pour the ore into ingots. Everyone has seen this many times in the movies and it is a spectacular sight to see . . . on screen. Sparks fly like fireworks and the molten ore flows like lava. In reality, it is a terrifying, dangerous place to be. It's a lot like working in hell.

Finally, I moved up to the floor where I made five dollars a day plus tonnage, which meant a bonus for a second pour per day. There, I was a member of a seven man crew feeding the ovens with scrap ore and various agents.

I worked in the mills for a total of three years. All the while the same thought plagued me until the sound of it reverberating in my head became almost unbearable. "This is where my life is going to end up." I tried to remind myself that I was lucky to have a job. It was still the Depression after all. At that time in Gary, you either worked in the mills, in a grocery store, a gas station, or maybe, if you were really ritzy, in a clothing store. Otherwise, you didn't work. It was hard to feel lucky laboring at backbreaking work that I loathed. I felt trapped.

After three years, giving my mother five dollars a week, I had managed to save three hundred and forty dollars.

I began to dream about a place I had never actually seen. I remembered that when I was in high school, there used to be an annual city-wide dramatic contest featuring one-act plays put on by the three local high schools. The judge was always a teacher from a place called the Goodman Theater in Chicago. How disappointed I had been that I had never participated in one of those contests. Between my basketball schedule and my nemesis, Miss Sandles, I had never made it into one of those plays. They'd wrangle me to build the scenery or do whatever else I could to help, but I was never on stage when that Goodman Theater judge sat in the audience.

I resolved that I was going to go to the Goodman Theater. Maybe, with a little luck, I could have some kind of a life in the theater. In the back of my mind I assumed I'd probably end up as a stage hand since I seemed to have no problem with physical work, but I had to give acting a shot.

Finally I had a plan, a destination. And, naturally, a new problem. How do I break the news to my father?

His reaction was predictable. He had let me have my little fling at college in Arkansas. Not again.

"Have you gone crazy?"

Deep down inside, I was thinking, "Yes. Yes, I have." But I never dreamed of admitting that. Instead I said, "No. I'm going to the Goodman Theater."

"What's that?"

"Acting school."

"You have a job. You are making five dollars a day. You should be happy to get that."

I said, "The mills will always be here."

"Maybe it won't be that easy next time," he warned me.

"So I'll do something else."

"Shta?" ("What?") he wanted to know.

I had no answer for that. What I was thinking was that he had hated the mills. He had quit them. Why did I have to stay? What he must have been thinking was that I had no idea how good I had it. He had escaped to America from a hovel where he had slept on a straw mat on the ground with pigs for company. What more could I want out of life?

Finally, my mother said to me, "Are you sure you want to do this?"

"Yes."

"Where are you going to get the money?"

"I've saved three hundred and forty dollars."

"If you think you want to do it, give it a try."

I told her I had to.

I watched my father as he walked out into the tiny yard behind our house and sat down on an old wooden bench. I had the feeling he had given up on me.

facing page:
With Mona as the Giant and Mrs. Giant
in *Jack and the Beanstalk.*

Chapter 2

I waited until I drew the four-to-midnight shift at the steel mills so that I would have most of the day off. Then one morning in September of 1934, I went into Chicago to find the Goodman Theater.

When I arrived there, I nearly passed right by it. The theater is not much to see from the outside. The Chicago Art Institute is an elegant, imposing structure boasting an entrance flanked by two massive stone lions. I spotted it immediately as I crossed the bridge to Michigan Avenue. But the Goodman, which was the dramatic arm of the Art Institute, looks like nothing from the street. All I could see on that September day was its roof peeking out from behind the rest of the Art Institute. But when I finally entered its doors, stepping into the small foyer, my heart was pounding like a triphammer. This was a real theater.

I noticed the two small box offices on either side of the foyer and walked up to one. A young lady directed me down some fifty steps to the main lobby of the theater. That sight was really something. It more than made up for the modest exterior of the building. The lobby was decorated with fabulous antiques. Museum quality tapestries covered the walls. I followed the directions the receptionist had given me. A left, then another left. There, a girl in an outer office sent me in to meet the head of the school.

I knew immediately that this very short, little man was unlike anyone I had ever met before. His name was Doctor Gnesin. Though he was from Kiev, he spoke with no trace of a Russian accent, only a very precise British clip tinged with a Yale education. Mostly, he had an unmistakable brilliance about him. He also possessed a warmth that he tried to hide beneath an authoritative air. It would take me a while to discover that warmth, but it was there. However, as I stood that first day in his book-lined office, I just felt enormously intimidated.

But there I stood. Once again, I had not sent a letter of inquiry ahead. I held in my hand no letter of introduction. I had not even submitted an application. I just showed up dressed in my finest—one of my three letterman's sweaters. I was so nervous I felt sick, but I was there. I had taken the first step.

I will never forget what I said.

"I'm from Gary, Indiana and I'd like to go to school here."

Dr. Gnesin knew right away what he was up against. A kid so

ignorant of how things are done that he would just show up in his office, hat—and future—in hand.

He looked me up and down and said, "What do you want to do here?"

"This is an acting school, isn't it?"

"Yes," he replied, "but we also have set design, costume design, everything."

"I built scenery in high school. I know something about that," I answered. "But I'd like to act."

I racked my brain for my best acting credit: *Arms and the Man*. I didn't think that all those years behind a bushy black caterpillar of a mustache, half-hidden under a fez, portraying an evil Turk would impress him.

Finally, he said, "Good." Then he added, "You know it costs nine hundred dollars a year to go to school here."

"I don't have that kind of money."

"Well, how much do you have?" he asked me.

I'm not sure if I ever really thought about exactly what I had been saving for all that time I had been working in the steel mills. But as I stood there, I suddenly knew.

"I saved three hundred dollars in the steel mills to come here."

Dr. Gnesin smiled and asked, "Do you gamble?"

"No."

"Would you gamble on yourself?"

"How?"

"You spend your three hundred dollars for the first term, three months," he proposed, "and if you don't belong here after that, I'll tell you so. If you do, I'll give you a full scholarship for the whole three years."

It took me a long moment to answer. It had taken me three years to save a little more than three hundred dollars. I could blow it all in one word.

Finally, I managed, "Okay."

With that, I became a student at the Goodman Theater.

On the way home, riding the South Shore electrical line, it suddenly hit me. What had I done? I tried to find some confidence, flattering myself by thinking that Doc Gnesin saw something in me, some small glimmer of talent, of something special. I now believe he was merely being pragmatic. There were only about one hundred students in the school at that time, no more than twenty-five of them were male. He needed men. Especially ones so green and eager that they would appear in your office out of nowhere insisting, in effect, "I've got to try this. Even if it's just to get it out of my system. Let me try."

I was in heaven to be there. I had absolutely no money, but that never bothered me because I was finally doing something that could lead to a real career, not just another job to get by. Maybe I wasn't going to end up a laborer after all. Maybe I was going to get out of Gary for good. Ensconced at the Goodman for the first time, I felt the energy, ambition, and drive I had been pushing down inside of me rush to the surface. I felt ready to conquer the world. And the fact that so many people, especially my parents, thought I was insane for trying lit the fire in my belly even more.

The Goodman Theater had originally opened in the mid-twenties. The Goodman family had built it as a memorial to their son, Kenneth Sawyer Goodman, who had been a playwright and had died in World War I. The theater had originated as a repertory company, but had closed after a couple of years and remained "dark" until Doc Gnesin decided to reopen this marvelous theater as a school.

The Goodman offered a perfect facility for a school. The main theater was spectacular, large enough to seat eight hundred and all wood paneled. It was designed on a modified stadium plan with no aisles, yet with plenty of room between the rows. The centerpiece of the main theater was the large stage, draped by a red plush curtain, but there was also space in the wings on either side of the stage equal to the size of the stage itself. The stage did not have the usual grid from which to hang scenery. Instead, a tremendous plaster dome vaulted over it, and a pit extended down five feet to light the dome from below. Legend had it that the pit was three feet deeper than Lake Michigan. The constant cold and dampness attested to that fact.

The first time I laid eyes on this theater it took my breath away. And it still does. If someone had told me I could have been a working actor in that theater for the rest of my life, I would have been a happy man.

The Goodman was particularly actor friendly, probably because it was conceived as a repertory theater. There were three or four dressing rooms on either side of the stage, men's and women's, each spacious enough to accommodate two or three actors (though they often assigned six to the same room). Whereas most dressing rooms, even on Broadway, are shabby and dreary, the Goodman's dressing rooms were very comfortable, downright beautiful, furnished with chrome dressing tables like those found in elegant drawing rooms in movies of that time.

On the other side of the lobby from the main theater was a small theater that sat about two hundred. This was ideal as a workshop theater for student produced and directed efforts.

Doc Gnesin was determined to make the Goodman one of the preeminent theater schools in the country. And he did. The Goodman was not a place where you dropped in on an acting class for a couple of hours a few times a week. The rigorous program often demanded eighteen hour days. The curriculum included Voice and Diction, Pantomime, Dance, History of the Theater,

Set Design, Makeup, and of course, Acting I and II (scene development classes). There was also a workshop with a full array of power tools for building sets. I felt quite at home in there.

We worked in class from nine until one every day. Then, from two in the afternoon until the wee hours of the next morning, we would rehearse at least one play, build scenery, do whatever needed to be done. The Goodman offered nine membership series plays, one a month, between September and June. Though each play ran for two weeks, meanwhile we would be prepping the next production. Since there were two full series of plays running simultaneously—the regular series and the children's series—we might be working on a total of four plays at any given time. If we weren't rehearsing, we were building a set, organizing wardrobes, or making props. It was a frantic schedule but I never minded. It sure beat the mills.

In order to save money, I started out by living at home even though Gary is an hour away along the south shore. The electric line that ran from Michigan to Chicago stopped only half a block away from the Art Institute, but that train was expensive. The New York Central line, on the other hand, offered a monthly pass. The stop was farther away, making it much less convenient, but far cheaper, which always won out.

When a play was running and we were working on crew, we had to stay after the curtain (usually around eleven o'clock) to clear the stage every night so that it would be bare and ready for classes the next morning. I was on crew for the first production of my first year. I would skip out on crew a half an hour early, run like a bat out of hell to the station to catch the train and, if I was lucky, get about four hours sleep until I had to catch the first morning train back.

One night early on, I didn't make the train so I ended up sleeping in the railway station. As I curled up on a bench, I couldn't help but wonder if my father's unspoken prediction that I would become a bum was coming true.

I arrived at school the next morning wondering what I was going to do. Could I possibly ask to be relieved of crew duty? Absolutely not. So the next night I slept in one of the dressing rooms. And the next as well. I showered in the one shower in the whole theater and filched one of the actor's towels. I wore the same clothes for a good five days and lived out of that dressing room for at least a week.

It turned out to be the dressing room belonging to Jimmy Russo, a second year student. Jimmy was a good-looking kid from Kenosha, Wisconsin—short, wavy black hair, a killer smile that flashed a mouthful of white teeth, and a heavy dose of Italian macho. Finally, I confessed to him, explaining my situation. Jimmy invited me to come and live with him in his hotel room. I declined, admitting that I didn't have enough money for even half of a hotel room. Jimmy said the offer stood anyway. The room had twin beds and, after all, he could only sleep in one. So I lived rent free for that first year at Goodman and have felt forever grateful and indebted to Jimmy Russo.

The first play I performed in was one of the children's series, *Aladdin*. I had one line, addressing the king. I had no idea what I was doing, right or wrong. I only knew that every time I made my entrance, the other students would stand in the wings and watch. And laugh. To this day, I haven't a clue as to what they were laughing at. But it didn't stop me.

Every year, Gnesin insisted that we do a Shakespeare play, an Ibsen, and a Russian drama (which he always translated personally). I had two scenes in that year's Russian selection, Tolstoy's *Redemption*. One was just a couple of lines, but the other was actually an important scene in which I had a long speech that articulated the theme of the play. I tried my best but I had absolutely no idea whether I was working properly. Finally, I got a hold of a fellow named Sydney Breese, one of the younger teachers there.

Syd was a few years older than I and, in my opinion, he was the best actor that school ever put out. Whenever a professional company came to Chicago with a production, they always asked him to be in it, but he never had the courage to go to New York himself. He preferred staying at the Goodman and teaching.

I did my speech for Syd and he listened intently, offering pointers along the way. "When you reach this moment, try to impress him with your knowledge. . . ." That kind of thing. When opening night came, I delivered the speech. The audience burst into applause when the scene was over. That sound washed over me with a feeling I will never forget. I felt that even if I never stepped onto a stage again, the sound of that one good hand was worth the entire three hundred bucks.

The next day in Dr. Gnesin's History of the Theater class, Doc spoke about how well I had done. But then he went on. He said that I had given just the beginning of a performance. What could I have done with that part if I were a third year student instead of a first? He certainly was one to make sure that none of his students would ever suffer from a swelled head.

Much to my amazement, my parents actually came to see this production. I'm sure they really just wanted to see what I was up to, what this Goodman Theater was all about. Since each student was given four tickets, they had a good—and free—excuse to check it out.

They brought my godparents, and I remember being so proud to show them all around backstage. I gave them the grand tour, particularly showing off the shop with all its professional caliber tools. The message was clear; this was several steps up from the Croatian Hall. All the while I was waiting,

waiting for someone to say something about my performance. I waited and I waited; I was determined not to ask them what they thought.

All my mother wanted to know was what I was doing with my laundry. (She ended up arranging for me to mail it home to her. The return packages always included some wonderful food along with my clean shirts.) My godfather admitted that this was better than the run-of-the-mill Serb productions. Then my father took me aside and asked me a question.

"Why you come on stage?"

"Well, I have to play the scene."

"No," he pressed. "Why you come on stage?"

"Because I want to tell him that . . . ," I began.

"No," Pa insisted. "You're not listening to me. Why you come on stage?"

"All right! Why?"

"You are professor, smart man. But you are drunkard. You drink too much. You come from bar where people buy you drinks because you got no money. So you go to other bar. That brings you on stage. To go to other bar you must come on stage. When you are on stage you see that man sitting by table. He has bottle of wine. Ah-ha! That man, maybe he give you drink. So you go talk to him. Philosophy. You are professor, so you talk philosophy. But you don't want to talk philosophy. You want to drink wine. You keep talking 'cause you are bum. You drink free wine."

What a revelation! My father really did know the theater. He went on. "All this while you tell him great things from Tolstoy's speech. Man is all of us all together. But don't forget, look at bottle. Look at bottle of wine. He never give it to you. So finally you have no more talk. You must go someplace else."

He didn't know it, of course, and I hadn't even learned the vocabulary to articulate it as yet, but he was talking about the subtext of the scene. It proved to be one of the best pieces of direction I would ever receive, no doubt helping me to create a better, more complex and interesting performance than Dr. Gnesin could have imagined my ever giving even after three years at his school. That was all my father said about the play. No comment on whether I had been good or bad. And certainly no comment on whether maybe, just maybe, I hadn't made such a foolish decision in going there. Only a comment on how to make my performance better.

Frankly, that is really all that I cared about, too. I worked the long hours like everyone else, and basically had no social life whatsoever. When I arrived at the Goodman, the first people I hooked up with were two second year students, Mary Elizabeth Aurelius (known as "Sis") and Jack Hubbard. They both had gone to high school in East Chicago, Indiana, and seen me play basketball against their team, so they introduced themselves to me. When the word got around the Goodman that I was a pretty decent ballplayer my stock rose a bit, but I didn't venture into new social circles easily. I latched onto Jack and I guess Sis and I became a sort of a couple for a while during that first year.

But there would soon be one member of my own class with whom I would find myself thrown together time and again. Her name was Mona Greenberg. She was the tiniest girl in the class—a shade over five feet tall and all of ninety-three pounds. Having graduated from high school at the age of sixteen and then attending one year of college, she was only seventeen when she arrived at the Goodman, but she looked about twelve. A scholarship student, Mona was the youngest in the class and the best. Already the word was that Mona was going to be the one who would make it. That's what I kept hearing from everyone before I even had the chance to work with her.

The first year class of sixty students was divided into two

groups. Mona was in one. I was in the other. Almost immediately, Mona's size and looks, as well as a talent that belied them both, qualified her as the queen of the children's theater.

The Goodman was renowned for its children's theater, which was run by a woman named Charlotte Chorpenning, known as "Corpy." Corpy looked like someone straight from the Kentucky hills, short and squat, but she had actually been a practicing child psychologist for many years. She continued to teach child psychology at Northwestern University in the mornings, while presiding over the children's theater at the Goodman in the afternoons. She wrote many of the children's plays herself, adapting them from familiar fairy tales and stories, but always in a novel, unexpected way that consistently delighted and positively captivated every child in the audience. To this day, hers remain the most outstanding children's productions I have ever seen.

After *Aladdin*, the next children's play I was in was *Little Red Riding Hood*. Finally, I got to work with Mona Greenberg who was, of course, Little Red herself. I played the Woodsman who saves her at the end, after what Corpy envisioned as a spectacular chase. The Wolf was to leap out of bed and chase Little Red Riding Hood until her only escape was to clamber up the side of the fireplace. There, he would have her cornered when I, the Woodsman, would burst in and Little Red Riding Hood would leap into my arms. And I mean leap.

The fireplace was six feet high and at every single rehearsal Mona was paralyzed with fear, unable to make the jump. Mona and I went into the rehearsal room alone one afternoon, determined that we wouldn't leave until she could jump. She climbed the stepping stones up the side of the fireplace and stood on the mantle. I started out close to the fireplace so that she could almost step into my arms. Gradually, I began to inch back little by little until she was finally leaping off. After a good long session, she could dash up the side of that fireplace and leap right out into my arms with no hesitation.

Then came dress rehearsal. Mona ran up the fireplace . . . and froze. I held out my arms, but she didn't budge. We had not realized that the entire fireplace set would be resting atop a platform that raised the fireplace a good eight inches. From where Mona stood, that extra eight inches made eight feet of difference. We had to start the process all over again. But, finally, she did it. And, with my coaxing her over and over to literally fall into my arms, we got to know each other.

By this time my three-month trial period was over. I had been so busy and enjoying myself so much that I honestly hadn't given a moment's thought to my agreement with Dr. Gnesin. When he called me into his office one day, I thought it might be all over.

Instead, he said, "Your gamble paid off. I'm going to give you the full scholarship." It was one of the great moments of my life. I thanked him profusely.

He said, "Don't thank me. Just keep working."

And that is exactly what I did. Doc knew that I always needed money, so he made sure that I was scheduled for crew whenever the theater was rented out for concerts or lectures. After our Saturday performance I would stay to strike the set and put up whatever was needed for the Sunday rental. Then on Sunday, around eleven in the evening, I would strike that set and prepare the stage for Monday classes. It was a long weekend but it was worth it. I could make five bucks.

In exchange for the scholarship, Dr. Gnesin assigned me to check students in each morning. I had to arrive early but that was no problem for me. I would sit there at the entrance to the lobby and take attendance, all the while practicing my Voice and Diction exercises.

"Good morning. How are you? Did you have your toast, orange juice, and hot coffee this morning?" I sounded like a Howard Johnson's John Gielgud.

Mary Agnes Doyle, the Voice and Diction teacher, had pulled no punches in telling me that I was going to have to work extra hard to get rid of my accent.

"What accent?" I asked her.

"You have an accent," she informed me. "Your d's and t's are very bad. Your speech is very sloppy." (I just kept thinking she should have heard the way people talked in the house I grew up in.) I guess every school has a Mary Agnes Doyle, the teacher who holds up the morale of the school, maintains its dignity, and by extension, the dignity of the profession she taught. She had a starched, Sunday school appearance, always wearing high-necked dresses that reached almost to her ankles and a tight braid twisted around her head. A huge cross always hung around her neck so that she ended up looking like a nun. (You could spot the girls who wanted to get on her good side; they always wore crosses, too.) Mary Agnes Doyle was the kind of woman who commanded attention.

So I practiced and I practiced until I sounded so affected and British that you never would have thought I was born in this country, let alone four houses from the wrong side of the tracks in a Serbian ghetto in Chicago. Of course, upper-crust British didn't exactly go with my open-hearth looks, so I ended up having to unlearn most of what I had learned.

By the end of my stint at the Goodman I finally got up the nerve to approach her. I said, "Miss Doyle, with my face, how can I speak like that?"

She answered, "Mladen, when you leave here, I'll be happy if you keep just a little of what I have taught you." She was right. And I remained grateful to her for having exacted such discipline from me. To this day, I often find myself driving along, saying, "It did, didn't it? Didn't it, it did." You can never work too long or hard on those t's and d's.

Fortunately, I didn't have to worry so much about the diction aspects of the characters in the children's theater. When the second year rolled around I was thrilled to play the Giant in *Jack in the Beanstalk*. In an unexpected (though brilliant) Corpy turn, petite little Mona was cast as the Giant's wife. Mona made me seem all the larger when I made my entrance. From offstage, in a big, booming voice, I would shout, "Fee fi fo foy, I smell the blood of a little boy . . ." and then I would walk on. The kids would gasp. I wore enormous boots that made me six inches taller and I padded my skinny body with three sweatshirts and a few pair of pants underneath my costume. By the time the show was over, I would be absolutely wringing wet, but the kids loved it. The children's audiences, who could go from chatty and squirmy to wide-eyed and mesmerized, provided a litmus test for young actors that was unbeatable.

Corpy felt it was crucial that there be funny moments in every play to counteract the inevitable scary villain. In *Jack and the Beanstalk*, the Giant, of course, was the villain. Together, Mona and I worked out all kinds of routines that made the kids laugh hysterically. I would start out demanding that she bring me my bags of gold in my big, giant's voice. But she would refuse. Each time I asked for the gold, my voice would get higher and whinier—like a child's—and my face would fall more and more. And the tiny Giant's wife still refused. This little woman knew exactly how to control him, and the kids loved it. They all knew what it was like to have your mommy put her foot down no matter how badly you wanted to get your way.

Finally, I would end up crying like a baby. Mona would break down and say, "All right, all right, don't cry," and she would bring me my gold coins.

Jack and the Beanstalk was one of Corpy's trademark productions. When she had first mounted the production a few years earlier, the play contained two scenes in the Giant's house, one immediately before intermission and the next immediately after. The first act ended with the Giant chasing Jack and was so scary that the children often refused to come back for the next scene, so Corpy wrote a new scene in which Jack meets the Man in the Moon. She added some lovely, soothing music to be played during intermission and then this lullaby of a scene unfolded where the Man in the Moon assured Jack that nothing bad would ever happen to him. The kids would relax enough for Jack to return to the Giant's house. This was Corpy's genius.

The set for that production included a magnificent beanstalk. Before the second act, "Jack," Mona, and I all had to climb up a thirty-foot "A" ladder to a platform suspended by four cables from the plaster dome. (Mona wasn't too crazy about climbing the ladder, but she did it.) Once we were up there, they would take the ladder away and we would make our entrance from high above the proscenium. Jack was supposed to start chopping the beanstalk when I was almost to the ground. Then I would collapse and fall onto the stage.

One afternoon, the technician who released the beanstalk climbed up the ladder, then I went up, then Mona, then "Jack." All as planned. The tech climbed onto the platform and they removed the ladder from below. Suddenly, moments before the curtain was to go up, two of the four cables completely snapped. The platform dropped, but remained hanging by the other two lines. The technician and "Jack" hung on. No one had time to think. I just wrapped one arm around Mona, grabbed a line with the other, and hooked my legs around the dangling platform. We hung there for what seemed like an eternity, a good four or five minutes. Mona couldn't even speak. I just kept yelling for them to bring the ladder in, and then when they did, to push it closer so that I could reach it. Finally, I could feel the ladder with my enormous boots and I managed to get Mona onto it. I'm sure she was never so happy to be on that ladder which she normally hated. I followed her down and we all made it safely.

I barely had time to catch my breath when Corpy told me to get out there and entertain the kids while they fixed everything behind the scenes. I ran out front, actually down among the kids, and played games with them, anything to pass the ten or fifteen minutes it would take to get the third act up and running. I ended up switching from Mr. Giant to the Pied Piper, leading the entire audience on a parade around the theater out to the lobby and back to their seats. Then I climbed up that ladder again and perched myself at the top of the beanstalk, while Mona and "Jack" took their places—on the ground—and we began the third act three pages in from the usual beginning.

We didn't really have time to catch our breath and realize how shaken we were until the final curtain. The show had to go on. But it was the second time that Mona had fallen into my arms. Fate must have been trying to tell me something. (As the passing years embellished the story, I would end up telling our daughters how, as we hung there, I said to Mona, "Marry me or I'll drop you.")

Mona and I played together again in a play called *Dear Brutus* by Phillip Barry. Our big scene took place in the Land of Might Have Been (if things hadn't been what they were). I was a drunk and my "might have been" was that I could have been a painter. Mona played my daughter. Since there were so many more girls than boys in the school and the plays ran for two weeks, often they would double cast a female part. Such was the case in this play. Mona played the part for the first week and another girl for the second.

The other girl complained bitterly during rehearsals, protesting that I was paying more attention to Mona, that I was giving more to her in the scene. I denied it vehemently. Mona did things instinctively, I insisted, that the other girl couldn't do. Mona came running out onto the stage and instead of just stopping, she would jump on me like a child would do. Then I held her on my lap and we played the scene. The other girl not only didn't think of this, she couldn't have pulled it off if she had. Besides, if she had jumped on me she would have knocked me over. Beyond that, I was not yet willing to acknowledge any special chemistry between Mona and me—on or off stage.

Temperaments often ran amok at the Goodman. I suppose that must be true at all acting schools where the students' dreams are at once so fierce and so precarious. I remember how many kids were disappointed and furious when cast lists would be posted on the bulletin board. Some of the girls would weep. Other kids would storm Doc Gnesin's office. Not me. I think in some ways I was fortunate not to have gone straight to the Goodman from high school. Three years of the steel mills under my belt helped to curb any ego I might have had. In general, as long as I had a part—any part—I was happy.

I developed that attitude early. By my second year at the Goodman, I realized that I was never going to be a leading man. Even there the other boys were cast in leads, while I was always the friend, the father, the brother, the second part. But it honestly never bothered me because I was always working and that was all I cared about. Frankly, half the time, I thought I had the more interesting role anyway.

This would prove to be an attitude that would serve me well

when I got to New York. If leading-man parts did not come my way at the Goodman, I knew when I arrived in New York that I was never going to be a big star. I'm sure that this realistic point of view saved me a lot of heartbreak. I remember thinking that with some luck maybe I could be like a Walter Huston, and that was a pretty decent goal.

It was also an attitude that, I believe, ultimately helped me to become a better actor, a better craftsman. God knows I didn't have a pretty face to help me get parts, so in order to stay in this profession, I realized early on that I'd better know my business. I decided I needed to act better than anybody else and I have always been competitive enough to think that if I worked at it, I could. I strived to be number one in the number two parts I knew I was destined to get.

It was also during my second year that I really began to feel secure in what I was doing on stage. Dr. Gnesin used to take a company out on tour every year for eight weeks during the summer. Often, it was Gnesin himself and ex-student Syd Breese playing the leads. Sometimes the pantomime teacher, Peggy Osborne, would go along. Usually they rounded out the company with recent graduates. When Dr. Gnesin came to me during my second year and invited me to join the company, I was elated. When he told me that I was the first second year student ever to be asked, I thought, "This is for me."

We headed from Chicago straight down to Corpus Christi in two cars and a truck. From there we worked our way back up to Chicago playing college towns throughout the Midwest with productions of *Dover Road* and *The Late Christopher Bean*. Along the way, we played Emporia, Kansas, Mona's hometown.

I borrowed one of the company cars and picked Mona up at Kansas State Teachers' College where she was taking a summer class. She showed me Peter Pan Park and told me all about how they used to have sunrise dances there when she was in high school. It really was one of the corniest little towns you could ever hope to visit.

I kidded her by saying it was such a two-bit town that I expected to see a cowboy riding down Main Street. She insisted she had never seen a cowboy in her entire life. I said, "Take a look." Sure enough, four cowboys were riding right down the middle of the street behind us. She never knew that I had seen them in my rearview mirror before I made my crack.

After the tour, as my third year got under way, Dr. Gnesin continued to support me, make me feel special, which was something I had never felt before. I remember when I was playing Satine (the part that Stanislavsky had played in Gorky's *Lower Depths*), one day during rehearsal, Doc came up to me and said, "Do you speak Serbian?"

I told him, "I spoke it at home."

He began to speak to me in Russian. In Russian, he said, "What I am telling you now is that I want you to capture the Slavic flavor. Be a Serb . . ." Every now and then he would interrupt himself and ask, in his British clip, "Do you understand what I'm saying?" I would nod and he would continue in Russian. I was flattered that he took it upon himself to direct me in his mother tongue, that he wanted to reach out for what was different about me—my heritage—in such a personal way. Subconsciously, I think this made me wonder if maybe what was different about me might actually be something good, that maybe it was also what might be special about me.

As I began to get my sea legs on stage, socially I was still very much the boy from Gary, even in my second year at the Goodman. I still had no money, of course, which didn't help my social life any. I had gone back to work in the mills during the summer break as part of the most menial labor force the mills had to offer, the labor gangs, but I couldn't make it through the year on what I had managed to save of my eighteen dollars a week. I broke down and asked my folks for a little help and somehow they came up with the figure of seven-fifty a week. That broke down into five dollars a week for food and two-fifty for rent. I was still sharing a room—bathroom down the hall—with Jimmy Russo at the crummy old stone castle of a place called the Albany Hotel on Rush Street.

I stretched the $5 for food by pilfering sandwiches from other people's brown bags. About thirty kids lived at home and brought homemade lunches every day. They'd toss them on top of the lockers and when things would get a little tough for me, I'd find a bag, check it out, and take out a sandwich. Only the sandwich. I figured they'd still have their piece of fruit, cookies, whatever. Besides, these were the kids who were going home to nice hot meals. I developed my sandwich snatching into a fine art. I began to know which bags held two sandwiches and I would take only one.

After a while, I could spot the bag belonging to my friend, Ralph Alswang, who later went on to become a magnificent scenic designer in New York. His brown paper bags were always a little greasy, which was a good sign. That signaled nice juicy leftovers in the sandwich. Roast beef was a good day. Corned beef was the best day. I ate his sandwiches for a good year and Ralph never said a thing.

Years later I met his mother for the first time in New York. I thanked her and said, "I'm so pleased to meet you because I used to eat your sandwiches every day."

Ralph was amazed. He never had any idea. Mrs. Alswang said, "If I'd known I would have packed extra."

I wonder if she would have pitched in and bought me a pair of coveralls, too. All the kids had to buy white coveralls for crew work. I think they cost six or seven dollars, but I didn't have that kind of money, so any time someone wasn't using theirs, I'd swipe them.

Once during the year, I worked crew on a play that was so well received that we were invited to bring it to a high school in a suburb of Chicago for two performances, matinee and evening. It happened to be the wealthiest suburb of Chicago. The plan was to save money by feeding all of us—actors and crew—at the homes of local families, two per home. My "partner" was a fellow named Frank Callendar who played the lead.

After the matinee, he and I were introduced to our "family" for the evening and returned home with them. We talked for a while, sitting in the poshest living room I had ever seen. Then dinner was served. I will never forget the seating. The mother and father each sat at a head of the table. Their two children sat on one side of the table, Frank and I on the other. The maid entered carrying the serving platters. Wouldn't you know it? I was the first stop on her route around the table. Everything was going fine at first. The meat. The potatoes. I managed to serve myself without making any heinous faux pas.

Then she emerged from the kitchen with the dessert. I must confess that I've had a big sweet tooth all my life, and when I laid eyes on this creation, my mouth began to water. It must have been eighteen inches high—a tiered masterpiece of meringue, strawberries, and whipped cream. I will never forget what that dessert looked like as long as I live. I stared at it for a long moment. I didn't know whether to start at the top or the bottom. I was lost. I wanted to dig in, but more than anything, I didn't want to make a fool of myself. Claiming that I never ate dessert, I declined and didn't take any. Instead, I watched as this bombe went all the way around the table and then disappeared out the dining room door back into the kitchen. I don't know

71

why I have never forgotten this incident. God knows I've made up for it in my time. But somehow that spectacular dessert symbolized everything I didn't know how to do, all the ways I felt uncomfortable and inferior. Twenty inches of whipped cream that took me a lifetime to climb.

I was afraid to cut into that dessert, and I was afraid to open my mouth for at least a year when I first arrived at the Goodman. Constantly hanging over me was the feeling that if I didn't make it I would be stuck in the mills forever. Also, aggravating that pressure was an underlying sense in everything I did—everything off stage, that is—that I didn't fit in. I was afraid that my poor education and shaky command of the language would give me away. I lived in fear of a malapropism. And I simply didn't have the tools to take care of the problem.

Consequently, I never became part of any of the little cliques that inevitably form in a school. Just as in high school, I was still not a joiner. At the Goodman, that was just as well. The second and third year schedules were even more hectic than the first. The children's series, the membership series, and classes kept me more than busy. But it never felt like work. By that point, I knew that I was doing what I was supposed to be doing.

Even when I felt the need to get away from it all, I was not one for gabbing with a group of kids. That only made me more uncomfortable. Instead, I would go down to the boiler room in the theater basement and sit for an hour or so with the janitor, a wonderful black man by the name of Harry. We all knew his name because one of the diction exercises that Mary Agnes Doyle forced us to practice ad nauseam was, "How did Harry's hat happen to hang in the hall?" The recurring "h" sound was excellent for breath control. Harry, the janitor, used to hear us practicing in the halls and would always answer, "Because Harry put it there."

Harry was a closet musician and I would often come upon him playing his saxophone. He would play it with some sort of muffling device on the bell so that he could work on his fingering without bothering anyone. And I would listen. Sometimes we'd talk about music. Or whatever. He offered me a great escape from the atmosphere of the school, which sometimes got to be a little too hoity-toity for me with all the kids putting on airs and practicing to be big stars. Sometimes I just couldn't take it any more.

Of course, I did my share of pretending to know more than I did. Syd Breese taught a makeup class to first year students. It happened to be scheduled first thing in the morning and he hated getting up early, so he offered me two dollars a week to teach the class for him, one dollar a session. I didn't know any more than the students who were just one year behind me, but I put on a good show.

That was one of the lessons you learned early at the Goodman: give it a hundred percent even when you were faking it. We did a lot of crazy things—drama school versions of typical college hijinks—but we always tried to pull them off with style. Once, a buddy and I took a curtain call for a play we weren't even in, *Heidi*. We strutted on out there, stood tall in our elaborate Tyrolean gear, and bowed deeply, smack in front of Heidi herself, Mona.

I guess it took the curse off all the hard work and long days on crew. At the end of one of those long days, Corpy asked me if there were a part in any particular children's story I might want to play. I told her, "Rip Van Winkle," and soon after, she presented me a script of Rip Van Winkle.

The one or two minutes I spent as Rip Van Winkle waking up after twenty years asleep offered some of the most fun I have ever had on stage. I came to life extremity by extremity; first one hand stretching through the overgrowth, then the other, then a leg, and finally my head. I whistled for my dog but I had no teeth. I tried to straighten up but my back was too stiff. I reached for my rifle, but it fell apart in my hands. I pulled no punches. It was children's theatre; all for fun. That gave you permission to play.

Though the Goodman curriculum was designed as a three year program, they were beginning to initiate a fourth year, mostly for people who intended to stay on and teach. I think Dr. Gnesin was hoping to develop a repertory company. I was flattered when he invited me—and Mona—back for the fourth year. It was an almost irresistible offer: teach a class and get the chance to play some leads for fifty dollars a week. Dr. Gnesin even suggested I take a few courses elsewhere and earn my teaching credentials.

I was more than tempted. I was finally happy somewhere. I was doing what I wanted to do. Yet something gnawed at me. I think deep down I was afraid the Goodman could end up trapping me, just in a different way from Gary. I was afraid of ending up complacent and unchallenged. If I was going to be a professional I would have to take the next step. New York or Hollywood. This time no one was daring me to gamble on myself. No one except me.

I knew that my decision to come to the Goodman, made rather tentatively and without any support three years earlier, had been the right one when Dr. Gnesin came to me right before graduation. He informed me I was the only one in my class who had gotten straight A's. Since I had always felt that I could never achieve anything academically, this meant more to me than Doc could have known. It also proved to me that the theater was really where I belonged because I had so enjoyed all the work. Not one minute of what could have been three brutally exhausting years had felt like a struggle.

I remember the graduation ceremony at the Goodman. Since we were a part of the Art Institute, we were officially part of a graduating class of some two hundred people. But only fourteen of us Goodman kids from my original first year class had made it to graduation. Some couldn't take the grind; for others, it was suggested at various points along the way that they leave if the faculty decided they were just wasting their time.

Dr. Gnesin delivered the commencement speech. "Years from now, when you people are reaching your peak, if by some chance you see us somewhere, don't stop, but give us a wave as you pass by . . ." Today, I give him a little nod nearly every day when my eyes fall on the picture of him that hangs in my study.

But in June of 1937, I couldn't envision my future. I walked up to Dr. Gnesin, this man who had challenged me to take a gamble on myself. He shook my hand and handed me my diploma. Then I continued across the stage to where a girl was waiting just in the wings.

She put out her hand. "Five dollars please."

"What for?" I asked her.

"For the sheepskin."

Who had five dollars? I barely had the sixty cents to get myself back home to Gary on the South Shore. I handed her back the diploma.

In 1978, the Chicago Art Institute presented me with an honorary doctorate. As I stood before the graduating class, I told this story. I closed by saying I was still afraid to walk across the stage for fear that someone was going to ask me for five dollars. No one did, of course, but I still don't have my original diploma.

Chapter 3

1937. October came. If Gary has a pretty time of year—which is a big "if"—October is not it. The weather begins to match the constant rain of gray soot. Gradually, everything around me began to look the way I felt . . . bleak, colorless, and full of despair.

I had graduated from the Goodman four months earlier, but I wasn't taking the theater world by storm. Instead, there I was, working at the Cloverleaf Dairy Company driving a special delivery truck. No particular route. When a grocery store was shy a few quarts, I ran them over there. When unexpected company arrived on a customer's doorstep, I delivered the extra cream for their coffee. My dad had gotten me the job. He figured it was better than the mills. It had been good enough for him all those years. It would be good enough for me.

I couldn't help but think that maybe my father had been right, maybe acting school accomplished nothing more than postponing the inevitable. Maybe I was destined to drive a milk truck for the rest of my life. That horrifying thought began to eat away at me. But I kept plugging away at the dairy, trying to save up enough money to get to New York. I gave myself a deadline. The first of the year.

Miraculously, I didn't have to wait that long. "Sudbina," fate, stepped in. A telegram arrived for me from Robert Ardrey, a Chicago playwright now living in New York. He had seen me in a few plays at the Goodman where his sister was a sometime student. Once, she had introduced us backstage after I'd been in *The Show-off* and I remembered him mentioning that there might be something for me in one of his plays if and when he could get it off the ground in New York. He had written a play that had actually run on Broadway for a short while; so being young and naive, I had no reason to think his next play wouldn't be produced, too. He said he'd contact me and he did. Isn't that the way it always works? I presumed it was.

The telegram said that Herman Shumlin, a producer who was riding high on the success of *Grand Hotel* and *The Children's Hour*, was going to produce his new play. It was called *Casey Jones*, and Ardrey thought there was a small part in it for me.

I was on my way. My folks knew that I had been saving to go, but they were disappointed—shocked actually— when it happened so fast. My dad must have thought that the more time that went by, the more hours I logged on that milk truck, the harder it would be for me to leave. He was hoping I would give in to a steady paycheck. But neither of my parents said a word. As for me, I couldn't give my notice at the dairy fast enough.

A few days later I boarded the Greyhound at the Gary station in the afternoon, traveled the rest of that day, all night, and into the following evening. I don't think I said two words to the man sitting next to me. I know I didn't sleep a wink. I couldn't believe I was headed to New York and that a part was waiting for me! I must admit I was terrified and profoundly impatient. Every rest stop irked me. If I didn't get there right away, maybe they'd give my part to someone else. Already I was calling it "my part."

As I jostled along on the bus, I kept hoping that Jimmy Russo, my former Goodman roommate now looking for work in New York, had received my letter and would be at the station waiting for me. I was thrilled to find him and his girlfriend, Cam Staneska (another Goodmanite), waiting there. They took me to their building where they had reserved a room for me. It was above a pawn shop, about a block from Bloomingdale's. A room with a bed. That was it. But that was all I needed.

We spent the night talking. Jimmy had been in town six months; he knew the ropes. Playing the old-timer, he filled me in about how everything operated.

"No reason to get up early. No one's in their office before ten."

That made no difference to me. I barely slept and was dressed by six A.M., ready to tackle the big city.

It may have been October, but fall hadn't hit New York yet that year. It was hot. Sweltering. I wore my one dark suit and tie, and it didn't take long before the heat and my nerves had me perspiring like mad. The sweat began pouring off me the minute I stepped outside. Jimmy came with me. Like every young actor, he'd get in the door any way he could.

We made our way down Forty-second Street, a street that saw a lot of action at one time but, by now, had lost all its real glamour. We passed burlesque houses, hot dog stands, gaming arcades—all run down.

By the time we entered Shumlin's second floor office between Broadway and Eighth Avenue, all I hoped was that I wouldn't leave a puddle of sweat on the floor. Posters from his big hit plays decorated the outer office. I walked up to the receptionist. No appointment. Nothing. (This was getting to be my usual routine by now.) I just showed up in my cheap suit, which now stuck to me like a clammy second skin.

"Robert Ardrey sent me a telegram." I handed it to her.

"Just a minute," said the secretary.

She disappeared into the inner office and came back out a moment later. "Mr. Shumlin will see you in a minute."

Jim looked at her and had an idea.

He whispered, "You know what? It's so hot, I'll go downstairs and buy us a Coke and I'll buy one for her, too. And she'll thank us. And then she'll put in a good word. That's the way you do things here. That's how you make things happen. If you can get to the girl, you're in."

I was mortified. I begged him, "Jesus, don't do that. Please don't embarrass me." I just didn't want him to blow it for me. That's all I cared about. I wasn't thinking about anything else. I was just sweating.

When I finally stepped inside, Shumlin looked me up and down, then said, "With a name like yours, I expected to see a great big Russian with a beard. And here you are. An American boy with an American face." I guess that pegged me. Good ol' Mladen Sekulovich from the heartland of America.

It baffled Shumlin. Finally, he asked, "What nationality are you?"

"Serbian. First generation."

He didn't much care. "Well, it doesn't matter," he said. "I'm not doing the play anyway. Walter Huston refused to play the lead and I won't do the play without him."

First interview. First rejection. My heart sank. I was totally unprepared for failure, especially so fast. After all, I had my telegram. I was healthy and strong and ready for work. I had quit a perfectly good job. Shumlin must have seen the dejection on my face. He asked, "Do you have an agent?"

"No."

"See Jane Broder in the Times Building. I'll call her and tell her you're coming."

I thanked him, but got out of there as fast as I could. I couldn't stand the humiliation of being rejected. Little did I know how bad it could get. At least this time it didn't have anything to do with me personally. He couldn't cast me in a play that wasn't going to be produced. But my stomach turned anyway.

That was a feeling I would never learn to get over. Through the years I learned to deal with it a little better, I suppose. You have to grow more philosophical; you learn to put things in perspective. But to this day, the thought of being humiliated just because you want to work is still the worst thing I can imagine happening to a human being. And when it is you yourself that you are selling, the humiliation cuts deeper than anything else.

I barely looked at Jimmy waiting in the outer office.

"Come on," I told him, but he was still trying to make his pitch to ingratiate himself with the secretary. While he was thanking her, turning on the charm, I stood at the door thinking we'd never get out of there. I couldn't breathe until I was out of that office.

Jimmy knew where Jane Broder's office was, so we headed straight there. Some ten other actors were waiting in her outer office when Jimmy and I arrived. Finally, Broder herself came out.

"Nothing for you, nothing for you, nothing for you . . ." She went right down the line. She came to Jimmy. "Nothing for you . . ."

I was sitting next to him. She hardly looked at me. "Nothing for you."

I have no idea whether or not Shumlin had called to say I was on my way. It all happened so fast that I didn't have time to tell her he had sent me. I didn't have the nerve either. We were out of there in record time.

I was on a roll. Two rejections on my first day in New York. In the first hour! I was reeling. Is that it? Is that what I've come here for?

I met Bob Ardrey at a little Italian joint for lunch. I wanted to yell at him for bringing me to New York, but I knew it wasn't his fault. Besides, he was already depressed that his play was not going to be produced. I was too baffled to be depressed. I was still trying to figure out what had just happened to me. Over a cheap dish of spaghetti, a 7-Up, and a lot of bread, we started talking about what to do next.

He asked, "How long can you stay?"

That was easy. "As long as a hundred and seventy-five dollars can last."

Bob said, "Stay."

He promised he'd call. I'm sure he felt responsible for my being stuck with no work.

I retreated to Jimmy's apartment. In those days we all did everything out of financial necessity, so in order to save money, Cam moved in to Jimmy's two-bedroom and I took her room. That made the whole arrangement cheaper for everyone.

I spent the next few days making the rounds with Jimmy. We

would read in the paper whoever was casting a play and we'd arrive in their office bright and early. Then around noon, a bunch of us out-of-work actors would congregate at Walgreen's and swap information. We'd send our friends to the offices we had been to that morning and we would go to the offices they had already visited in a sort of round robin of pounding the pavement. I saw a lot of outer offices in those few days: George Abbot, Max Gordon, Brock Pemberton, George S. Kaufman, The Theater Guild. I met a lot of secretaries. I learned to say the horrible phrase that sticks in every actor's throat: "Anything for me?"

Finally, after several days, Bob Ardrey called. He said I should meet him the next day at the Sardi building where the Group Theatre had its offices. He would introduce me to two Group members, Harold Clurman and Elia Kazan.

I had never heard of those two men specifically, but I knew of the Group Theatre. They had brought their groundbreaking production of Clifford Odets's *Awake and Sing!* to Chicago when I was at the Goodman, but I had not been able to afford a ticket. What I did know was that the Group Theatre was as close to an American repertory theater as you could get. And they were a company who put on plays continually. If you could get in with them, you were working. I didn't really know anything about their philosophy as yet, and I certainly didn't know anything about their politics (nor would I ever really care), but I did know that they were a company that most New York actors were dying to work with. What would they want with me?

I thought, "Here goes. Another rejection." I went to bed that night racking my brain over how to make a good impression. I couldn't come up with a single thing.

The next day I walked into the Group Theatre offices on the fourth floor of the Sardi building on Forty-fourth Street. I left Jimmy behind. I didn't want any more arguments about bribing secretaries with Cokes. I was shocked to find Peggy Osborne, a teacher of mine from the Goodman, sitting in the waiting room. She intended to go back to the Goodman, but had always wanted to be part of the kind of theater that the Group was becoming. They called her in for her interview and I sat there in the waiting room . . . and theatrical waiting rooms are not like doctors' offices. No magazines to distract you. You just sit and wait and stare at the competition. It seemed like forever before Peggy came out again.

She only said, "Good luck, Sukie," then left me to wait some more.

Finally, it was my turn. I steeled myself for another rejection, walked in ready to turn around and walk out. Bob Ardrey was already sitting in the office and he introduced me to Clurman and Kazan. Clurman was on his feet the whole time, pacing energetically. He asked me a lot of questions. Why had I chosen the Goodman? Why not the American Academy in New York?

Kazan sat quietly and listened. Though he didn't say anything for the longest time, he had an intensity about him. His short, stocky body had a different energy from Clurman's; he was more like a coiled spring. After about twenty minutes he finally said, "Bob tells me you worked in the steel mills." I said, yes, I had, and Kazan fell silent again. Nothing was said about me personally. Nothing was said about a job. So, I figured, this is just a different method of rejection. The easy letdown.

But when I was about to leave, they mentioned they were mounting a play called *Golden Boy* by Clifford Odets. They thought there might be something in it for me. They would call in a month. I wondered if my friend, Peggy Osborne, had put in a good word for me, or whether they were just being polite.

That was one very long month. Even in those days, one hundred and seventy-five dollars did not last forever. I was running out of money and intestinal fortitude. My gut wrenched every time I walked into an office only to hear a girl behind a desk tell me, "Nothing today." Half the time, she didn't even look up. That month was filled with a chorus of: "Come back in a few weeks," "Not casting today," "Sorry."

I ached to hear just one of those office girls say, "Stay and meet the director," "Come on in and talk to the producer," "I'm sure there's a part for you." Instead I met a whole new kind of rejection. Rejection so impersonal, so matter-of-fact, that I was angry with myself for letting it get to me. These girls obviously had nothing against me personally, so why did their offhand rebuffs turn my stomach so badly? I realized that job security for these office girls meant saying "no." Taking a chance on a new face meant running a risk. No one wants to be the first one to gamble on an unknown. But that didn't make hearing the "no's" any easier.

Finally, a card came addressed to me, Mladen Sekulovich. It read: REPORT TO REHEARSALS OF *GOLDEN BOY* AT THE BELASCO THEATER AT 2:00 P.M. Signed MICHAEL GORDON (a Group member).

I arrived at the theater a little early. An elderly man sitting inside the stage door asked what I wanted. I held up the card for him to see as though it were a magic ticket. He looked at it and told me to wait in the green room.

I thought, "At least I'm in the green room. At least I'm backstage in a New York theater. This is the big leagues." But in the back of my mind I wondered if this was going to end up just a different road to another rejection. A short, roly-poly young man, almost bursting with energy, was also waiting. He said, "I'm here to see about a part in *Golden Boy.*"

"Me too." I wondered if it was possible that the two of us could be up for the same part. I'm sure he was probably wondering the same thing.

Not so. We both wound up getting parts. And when we began rehearsals, I learned his name. It was Martin Ritt, and he went on to become a brilliant and renowned film director. I don't know about Marty, but I felt so lucky not to have to read for the part. My mental block about reading left over from my grammar school days still handicapped me. I don't think I ever got a job in my life that I had to do a cold reading for. But at the end of 1937, Marty, like me, was absolutely thrilled simply to have a job.

The next step for both of us was to join Actors' Equity. As usual, I didn't have enough for the fee. I opted for the installment plan, but I would have gladly skipped lunches to be able to carry that membership card in my wallet.

I imagine both Marty and I made the same salary: twenty-five dollars a week, rehearsal pay, to be upped to forty dollars when the play opened. Who cared? I was a working actor. A professional.

The Belasco Theater became my home away from home. And it was magnificent. Belasco had built the theater as a real working plant. It had the stage proper, one rehearsal hall upstairs on the third floor, and another downstairs in the lounge. It also held enormous space for costume storage backstage and for electrical equipment in the basement under the stage.

Most of the players in the Group knew each other well, so there was none of the usual lag time when everyone has to feel each other out, get adjusted. Rehearsals began with our director, Harold Clurman, giving us a pep talk. He had enough energy to propel everyone in the room. He pounded himself on the chest, pulled at his cheeks, and rubbed his hands together until you thought flames were going to shoot from his body any minute. As he analyzed the play, the characterizations, the relationships, he inspired us all. I had a total of four lines in the third act, but I felt ready to get out there and play Hamlet.

Clurman declared that this play had to be a hit. The future of the Group depended on it. I kept thinking, "What group? Am I a member of the Group? I just got here." The word "group" had always terrified me anyway.

But I was in awe of names like Frances Farmer, Morris Carnovsky, and Luther Adler. Photographs of two other members, Art Smith and Roman "Bud" Bohnen, had hung in the green room of the Goodman. They had been members of the Goodman's original repertory company from before it had become a school, so their faces were familiar to me; I had spent three years passing their photos.

Harold Clurman, this debonair man unlike anyone I had ever met, possessed both the best wardrobe and most brilliant intellect I had ever encountered. He carried on for two whole days. Two days of talk. He was a great scholar of the theater and could light a fire under you like no one else.

However, he—like everyone in the Group—used a vocabulary that was a foreign language to me. I didn't know what they were talking about half the time. The terminology whirled around my head as I struggled with how to tackle my tiny role. The spine of the character. The action. The physical action. A beat. What the hell was Clurman talking about?

After the two days, we got on our feet to get to work. The first week went by and I still hadn't done anything. Then the second week. I was still observing.

Finally, the third week came. My day. I was playing the manager of a fighter killed by the Golden Boy in a championship fight. I was just about to make my entrance when Clurman stopped the rehearsal and took me aside.

"You told me you came here by bus from Gary, Indiana," he began.

"Yes," I said. "That's right."

"The bus is full. You're riding along all afternoon having a

87

great conversation with another young man. You don't know him but it's relaxing and the time is going by. Night falls. You try to sleep a little. Suddenly the bus is in a terrible accident. It rolls off a cliff. There are no lights, but you manage to climb out a window. You start to help others, pulling people out one by one, then finally the police come. Then the fire trucks. Ambulances. Later, after about three hours, another bus comes and they ask you all to get in. The new bus will take you to New York. Everyone gets in and takes their same seat. You do, too. You ride along for an hour or so when you suddenly realize that the seat next to you is empty. That was the one person they took away in the ambulance. Covered with a sheet."

Clurman looked at me. "That's the moment I want. The realization. No histrionics. No shouting. No screaming. Just that moment."

That was my first bit of professional direction. And it worked. He dropped all the Group talk and painted a picture for me with a vocabulary that meant something to me. He made it vivid and real.

Elia Kazan, at that time, was an actor with the Group. A few years earlier, before I arrived in New York, he had played the taxi driver, Gadget, in Clifford Odets' *Waiting for Lefty*. He had made such an impression that the nickname "Gadge" would stick with him forever. In *Golden Boy*, Kazan played Fuseli, the gangster. His acting fascinated me. He had a quirky, stylized quality, yet he made everything he did believable. His performance was real and honest, yet full of sharp edges. I marveled at how he managed to pull this off. I watched as he made his entrance. He looked at Luther Adler, the Golden Boy, and stood at a jaunty angle with all his weight on one foot. Then when he took his hat off, as though to a lady, his hand came up slowly with a loose wrist, took the tip of his hat, removed it from his head and held it at arm's length from his body. There was a grandeur in his movement on stage, his carriage, that was completely opposite from how he appeared in his daily life.

It was Kazan, along with another Group actor, Roman Bohnen, who approached me one day after about two weeks. "Did you ever think of changing your name?"

"No."

"Would you change it if we asked you to?"

I thought for a minute. "Why?"

"Well," Kazan went on, "everyone thinks the Group is a Jewish organization and Sekulovich sounds Jewish."

"But I'm not Jewish," I explained, figuring that would take care of the problem.

It didn't. Whether or not I really was Jewish didn't seem to be the point at all. They wanted me to change my name. I asked to have some time to think about it, but it didn't take long. Insecure beyond words, I immediately suspected that this was just another way of letting me down. Maybe I wasn't delivering and they had concocted the plan of dropping me if I wouldn't change my name. I wasn't about to give them that excuse.

I suppose it would have happened sooner or later. After all, Mladen Sekulovich would have left no room for anyone else's name on a marquee. So I flipped the "l" and the "a" in my first name and came up with Malden. My first inclination was to steal my brother's name and make it Milo Malden, but I decided that sounded too pretty, too artsy, so I went with Karl, which had been my mother's father's name. It seemed to work. And that was that. But in the back of my mind, I worried about what they would think back in Gary. Specifically, what would my father think?

Underneath my agreeability, I felt enormously guilty. I would spend most of my film and television career trying to make up for that guilt by interjecting the Sekulovich name wherever I could—engraved in a nameplate on someone's desk, called out as part of army roll call or to a detective in the station house in *The Streets of San Francisco.*

Golden Boy opened in December. The play was not a smash hit, but received a lot of favorable notices. I felt that we were in for a good run and that was a marvelous feeling.

Of course, even in those days you couldn't do much with forty dollars a week. It paid my rent and bought me food. I managed to send my clothes to the laundry on occasion, but there was certainly nothing left over to save.

I indulged myself in one luxury, if you could call it that. Every so often, I would buy myself a ticket to the Paramount Theater. They let you in for fifty cents before noon. I would go all by myself and spend a few hours there. First, the movie. Then the major attraction as far as I was concerned: the big band. Oddly enough, that was the draw for me—not the movies. I heard all the greats there: the Dorseys, Benny Goodman, Gene Krupa, Harry James, Glenn Miller, Duke Ellington. All of them. Sometimes, the show included a dance act. Or a singer. Once I even got to see a skinny kid with a big voice drive the crowd wild. His name was Frank Sinatra. The big bands were my one great treat.

That, and the work.

I have never in all my career witnessed more dedicated people than the members of the Group. Organized in the late twenties and early thirties, the Group Theatre devoted itself to putting on plays for the people, proletariat plays. They believed that the play came first, the actors second. Even their curtain calls were democratic. In Group productions, everyone stood shoulder to shoulder together. There were no star turns.

Three months later, Bob Ardrey called me once again to let me know that he had just sold a play called *How to Get Tough*

About It, which was going to be directed by Guthrie McClintic. He hoped I would be in it. I was so grateful for all that Ardrey had done for me that I couldn't turn him down, though I hated to give up a sure thing. A bird in the hand and all that. Besides, I didn't know how to get out of *Golden Boy.* Too much work— that was a dilemma I never thought I'd have to worry about.

I asked Bob, "How do I get out of the play I'm already in?"

He was kind enough to speak to Clurman on my behalf and Clurman gave me his blessing to leave. The part in the Ardrey play was a breeze for me. A steel worker. I didn't have to dig too deep for that. The whole experience was far less grueling than working with the Group. Whereas Clurman could analyze a character brilliantly, he could not move actors around on a stage. Maybe that aspect of directing simply didn't interest him. I don't know. But if you were not free enough to move on your own, he left you utterly lost.

McClintic, on the other hand, was a more traditionally commercial director. He had no problem with blocking, but could not have been less interested in character analysis and motivation. After coming from the Group, my head swam to find myself landed under his direction.

McClintic ran an infinitely more carefree rehearsal than the Group. No pressure. A lot of joking, a lot of laughter. Being young and intent on learning as much as I could, I preferred the Group's style. I was still feeling my way and the lightheartedness of McClintic's rehearsals distracted me. Rather than making me feel relaxed, it made me nervous. I was all wound up and concentrating every fiber of my body on the task at hand. It was serious business to me, so I felt out of sync with the atmosphere.

Bouncing from one school of working to the other, as I would continue to do for the next few years, offered me an invaluable training ground. The Group steeped themselves in a gritty reality. McClintic's whole organization had big-time Broadway class, symbolized by McClintic himself who was married to Katherine Cornell, a first lady of the theater.

However, McClintic's golden touch didn't work with Bob Ardrey's play. It failed miserably and closed after a couple of weeks.

I was just beginning to panic about where my next job would come from when I got a call from the Group. *Golden Boy* was still running and they were asking if I wanted my old job back. Needless to say, I jumped at the chance. Once through my lines with the stage manager and I was back in the old routine.

I was especially glad to be back in *Golden Boy* when they announced that the play would be going to London that summer for a three month run. Marty Ritt and I were all ready to splurge on a couple of tailor-made Savile Row shirts. At the last minute, word came down that two official Group members (as opposed to peripheral unofficials like the two of us) would be stepping into our parts for the trip.

As the Group was packing up, so was I. It was the beginning of summer and no one would be casting again until early fall. Basically, I was stupid. I didn't have a clue about summer stock or other avenues of work. I couldn't afford to stay in New York, so it was back to Gary. That's what I had always done after each school year at the Goodman, so I figured that's what I had to do now. Back to the dairy or, God forbid, the mills.

The mills it was. A labor gang. Backbreaking work. Cheap pay. But it didn't matter to me. Right before I left New York, McClintic called me to say he had optioned a play called *Missouri Legend*. His parting words to me were "See you the first week of September." The promise of a job back on Broadway kept me going through that long, miserable summer back home at work in the mills.

September couldn't come fast enough. And when it finally arrived, I was off—on a train this time. The speed was worth the extra money.

I knew my way around New York a little better this time so I checked into a cheap hotel and immediately headed for McClintic's office. McClintic asked me, "What did you do this summer?"

"I went home and worked in the steel mills."

He threw back his head and laughed. A good, long laugh. "You're the only actor I know who works in the steel mills between engagements."

I signed a contract for seventy-five a week. I was coming up in the world. My part was a little bigger this time, too, and it was a good cast. Dean Jagger, Dan Duryea, Mildred Natwick, Dorothy Gish, and José Ferrer whom I already knew from *How to Get Tough About It*.

The play had all the earmarks of a hit. It was well researched and José was very funny in it. The audiences loved him. Duryea was perfect. When we opened on September 19, we were ready to make the beautiful Empire Theater our home for a long time.

I was back knocking on doors by the first of November.

My head was spinning. This is what I had been looking forward to all summer?

Around this time, I ran into a Goodman classmate, Kenneth Helmbach, on the street one day. He wasn't having much luck finding work either and he invited me to share his tiny apartment with him. Again, the bottom line was saving a few bucks. So I moved into his Ninetieth Street room with the bath down the hall. But I was even lonelier there. Kenny was a fine person, but he put considerably more energy into drinking than acting. He would come in at two or three o'clock in the morning; I'd be up and out by eight. We never had anything against each other; we were sharing a room but living very different lives.

I was impatient with the transplanted Goodman crowd who were more focused on having a good time than getting a job. I was probably a bloody bore, absolutely single-minded, but I felt that I had only so much energy. I did not want to dilute it with a social life. I didn't even allow myself a fallback position. I never considered getting a job in Macy's basement or flipping burgers while waiting for the next part to come along. I would only work in the theater.

I found a kindred spirit in another familiar face from Goodman—Mona Greenberg. Now calling herself Mona Graham, she was looking for work in the theater, too. She was living with her aunt and uncle in Brooklyn, trying to get auditions just like me. Occasionally, we'd run into each other at the out-of-work actors' hang-out, Walgreen's. I was surprised by how happy I was to see Mona and we began to see more and more of each other. We were two lonely people looking for companionship, but it was more than that. I was comfortable with her, a feeling I had experienced very rarely in my life. I suppose on some level, I felt she understood me and that allowed me to relax and be myself around her in a whole new way. She wasn't impressed with herself like so many of the struggling actors were, so I felt like I didn't have to try to impress her.

We both knew the agony of pounding the pavement. I was in the depths of a depression, convinced I would never work again, when a telegram arrived one day. It was from the Group. They were still on the road with *Golden Boy*, but wanted me to rendezvous with them in Philadelphia to start rehearsing a new play, Irwin Shaw's *Gentle People*. I could have the part of an Irish cop.

My return telegram said, "When?"

Their answer came, "Now."

I was off to Philly.

Already rehearsing the new play were Sam Jaffe, Lee J. Cobb, Franchot Tone, Harry Bratsburg (now Harry Morgan), Sylvia Sydney, Marty Ritt, and Kazan. To make it worth my while, they gave me back my old part in *Golden Boy* (now for the third time)! We finished the run in Philadelphia and returned to New York to begin rehearsals in earnest.

Gentle People meant back to ensemble acting. Whereas Mc-Clintic's focus had been to create star vehicles, the Group didn't view theater in that way. The play came first. They saw themselves as artists, all equally engaged in the artistic process regardless of their status within the Group or the particular production. McClintic was in the business of Broadway. I consider myself enormously lucky to have had to adapt to both ways of working so early in my career. Somewhere between the two schools of thought, I was forced to discover what worked for me personally.

Although I adored working with the Group, their holier-than-thou philosophy about the theater annoyed the hell out of me. I admired that they were striving to perfect the art of the theater and I agreed with them that the play came first, but I resented that they poo-pooed everyone else's approach. If you weren't doing it their way, they demeaned you. To me, it was all theater, all part of the same tapestry.

So, once again, I found myself part of a group—this time, literally the Group with a capital "G"—but looking in from the outside, from the edges. Here I WAS the common man the Group wanted to praise, maybe more than any of them. However, I just couldn't go along with their attitude one hundred percent; not when it left so many people out. Besides, I was never one for participating in their philosophical or political discussions after work.

But miracle of miracles, I clicked with Mona. She was more

gregarious than I, but she, too, wasn't comfortable with a lot of the Goodman kids and their hard partying. We were the two squares. Mostly, we kept to ourselves. But that was just fine. That's what you do when you are falling in love.

The two people we did socialize with on occasion were Jim Russo and his girlfriend, Cam. We came up with the idea that the two girls should get an apartment together while Jim and I were living in the Sharon Hotel. The girls would cook for the four of us and, once again, we would all save money.

That plan lasted one night. Jim and I helped the girls move into their fourth floor apartment above a greasy Chinese restaurant on Forty-sixth Street. The girls ignored the strange looks the janitor shot their way as they passed in the hallway and didn't even give it a second thought when he asked them, "What are you girls doing here?" They would figure out what he meant before the night was up.

Later that evening when Cam was taking a bath, she overheard a conversation going on in another apartment through the air shaft. One girl was yelling to another, "Don't let that son-of-a-bitch out of here! He didn't pay!"

When Cam told Mona what she'd overheard, Mona, true to her good ol' Emporia upbringing, had absolutely no idea what she was talking about.

"Paid for what?" Mona asked.

Cam gave her a crash course in "business," and they immediately began piling furniture in front of the door to make sure no unwanted customers burst into their apartment during the night. They called Jim and me at the break of dawn and before we knew it, we were back over there moving them out. The janitor had the last word. "I told you girls you didn't want to be livin' here."

Mona was devastated to have lost the month's rent, sixty-five dollars.

She moved in with her mother who had come to town, but life got no easier. Mona hated the demoralizing process of looking for work. It may have sickened me, but it absolutely terrified her.

Socially, she was like me, out of her element. I was rehearsing at that time, but more and more at loose ends whenever I was not at the theater. Already, I loved everything about the theater except the lifestyle of an actor. I hated partying after a show and had no desire whatsoever to see or be seen at Sardi's or any of the other hangouts. The only thing that depressed me as much as carousing into the night was coming home to my dingy, god-awful room.

Mona and I were two miserable people trying to find something solid. I don't remember ever really "setting my sights" on her. We just kept gravitating to each other. If ever "sudbina," fate, was on my side, it was that Mona and I should find each other. I knew that I might never find that again. There was only one thing to do. Get married.

I remember when we announced our plans to Mona's mother, Marian. She absolutely froze. To her credit, she said nothing, but I knew what she was thinking: that she was going to have another mouth to feed. Mine.

Mona's father had died when she was a baby, and her mother had toted her from relative to relative throughout her childhood. They had no home of their own. Growing up, Mona was always the unwanted visitor who invaded some cousin's territory or slept on a cot in the hallway. In a childhood right out of Dickens, she went to thirteen schools by the time she graduated, two years early, from high school. But her mother had done the best she could for her and they always had each other. I'm sure the last thing Marian's dreams included for Mona was a starving actor with a face like mine.

My family, on the other hand, did not swallow their dismay quite so readily or silently. Once I told them I was getting married, the letters started arriving, one after the other. First from a close family friend, Aunt Mary of the Nikchevich clan, who was the most educated of our "kumovi" or extended family, and who, I'm sure my parents believed, could make the most persuasive case. She begged me to come home before rushing into anything, to have a face to face with the family. She warned me that I would be breaking my folks' hearts.

When that didn't work, my parents appointed my younger brother, Milo, to try his hand. I cannot remember whether his letter actually mentioned Mona's being Jewish or whether my parents' horror about the religious issue just spilled out between the lines. They reminded me of the Maravich girl I had seen quite a bit of while I was working at the dairy. When we were actually dating, they thought she wasn't good enough for me because she was an orphan who lived with her aunt. No dowry. But suddenly, the name Maravich sounded pretty good in comparison to Greenberg, dowry or no dowry.

So, without my parents' blessing, Mona and I planned to get married on December 18, 1938. Mona wanted to have the ceremony in the courthouse, but I insisted on some kind of chapel. I didn't care what denomination: Baptist, Catholic, anything. I just wanted a religious place, something spiritual.

There was no Serbian Orthodox church in New York then, and at that time, no priest would have married a "mixed" couple anyway. Mona's family had been one of the four Jewish families in the entire town of Emporia, Kansas, and she had no religious upbringing whatsoever, but the only religious place she would agree to was a synagogue. I didn't care. That was fine with me.

Mona's aunt and uncle had tried to dissuade her. They

worked the guilt angle. Mona's mother had recently moved to New York and how could she be so selfish as to leave her all alone after all Marian had sacrificed for her? But Mona stood up to them and set her Uncle Mitch about the business of finding a temple that would marry us. It wasn't easy. Rabbi after rabbi turned us down. This was just fine with Mitch; he thought a little adversity would persuade us to give up on the whole misguided idea. He was wrong. Finally, we found a rabbi in a conservative temple in Brooklyn who agreed. I have no idea why.

New York City law demanded we get a blood test. Somehow we ended up in a doctor's office on Park Avenue. I remember the nurse came out and asked us, "Who wants to go first?" With great bravado I said, "I will." I rose to my full six feet two inches, strutted on in and rolled up my sleeve.

I don't know what happened next. Mona said the next thing she heard was the nurse saying, "Now breathe deeply. Just breathe." Mona poked her head in to find me crumpled in a heap with the nurse waving smelling salts under my nose. I have never fainted before or since, and I have never been particularly squeamish, but that moment, that needle, meant, "Now you are a grown-up." Everything that had been overwhelming to me since coming to New York got me all at once. Needless to say, Mona stuck out her arm with no problem and the nurse finally drew my blood, too.

The next stumbling block was getting a day off from rehearsal to get married. I approached Harold Clurman. He asked, "Are you getting married in the morning or the afternoon?"

"In the morning," I told him.

"Okay. Be here after lunch around two o'clock."

Mona and I stood in the rabbi's study across from him at his desk. The rabbi was stuffing his mouth with a sandwich. He barely looked up as he said to me, "You'll have to take a Jewish name for the religious marriage certificate."

I looked at Mona.

"My grandfather's name was Marcus," she suggested. I had just changed my name—my Serbian name—because it sounded too Jewish even though it wasn't. Now here I was choosing a real Jewish name. I didn't know who I was anymore or what to call myself. I just said "yes."

The rabbi took a swallow of milk to wash down the sandwich before taking another bite. "Your children will have to be raised in the Jewish faith," he said.

Mona started to argue with him. Even at that young age, she was always ready for a juicy political or philosophical argument. He had no right; that would be our decision. But I just said, "Sure, sure." It was all going in one ear and out the other. All I knew was, I just wanted to get married.

Finally, he finished his lunch.

"Let's hurry this up. I just got back from a funeral and I have to go to another one right after this." He took a last sip of milk, swallowed hard, and rose to his feet.

We each had one person standing up for us. Acquaintances really, not even friends. Two of the hard-drinking, high-living crowd that Mona and I were always trying to escape. (Jimmy Russo was on the road.) Mona's mother was there, forcing a smile, as well as her aunt, uncle, and two cousins. I had no family by my side. There was no music. No flowers. Mona and I both wore the one suit we each owned. Hers was blue. I don't even remember what color mine was. Something dark. In our own way, I'm sure we made as unlikely a couple as my parents had.

The rabbi rushed through the ceremony. After all, the dead man couldn't wait. It was a lot like getting a shot. All this anxiety and buildup, then boom, it was over and we barely knew what hit us. At the end, we fell into each other's arms just as we had so many times before on stage at the Goodman.

We walked from the synagogue to Mona's aunt and uncle's for lunch. No limo, no tin cans, no rice. Despite the fact that she had been trying to talk us out of getting married only weeks before, Mona's Aunt Sophie really put herself out. Her best linens, china, silver. She tried to make it a celebration. Mona's mother, Marian, smiled weakly throughout the ordeal.

I could only stay about an hour, then I had to get back to rehearsal. But Mona didn't want her mother and her other relatives to know that I was going to work on our wedding day, so we left together.

They never knew that Mona headed for some friends' apartment to pass the rest of the afternoon while I headed for the theater. As I was walking to work, a slow, steady panic began to wash over me. What had I done? What if *Gentle People* failed? Would I ever work again? I could barely take care of myself and now I had the responsibility of taking care of a wife. What's more, I was in debt. I'd had to borrow fifty dollars from the Group to pay for our fabulous marriage ceremony.

I walked along Forty-fourth Street in a fog.

Kazan and I spotted each other approaching the theater from opposite directions.

I called to him, "You're late!"

"So are you!"

"I have an excuse. I just got married."

"So do I," Kazan explained. "My wife just had a baby boy."

Enough said. Together we walked through the stage door of the Belasco. Who had time to celebrate? We were so young and so passionate about our work that I suppose it was hard for us to figure out exactly where our real life was happening, inside the theater or out.

That night Mona and I rendezvoused back at the one-room dive of an apartment I had been sharing with Kenny Helmbach. Mona climbed the stairs of that ancient brownstone, stepped inside, and looked around the place. She didn't say a word. What could she say? The room was dark and dingy. There was no kitchen, no bathroom, just a couple of worn plush chairs and two twin beds. It was not the honeymoon suite at the Plaza. For at least one instant Mona must have wondered what she had gotten herself into. But she said nothing. Instead, as she had when we were Mr. and Mrs. Giant or Little Red Riding Hood and the Brave Hunter, Mona fell into my arms.

Exactly one week later—Christmas day—Mona and I had planned to have dinner at Schrafft's to celebrate our first holiday together. But first we had to dig through our pockets. She came up with forty cents; I had eighty. We decided on Chock Full O'Nuts instead. There was practically one on every corner. We stopped at the first one we passed.

We each ate a hot dog, a donut, and cup of coffee. But I remember that Christmas dinner more than any I have ever eaten before or since. I had a job in the theater in what promised to be a hit play. I was married to the sweetest girl I had ever met. And we weren't even broke. After our meal, we still had fifty cents left between us.

facing page:

Flight to the West

Chapter 4

Of course fifty cents didn't stretch too far, even in 1938. But at least I had a job. *Gentle People* opened the first week in January of '39 to good reviews. I was making seventy-five dollars a week. That was finally enough to think about paying bills and having a little left over, so Mona and I decided that we would make it our practice to try to save half of whatever we earned. That became our standard operating procedure.

Subtitled by Irwin Shaw *A Brooklyn Fable,* the play was about an old Jewish fisherman played by Sam Jaffe. When I first laid eyes on Sam I was stunned. I knew him as the beatific, ancient and eternal High Lama in *Lost Horizon,* which had come out the year before, but lo and behold, he looked exactly the same in person as he had in the movie. I had credited makeup for what was really Sam Jaffe himself. Lighting may have helped create that halo around his wonderful spun-sugar hair, but the serenity and wisdom he radiated came straight from his soul.

Co-starring with Sam in *Gentle People* was Roman Bohnen as the fisherman's Greek friend. These two characters are desperate to get out from under the thumb of a small-time hood played by Franchot Tone. Finally, they can think of no way out other than murder. I played a cop on the beat who passes by and stops to talk to the two old men, waiting for them to offer a sandwich.

I also understudied Franchot Tone, but I never gave that assignment much thought. I was too busy worrying about my little scene, never imagining I'd have to go on for the lead. I was never called to an understudy rehearsal and I was sure I was safe. Franchot Tone seemed to be the one cast member who never missed a performance. Sam Jaffe was out for a few days, then Sylvia Sydney, but never Tone. However, a few months into the run, Jaffe and Sydney both fell ill at the same time. Franchot Tone began to grumble. He was miffed that he was carrying the burden of the show. (He had also put some of his own money into the production and hoped that the star power would bring in fast profits. I can only wonder what Joan Crawford, his wife at the time, had to say about his ailing costars.)

One Friday night, he got fed up and threatened to be sick himself. He felt an unusually specific bug coming on; it was going to strike on Monday at eight P.M. Curtain time. I was scared stiff. Like an idiot, I had never looked at the part. And it was the lead. I spent the entire weekend memorizing that part. Mona cued me for so many hours I think she could have played any of the parts herself.

I arrived at the theater at five o'clock on Monday. Sure enough; no Sam Jaffe, no Sylvia Sydney, and no Franchot Tone. I began to feel a little woozy immediately; by the time I began running lines with the stage manager the room was practically spinning. The understudies for the other two actors were helpful. Having no roles in the play themselves, they knew their lines and were calm and ready. I was huffing and puffing through the scenes with the stage manager, absolutely sick with fear.

To add insult to injury, I couldn't fit into Tone's costume, which happened to include an elegant set of tails among his high-priced suits. Hysteria broke out backstage as everyone tried to find me something to wear. The poor stage manager who had to step into my little part was as hysterical as I was because he didn't fit into my policeman's uniform any better than I did into Tone's monkey suit. The whole backstage was in an uproar because of these stupid costumes. Of course, it was bigger than that. What it meant was no one was prepared. I ended up phoning Mona who hurried to the theater with the one suit I owned.

By the time she arrived, the sign required by Actors' Equity regulations had been posted outside the box office announcing that all three leads were going to be played by understudies in that evening's performance. There was nothing left for me to do but sweat it out and wait, changing into the one suit I would wear through the whole play.

By seven-thirty, a half an hour before curtain, people had begun to approach the box office. First a single. Then a couple. Then another party. Of the first fifteen people who walked up to buy tickets, ten walked away after reading the sign. Others turned in the tickets they had already bought.

The decision was obvious; they closed down the show for the night. I was never so relieved in my life, never so thrilled not to have to go on stage. After that night they shut down for two days while they hired Leif Erickson who was enough of a name to attract a little attention, certainly more attention than I could have.

❦

Basically, the next five years were a mess. It was a period of such chaos and confusion that I honestly have trouble recalling the sequence of events. Mona and I moved so often, it's hard to remember where we were living when.

It was a chaotic and frightening time, hysterical really. I always felt like everything was just on the verge of flying apart in all directions. I managed to get work in a series of plays—eight to be exact, most of which ran for less than a month. But mostly I remember the long, dry stretches when it seemed like I would never work again. They call it making the rounds, a fitting expression in more ways than one because you always feel like you're ending up right back where you started. Nowhere. "Making the rounds" traces the most vicious of circles, one that can end up becoming a downward spiral into despair.

During this period, I was grappling with a conflict within myself that would plague me throughout my career. The attraction of the nine-to-five job versus my passion for the theater. Countless mornings I woke up bright and early, healthy and strong, raring to go and full of energy, with nowhere to go and nothing to do. I would decide once and for all (or at least for a few hours) that I was really meant for a steady job. Something reliable. Security sounded better and better. What could be more appealing than getting a job and working your way up? After all, I had a wife to support now.

My brother, Milo, led that life—forty years at Sears Roebuck.

He was at the same place, but he was constantly moving up the ranks, and it was a life he could be proud of.

He could also leave his workday behind when he came home. Not me. When I got a part, it was with me twenty-four hours a day, and when I didn't, I carried the rejection. Acting is the only profession I can think of where the rejection is so personal that it can consume you. It's you you're selling and if you don't make the sale, it's you who was wrong—not what you manufactured or created. Just you.

During that time, I wasn't making the sale anywhere near enough. When you're young you want things now, and it sure wasn't happening that way. In retrospect, the long, slow process worked for me. There's no doubt I made a better tortoise than a hare. Of course, at the time, inching along felt like standing still.

I tried to keep in mind that the only way you could move forward and learn was by working. I was always—and still am—trying to learn. A different word for it, a better and more honest word, I suppose, is "workaholic." My philosophy was: Take the part no matter how small or how little they pay you. I have always believed there isn't a part I couldn't learn something from. But I also had to make a living.

Everything at that time was a matter of economics. It was getting a little old by then, but the bottom line in making any decision remained "What's the cheapest way to go?"

The answer to that question pushed Mona and me to move in with her mother in Brooklyn not long after we were married. She had a decent two bedroom apartment and it made good economic sense for all of us, but the price of saving money was high. The tension in that apartment was so thick you could barely see across the room. I was mortified that I couldn't make it on my own, that I had to ask for help. I felt that my mother-in-law, Marian, considered me another liability. Since Mona's father had died when she was a baby, her mother had worked hard to make sure Mona could do whatever she wanted to in life. And I represented throwing all that away. Although Marian never said a word, I felt that I had taken away the only thing in life she had—her daughter—and now I couldn't even support her. Maybe it would have been better if she had said something, if we could have cleared the air, but no one said a thing. She probably felt that she was in the way and I know I felt that I was in the way. Poor Mona, my wife of less than a year, was caught in the middle.

We moved in with Mona's mother during the run of *Gentle People*. After that play closed I weathered a miserable dry stretch, made all the more humiliating by our living with my mother-in-law. I felt like a real prize. The son-in-law every mother dreams of: an out-of-work actor! The whole situation compelled me to doubt myself and my choices more than ever. Maybe this really was the time to cut my losses and get out. How much later in life could I realistically change careers?

During this time, Dr. Gnesin of the Goodman visited Mona and me in New York. Before the evening was over Dr. Gnesin looked me in the eye and said, "Would you be interested in coming to the Goodman and teaching?" I was stunned.

He explained that he was beginning to think about retiring, maybe in about five years, and thought that if I came back and taught it would be with an eye toward taking over for him as head of the school.

My first reaction was, "But I don't know anything about the financial end of running a school."

"I've taken care of that," he said. "There is someone working in the box office who manages the bookkeeping. What I'm looking for is someone to take care of the artistic side of the school."

I looked at Mona and she looked at me. After a long moment,

she smiled and said, "That would take care of a lot of problems."

I knew what she meant. No more looking for work. No more heartache. We could go back to Chicago, to the Goodman where life was a constant buzz of activity, not what felt like eternal waiting. It would be a busy life, not just life on hold between parts. It was so tempting I could taste it. I promised Dr. Gnesin I would give his offer some serious thought.

"Just don't take too long," he asked.

As Mona and I walked home that night we kept enumerating the pros and cons. Finally, Mona said it was a decision I would have to make myself. She offered her usual, "Whatever makes you happy." I'm not sure that was what I wanted to hear from her that night. I was so confused I really wanted to be pushed, but Mona wasn't going to do the pushing. I knew in her heart of hearts she genuinely did mean, "Whatever makes you happy" in a way that very few people in this life ever do, but right then, knowing that her happiness was so intertwined with mine felt like more of a burden than a blessing.

For two days I kept weighing the decision, turning it over and over in my mind, as I continued to look for work. Should I become a big man in a smaller world? Should I be a semi-pro? Or should I stay in New York and struggle to be a small man in what felt like the biggest world, with no guarantee of ever making it?

One phrase kept ringing in my head. "Those who can do; those who can't teach." I'm not sure I really believe that, but it frightened me terribly. Would going back to the Goodman be an admission of failure that would gnaw at me for the rest of my life or would it set me on a path to a "normal" life that would mean security and fulfillment?

A phone call settled it. After another sleepless night thrashing this whole decision out, Guthrie McClintic called. "Are you available?"

He was offering me a part in The Playwrights' Company production of *Key Largo* starring José Ferrer, Uta Hagen, and Paul
Muni, a major film star at the time. I had worked for McClintic
before so I didn't even have to read; the part was mine if I wanted
it. It was a very small part but that didn't matter. The decision
was made instantly. The prospect of returning to the Goodman
had not for one instant excited me like this call from McClintic.
The butterflies in my stomach knew where my passion lay even
if my head didn't. I answered with my usual, "When do I start?"

I called Dr. Gnesin and reminded him that several years before he had dared me to gamble on myself. "I think I'm going to
try that again," I told him. "I hope you understand."

I was ecstatic to be back at work. Rehearsals began at the
Barrymore Theater, which was to become a lucky theater for
me. Mostly, I was an honest-to-God Paul Muni fan and, like the
rest of the cast, was thrilled to be working with the man who
had played Émile Zola and Louis Pasteur so brilliantly in films.
I couldn't wait to observe him in action. Here was an actor, not
a personality.

I knew that he had had the script long before any of the rest
of us since his attachment to the play had helped to get the
funding, yet in rehearsals, he held onto his script longer than
anyone, like a child's security blanket. Gradually, the other actors let go of their scripts, but Muni kept his. One by one, even
the other actors who had long parts got rid of theirs. But not
Muni. This was an eye-opener for me. What he was doing was
releasing himself from struggling to remember the lines. He
was adjusting to the people he was working with. He was figuring out how to work with them, against them, off them, and he
didn't want to worry about the lines. He was feeling out the material he had to work with; not just the script, but the actors too.
Then, one day, Muni let go of his script. The character exploded.

It was so magnificent to watch that I will never forget that day, that transformation.

Everyone—the critics and the public—had anticipated Muni's return to the stage eagerly, but the play was not the success everyone expected. It ran for about twelve weeks in New York and then, because most stars at that time feared the stigma of being associated with a play that didn't make its money back, we took it on the road.

Standard procedure meant negotiating a new contract. The road usually meant more money to cover additional expenses. Having no agent, I had to march into the production office myself. Typically, I was hesitant to go to the business manager of The Playwright's Company (the producing entity) to ask for more. I was twenty-eight years old by then, but I was still that naive kid from Gary, Indiana, petrified about having to talk money. I remember sitting on the subway phrasing and rephrasing what I was going to say, how I was going to say it. Mona went with me and tried to calm me down, but I got myself so worked up that I had to get up from my seat and run to the end of the car. I got there just in time to throw up between the subway cars.

I was still green around the gills when I walked into Victor Samrock's office. You couldn't ask to have a dearer, more sensitive man across the desk. He knew what I was there for, took one look at me, and offered me ten dollars more a week. I accepted and got out of there as fast as I could.

Many years later I attended a memorial service for Jessica Tandy in New York and Victor Samrock was there. He came up to me and said, "You want to talk money with me?" We laughed about it, but obviously my terror had made an impression on him that lasted fifty years.

I got to know Muni a little better on the road. He was big on taking walks in new cities and he often invited me to go with him. We'd walk and walk, maybe grab a bite of lunch. I was surprised to discover that this serious man who had played so many distinguished historical figures was actually quite funny, a joker. I remember once he got so annoyed waiting for a traffic light to change in Washington, D.C. that he marched into the middle of a busy street and did his best imitation of a traffic cop for a few minutes, motioning for the cars to stop and for me to cross.

The play (which was related to the film *Key Largo* in name only) had a lot of long speeches about the Spanish Civil War, speeches that contained Maxwell Anderson's message. And Maxwell Anderson speeches were notoriously dense and difficult to deliver. It fell to Muni to deliver these, often to a great deal of coughing accompaniment from the audience. After a while, he would be delivering the speeches, but you could see in his eyes that all the noise in the house was getting to him.

I happened to be on stage with him when one day, he stopped in the middle of one of these speeches, walked down to the footlights, shoved his hand in his pocket and pulled out a handful of coughdrops. Smith Bros.' finest.

"Try these!" he said, and he threw them out into the audience.

I stood statue still, waiting to see what was going to happen next. After a long moment, he turned around, walked back, and picked up where he had left off.

Once, when we got to talking, Muni found out my real name and was interested to learn that I had come from Slavic steelworking stock. He was fascinated because he had played a Polish coal miner in *Black Fury*. He had come away from the part with a great fondness for the Polish dialect, that whole way of speaking, and he loved to laugh at the particular style of misusing the English language characteristic to people of that descent.

I would say to him, "Hey Stash, you go to work tomorrow. I meet you on the corner where the streetcar bends."

He would answer, "Okay. I got a deal."

Or I would say, "Hey Stash, throw my mother over the fence some clothespins, yah?"

"Okay, I got a deal."

Or, if we had walked a long distance, Muni would turn to me and say, "Hey, Stash, you get taxi. I pay price."

He was fascinated by the rhythms of speech.

Despite the strong cast, *Key Largo* never quite made it, on the road or in New York. Basically, there was no escaping the fact that the play was a thesis, not a drama, and audiences didn't want to be lectured to.

So . . . another dry spell.

Fortunately, I discovered summer stock. Mona and I jumped at the chance to join a stock company run by Malcolm Atterbury in the Adirondacks, especially since Atterbury had already hired two dear Goodman friends, Duane and Phyllis McKinney. What's more, Peggy Osborne, the friend from Goodman who kept popping up, had been hired to direct the plays. We had one leg up because she would be doing plays she was familiar with, the same plays we had done at the Goodman.

We took the train up to Albany and then drove two hours to the playhouse out in the middle of nowhere. When we arrived at the "camp"—and it was very much like going to summer camp—in upstate New York, we were surprised at how deep into the wilderness the place was. How would audiences ever hear about the theater, let alone find it? But they did. Every performance was sold out—we played only weekend evenings—in a theater that sat two hundred fifty people.

So Mona and I spent two summers, the first two of our married life, in this spectacular setting—a dormitory room in a "lodge." It was our version of a honeymoon. We each got forty dollars a week but had to pay twenty a piece for room and board so we ended up with forty dollars between us. Our work routine harkened back to the Goodman days of prepping and performing two plays simultaneously, only now they rotated by the week instead of by the month.

As I said, it was a lot like going to camp. We got reacquainted with old friends and made new ones. When we would set off from the living quarters to trek the quarter of a mile or so to the theater, the woman who acted as a sort of dorm mother would give us each a pan and send us out to pick whatever berries were ripe along the way. Blueberries, strawberries, raspberries. The homemade pies served at dinner were almost an even trade-off for having the bathroom down the hall.

By our second summer there, Atterbury had spent the year building a nightclub so that people could see the show and then spend some more money having a drink afterward. The actors would come and mingle with the audiences as an added "attraction." There was also dancing, of course.

That second year an apprentice actor showed up who turned out to be a wonderful ballroom dancer. That, along with his handsome face, kept the girls lined up. Not to mention a gorgeous build—like an inverted triangle. Girls gravitated to Izzy Demsky like a magnet. Every weekend, a couple of girls would show up to see him, having driven up from different colleges where he had dated them during his own college career.

Despite his obvious sex appeal, it never occurred to me that this kid would some day be a big star. When he left at the end of the summer, Isador Demsky was still just a broke, out-of-work young actor trying to figure out what to do. One early morning he and I were doing a little jogging together when he asked me for advice. Of course, he really came to the right guy; I was still trying to figure out the game myself. But I was a couple of years older and I must have seemed like a veteran to him. I'd been

knocking around New York for all of two years already. I told
him to get a job to pay for a room and food. He was a nice kid
and did a fine job playing the juvenile in a couple of the plays so
I was happy to dole out my words of wisdom.

Little did I know that some thirty years later I'd be offering
the occasional word of advice to his son, Michael. Isador Demsky nabbed a big part on Broadway a couple of years after summer stock. When I saw him in that, I knew he was headed for
the stardom that would match his new name: Kirk Douglas.

Before long, as often happens, Kirk and I were traveling in
different social circles. But I have always had a warm spot in
my heart for Kirk and I believe the feeling is mutual.

After all, we went to camp together.

And to this day, Mona, who is a great dancer herself, still
claims that Isador Demsky was the best ballroom dancer she
had ever danced with, any time, anywhere.

I suppose Mona danced with him quite a bit that summer because I got called away before the summer was over. I received
a telegram from Harold Clurman inviting me to join the
Group's retreat at Lake Grove on Long Island. Emulating the
Moscow Art Theater, whenever the Group had a good year they
would go off someplace in the country to work—on themselves,
on new productions, whatever. Mona and I discussed it and
Mona convinced me I should go. I was worried about leaving a
paying job for a non-paying workshop, but Mona was able to
put that aside and look to the future. The Group could mean
work down the line. Mona stayed at Tamarack so that at least
one of us would continue to get paid.

It was a two-month intensive. Voice, diction, movement, the
works. For the first time the Group's vocabulary became part of
me. The Stanislavsky method. Line to line. A beat. Moment to
moment. The spine. Nowadays anyone who has ever set foot in

an acting class is familiar with these terms, but in those days it was all new. The Group was breaking theatrical ground by developing a vocabulary that could help the actor BE instead of ACT.

I was placed in Bobby Lewis's class. Bobby Lewis was a little gnome of a man with a somewhat affected manner, but he knew how to run an interesting class. He would study the class list and decide who was "on his dance card" for the day. Although Bobby was a good teacher, it didn't take much to get this group going; everyone's passions ran high.

I remember one improv that Bobby gave to Johnny Kennedy (who would later go to Hollywood as Arthur Kennedy). He informed Johnny he was to be an auctioneer, then he handed him a quart Mason jar and told him it was a Ming vase worth at least a million dollars.

Johnny proceeded to tell us all about the Ming Dynasty—its history, culture, art—all the while handling the jar as though it were the most delicate and valuable object on earth. I was amazed at how much he knew or was faking so glibly about the heritage and craftsmanship of this make-believe piece. Finally, he asked, "Do I hear a bid?"

It started. Hands were flying in the air. People were calling out. The price got up to three million when suddenly Marty Ritt spoke up. "You're all crazy. It's just a lousy Mason jar."

Kennedy held his ground with more determination and kept on selling.

The class became a duel between Marty Ritt's Mason jar and Johnny Kennedy's Ming vase. Everyone was in such an uproar that Bobby finally had to call a halt to the session, but the discussion went on for weeks. Mason or Ming. The class was divided in half. Reality versus the imagination. I went for the Ming. I thought, "Why else are we here?"

That summer at Lake Grove I began to hone a way to work.

Start with the truth (which, of course, is sometimes easier said than done). What is the truth of the character? What is his connection to the overall theme? How does this character contribute to the play as a whole? What is his spine?

To me, the spine functions like the trunk of a tree. I see many people working on a part by starting with the branches. A leaf here, a twig there. But ultimately nothing is holding them up. The trunk is missing. The trunk must be there in the first place; that keeps you honest. Once you have that basic truth you can do anything in the scene and still be believable.

The evenings at Lake Grove were usually spent attending lectures by Harold Clurman. Clurman's focus was clear: not only theater, but the Group itself and its importance. He stressed that the Group must stick together, that it was a movement in American culture making as much of a political statement as it was a theatrical one.

One night Roman Bohnen stood up to announce that he had been offered a chance to go to Hollywood to be directed by the wonderful director, Millie Milestone, in *Of Mice and Men*. Of course, there was no such phrase as "politically correct" at that time, but the concept was clear. And going to Hollywood was as politically incorrect as you could get; Hollywood meant selling out. Bohnen was fighting an uphill battle with this group, though his case was strong. "If I could make this movie, I could get out of debt. I could pay all the bills I've accumulated since the birth of my child. I could buy my wife a winter coat. How can I pass up this chance?"

One by one, various people got up to challenge him. Kazan, Morris Carnovsky, and, most vociferously, Harold himself. I remember only Sandy Meisner defending Bohnen: "How can you expect him to give you good work when he has all this on his mind?" I was appalled that Meisner stood alone, but I didn't have the guts to support him. I'm ashamed to say I remained silent when Clurman screamed at him, "Sandy, I will destroy you for standing up for Bohnen like this!"

Emotions ran high because they were talking about an awful lot more than whether one man should accept one job. They were talking about loyalty and betrayal (at least what some people perceived as betrayal), issues that would preoccupy this group and the nation several years later. The implications made me very uneasy.

1940. Back in New York. Looking for work again. I started making the rounds in the usual way, by going to the offices that knew me. First, McClintic. Nothing for me there. Then The Playwrights' Company. Maxwell Anderson asked where I had been. I told him I'd been playing summer stock. About three days later, he phoned to say, "We've got something for you." As luck would have it, they had just let an actor go and wanted me to step into the part of a centurion in a play about Christ as a child called *Journey to Jerusalem*. A fourteen-year-old boy named Sydney Lumet was playing Jesus Christ. (Something in that part about telling people what to do must have appealed to him because he grew up to be a talented and very successful film director.)

The play was designed beautifully and Anderson had something timely to say about the Jews being chased out of Jerusalem by the Romans, but the play only ran two weeks.

Elmer Rice, who had directed the play and was a member of The Playwrights' Company, told me the Company would next be producing a play that he had written, so I should stay in touch. Those are words no one should ever say to an actor in vain. I was there at the Company office every other day, "keeping in touch." But it was another long month before *Flight to the West* went into rehearsals.

The United States was teetering on the brink of entering the war, so naturally it was a time when everything, most particularly the arts, was imbued with political overtones. Playwrights felt it was their obligation to raise their voices and that's what Elmer Rice was doing in *Flight to the West*. The play was about the problems of refugees fleeing Europe for America. Unfortunately, righteous indignation often took the form of dry drama.

The play featured Betty Field and a young Paul Henreid. Henreid had just arrived in the States from London and would, a few years later, become a big star in films when he lit two cigarettes at once, one for Bette Davis and the other for himself. But the real star of *Flight* was the set. The curtain rose on the interior of a Pan Am plane. Suddenly, you heard the motors revving and the plane took off. The brilliant designer, Jo Mielziner, achieved the illusion with water splashing against the side windows of the plane as it took off, and he did it so effectively that the audience always gasped.

I played the pilot in what was basically an uneventful run.

There was, however, one memorable incident during that run. Every actor's dream, in some ways, and every actor's nightmare in others, is to die—literally—while onstage. During *Flight* an actor by the name of James Seeley did just that. Throughout this play, of course everyone in the passenger compartment of the plane had to remain on stage. In the middle of a heavy political dialogue about the ramifications of the war, Seeley, playing the part of a Texas oil man, was to get up and head to the restroom. His cue came. Nothing. The actors ad-libbed a little, delivered the cue again. Again nothing. Finally, Hugh Marlowe got up, walked up to Seeley's seat and nudged him. We all

thought the old guy was asleep, but after a stronger nudge, Seeley just slumped over in his seat. Hugh looked offstage, mo-
tioned to pull the curtain, and Seeley was carried off. They
called the doctor on call for the theater, but everyone on stage
knew that it was too late.

We all wanted to stop the show but the stage manager, an
old-timer who'd seen it all, insisted that the show must go on. He
volunteered to read the part himself and we finished the performance.

Despite the play's good intentions and magnificent set, it only
ran about eight weeks. The management believed that it centered around such an important topic that more people should
have the chance to see it, so they moved the play to a bigger
house where they could charge less, but we only eked out another eight weeks there.

It was spring by the time we closed for good. Not the best
time to be looking for work in the theater. Luckily, summer follows spring, and that meant summer stock once again.

My friend, Duane McKinney, had met a man who ran a summer theater up in Woodstock. Duane had committed to be part
of the company and asked if I wanted to go, too. There was no
work for our wives, but they would be able to come with us
there to spend the summer, so off we went. What's more, Woodstock was just a few hours' drive from New York, so we figured
more people from the city (in other words, producers and
agents) would come to see our work there. For that very reason,
this was supposedly one of the more prestigious stock compa-
nies, but it couldn't compare with Tamarack.

Woodstock was all about featuring the big draw, the guest
stars. For the actors, that meant just supporting the stars the best
you could. The biggest star of that particular summer turned out
to be ex-stripper Sally Rand, who had made a name for herself as

the world's foremost fan dancer at the Chicago World's Fair. Her burlesque days were written all over her, especially in her hygiene habits. One could assume she rarely bathed, and the college kids who cleaned the rooms at the playhouse confirmed that the tub was never used. Instead she just kept dousing herself with perfume and shoveling on the makeup, layer upon layer, until it began to cake and separate so that you could see the dirt buildup in the creases around her neck.

She had made a deal to do two plays, *Rain* and *Little Foxes* in which she wanted to play the Tallulah Bankhead part. I was playing the oldest brother, Ben, in *Little Foxes*. She showed up for the first two days of rehearsals, then she disappeared. I kept reporting to rehearsal, but no Sally Rand after those first couple of days. Apparently, she had gone to New York to work on her costumes, which, true to her burlesque queen background, she believed to be the most essential element of her performance. Meanwhile, I was running scenes with the rest of the cast and with the apprentice stage manager reading her lines.

Come final dress rehearsal, Miss Rand appeared. Predictably, she didn't know a word and was muddling her way through the thing (though I must admit her costumes were pretty wonderful). After we broke, I noticed her walking around onstage with her assistant later in the day. I figured she was finally learning the part. Not until the last rehearsal did I discover that she was, in fact, spending that afternoon pinning her lines all over the place . . . on every article of clothing and piece of furniture she could get her hands on. Lampshades, the inner arms of the couch, every exit. She still didn't know a word. I kept thinking, "There's no way she's going to know her lines by opening night. What am I going to do when she goes up?"

Opening night came and there we were, Sally Rand and I, on stage together. We struggled through our first scene. Then came the next scene. Suddenly, I stared at her and she stared at me. And who should go up? Who else? Yours truly. Absolutely dry. Not a syllable in my head. I was so damn worried about her that I couldn't focus, not even enough to improvise. It was as if I couldn't speak a word of English. I looked to the stage manager in the wings, but she was just a young kid who was never on the book. She was nowhere to be seen. If it hadn't been for one of the other actors making his entrance two pages early, I'd probably still be standing there.

But it taught me a valuable lesson. Don't worry about what anyone else is doing. Just concentrate on what you're doing and hope that everything else takes care of itself.

Once again, I began to get that same feeling you have when you're a kid as summer is ending and you know each day means it's almost time to go back to school. Only now, in the real world, it meant back to looking for work, which was far worse than back to school.

The people in the offices of the Group Theater, McClintic, and The Playwrights' Company were nice enough to me, but if they had nothing, they had nothing. There was nothing you could do about it. I still had no agent, so that made the situation even tougher. Six months went by. Seven, eight, nine. Before this, I had always felt that no matter how bad things were, I was always meeting new people and somehow moving forward. But now, for the first time, I really felt like I was hitting a brick wall. Mona, always cheerful, laughed it off, but I was nearly ready to go back to Gary and the steel mills when I ran into Sam Jaffe one day while I was making the rounds.

We met on the street and just stood there chatting for a few minutes in front of Radio City Music Hall. I confided in him that I was ready to quit, that I hadn't even had a reading in nine months. Despite being in seven or eight plays I felt like I was back to square one, like no one knew me. I was still battling that purgatory known as the outer office. Sam, in his sweet, gentle way, tried to tell me that this was not unusual; long dry spells like this happened all the time. Then he took me by the arm and said, "Come with me."

Before I knew it we had walked a block or so, turned the corner, and were on our way up in an elevator to the fourth floor. Sam led me into an office—right past the secretary for once— and I found myself face-to-face with Joseph Schildkraut, Eva Le Gallienne, and a young director by the name of Lem Ward.

Sam presented me to them like a proud father. "Here is the man who should play the druggist."

Lem Ward looked at me. "But he's too young."

Sam answered without hesitation. "So make him the son of the druggist."

There was a long silence.

Finally Miss Le Gallienne asked me, "Do you mind reading?"

I was still trying to figure out what was happening, but I answered, "May I look at the script for a minute?"

They sent me into the outer office with a script. As I tried to collect my thoughts and concentrate on the pages in front of me, Sam emerged. He whispered to me, "Don't worry about a thing."

I went in and read, and when I had finished they asked me to come back the next day and sign a contract.

The play was called *Uncle Harry* and it ran for over a year. They did indeed change the part to be the druggist's son by adding two lines. Someone asked me, "Where's your father?" And I responded, "He's busy filling prescriptions." Not exactly sparkling dialogue but it meant the difference between a job and no job for me, so I was happy to say the line.

KARL MALDEN

Happy to say the line and forever indebted to Sam Jaffe who was not only one of the gentle men of the world, but a great and kind friend who went out of his way for me when I was at one of those low points that I think perhaps only actors experience.

The play had a decent run. The cast was warm and friendly and I was enjoying the part. I guess Joseph Schildkraut was having a good time, too, because he began to play with his lines. Actually, he began to grow more and more impossible with every performance. He tried every trick in the book to keep the audience's attention on himself. He even invented some new ones; at least they were new to me. In my scene with him I had a story to tell to several other characters on stage with us. I was to turn my back to him and address the other actors. Gradually, Schildkraut began to mumble behind my back. As the play ran, this mumbling grew louder and longer until it was full-fledged dialogue.

After a while I'd had it. In the middle of my speech, I stopped, turned to him and said, "What did you say?"

He froze.

I was on a roll. "I thought you said something."

Just a blank stare from Schildkraut.

By that time I was a little confused about where I had left off in my story. I turned to another actor, Johnny McGovern, and said, "So, where was I?"

He said, "You were just telling us about . . ."

And I carried on.

The minute the curtain fell, Schildkraut called me into his dressing room. He told me in no uncertain terms that I was never to do that again. I pretended that I had really thought that something had gone wrong in the scene, that I had forgotten an important line. But he saw through me, I'm sure.

When I left his dressing room, Miss Le Gallienne called me aside and told me she was so thrilled that I had called his bluff.

Even though he would never behave that way with her because he knew she was a big star and would tell him off, she couldn't stand that he did that to all the lesser players.

Despite this little episode with Schildkraut, I remained with *Uncle Harry* for about a year when Edie Van Cleve, a well-known agent with M.C.A., called out of the blue and said she had a wonderful part for me in a new play about Babe Ruth called *The Sun Field*. It was my first contact with an agent, and I thought it sounded pretty great when she promised she could double my salary to a big one hundred and fifty dollars a week. That was more money than I had ever made, so I had a tough decision to make. I read the play and forced myself to pretend it wasn't so bad. In my heart, I knew it was terrible, but I left *Uncle Harry* and went into rehearsals on *The Sun Field*.

I was out of work again before I knew what hit me, in one week to be exact. I ignored what I knew to be true: "The play's the thing." It has to be on paper. Otherwise, no amount of money, not even one hundred and fifty dollars, will help. Of course, *Uncle Harry* was still running in a nearby theater and continued to run for a few more months. Never again would I use money to decide whether or not to take a project.

So once again I was making the rounds. Gradually I got into the loop of reading for radio work. Eventually I landed a running part on a radio soap opera called *Our Gal Sunday*. The job was a godsend because they only used me two or three times a week, which meant it paid the rent and took a little pressure off, but allowed me to keep looking for work in the theater.

After about a year I got a job back on Broadway in a wartime melodrama called *Counterattack*, so, in the tradition of all good soap actors, I got killed off in the radio show.

Early in the run of *Counterattack* an actor playing a Nazi dropped out. I asked the stage manager to call my old Goodman roommate, Jimmy Russo. So Jimmy joined me and another Goodman alumnus, Sam Wanamaker. It was like old times. Jimmy and I were both playing Nazis. We knew this wasn't Shakespeare. We would pick up our guns and make our entrance. Not Sam. Along with Morris Carnovsky, Sam was playing a Russian soldier, and he took the process of preparation very seriously with the almost comical self-absorption of the very young, eager actor. Before Sam went on, there he was, backstage crawling around on his hands and knees in the dark like a soldier advancing.

One day Jimmy asked me exactly what Sam was doing.

"That's the way he prepares. He's been talking to Morris a lot," I answered.

Jimmy watched for a few more days. Then one afternoon before the matinee, Jimmy arrived early, changed into his Nazi uniform, and hid in the dark as Sam began his ritual crawl. After a minute, Jimmy jumped out of the shadows, stuck his rifle in Sam's back, and shouted, "Bang! You're dead. Now you can't go on."

Wanamaker was not amused.

Next came *Sons and Soldiers*, another lackluster show remarkable only for its cast. Geraldine Fitzgerald, Stella Adler, and in his first big part, a handsome young man named Gregory Peck. I knew right away that he was going to be a big star. He had a resonant voice and a winning, relaxed manner on stage. Peck and I were roughly the same age, but I played his uncle in this run-of-the-mill play about a middle-class family in New Jersey.

Though I knew from the start that the play had big problems, I was intrigued by the prospect of working with the famous director and German theater impresario, Max Reinhardt. Reinhardt was the big attraction for all the actors in the play. We found him to be mild-mannered and dignified, always well dressed and absolutely spic and span in his appearance.

The challenge lay in working with a director who had a difficult time with the language and generally needed an interpreter. When he had trouble expressing what he wanted in a scene he would say, for example, "Look at the girl. Count one, two, three, four. Look at the floor. Count one, two, three." It was directing by numbers.

Despite the work being done by the Group and others to bring a new realism to the theater, these were still the days when more was more, especially when it came to set dressing. In fact, the set designer, Norman Bel Geddes, was really the star of this production. He had just come off of designing the New York World's Fair and couldn't quite leave that grand scale behind. Reinhardt, who couldn't communicate his own ideas very well because of the language barrier, was a little intimidated by Bel Geddes and his suggestions. Consequently, these middle-class Jersey folks had a living room with a sweeping staircase and a huge grand piano topped off with a Tiffany silver bowl just as huge. Worst of all, the set made it very difficult to act.

The set was so cumbersome that I had to slither through a tiny gap in all the furnishings to make my entrance. And here I was supposed to be a bigger than life extroverted fella, a Flying Tiger pilot who had flown the "Hump," blustering his way in. I don't think I lose my temper easily when I'm working, but one Wednesday afternoon after the matinee I had really had it and I let loose. Was this show about people or their furniture?

The set was actually a massive insert twenty-five feet high. The stagehands would bring out a three-fold flat of black velour during the blackouts between scenes to redress it. For example, they would place a bench and potted bushes in front of it during the blackout to create a park. Then the guys would have to hold the damn thing up from behind throughout the whole scene.

One Wednesday matinee, they opened up the set and the lights started to come back up as Gregory Peck and I made our entrance. Peck was walking in front of me. All of a sudden I noticed that he was leaning to one side, farther and farther every second. I realized the set was falling down. He turned around and looked at me. I looked back at him. Finally, I just said, "Let's push it back." As we pushed it up, I realized that stupid set would have fallen right on top of us if it hadn't been for the light rail that happened to break its fall. Greg and I got it back up, and I called to the stagehands, "You fellas got a hold of it now?" I must admit I didn't care by that point. That was the end of that performance; after an incident like that, it was just say the lines, get it over with, and get off.

It was no surprise when *Sons and Soldiers* closed after a couple of short weeks.

Back to the old routine, which, by then, I had down pat. Make the rounds for theater and radio work in the morning. End up at Walgreen's on Broadway and Forty-fourth around noon. Those who could afford it would buy a sandwich in the little restaurant downstairs. We'd all swap leads. Today they call it networking; then we called it the "grapevine" or just helping out your friends. By midafternoon, you'd be in the offices where your friends had been that morning. Day in, day out. That was the drill. You just did as much of that as you could.

By this time, Mona had pretty much decided she couldn't bear it any more. She claimed that one actor in any family is enough and she may have been right, but the truth was she just didn't have the stomach for the rejection. I suppose you could say that if she had really had a burning desire to act, she would have stuck with it, but I'm not sure that's necessarily true. The process of looking for work can wear anyone down. Even today, I run into people who started out with me and find that they are still looking for work, looking for that break. It pains me and yet, at the same time, makes me feel so incredibly fortunate.

At this point, my life with Mona was in constant chaos. We were jumping around from one rathole to another. After Mona's mother moved back to Kansas, it seemed like we were moving constantly . . . Ninetieth Street, Jackson Heights, Fifty-fifth Street, First Avenue, and finally Sixth Avenue where we landed in a four floor walk-up above a deli. That was our first unfurnished apartment, so we had to buy a bed. That was it, all we had. Then one day I ran into an acquaintance, Wally Freed, who was the business manager for a producer named Oscar Serlin. Serlin had been boycotting the Schubert organization and therefore running *Life With Father* (one of the longest running shows ever) in vacant old theaters around the country. Freed told me Serlin had a warehouse full of cheap furniture that he used to set up in the lobbies. I told him I couldn't afford anything but he insisted I go over and take a look. Reluctantly, I chose a few pieces.

He asked, "Do you have a hundred dollars?"

"Yeah, sure, I guess so."

"It's all yours," said Freed, "for a hundred dollars."

I wished I'd picked a few more pieces for that kind of deal! We ended up with a coffee table, two chairs—one green velvet, the other some godawful print, I think—and a red satin sofa. Mona's uncle visited us shortly thereafter and sent us a hideous red carpet after he got home. The place looked like a thrift shop bordello but we had chairs to sit on and a table to eat off of.

By this point, Sam Jaffe had been recently widowed. He was nursing his broken heart by walking the streets late into the night. Then he would stop by the night club where his dear friend, Zero Mostel, was doing his own brand of comedy routines to make ends meet so that he could work on his true avocation—painting.

The two of them appeared on our doorstep countless times at two A.M. asking for something to eat. Mona would throw on her robe, cross from the tiny bedroom to the kitchen, and scramble them some eggs. They'd wolf them down with some toast and coffee and a lot of laughs, then they'd disappear back into the night.

Zero was a bigger-than-life character utterly without inhibition. He couldn't help drawing attention to himself. One day Mona was walking down Sixth Avenue when she spotted Zero approaching from the other direction. He stopped dead in his tracks halfway down the block from her and bellowed, "Mona! If you don't marry me I shall kill myself!" Then he took a long puff from his pipe, held the pipe to his head, exhaled the smoke, and fell to the sidewalk in an enormous heap.

Somehow their middle-of-the-night visits made perfect sense in terms of how our lives were going. Changes every five minutes. No permanent place to live. No permanent job.

That feeling of uncertainty has stayed with me all my life. I am a person who likes things to be orderly, and my life felt like one great big mess at that time. Even when I had a job during that period, I knew that sooner or later—usually sooner—I'd be back on the streets pounding the pavement, making the rounds, looking for work.

facing page:
My life saver, Sam Jaffe, got me this part
in *Uncle Harry.*

Chapter 5

Ironically, it was during the short run of *Sons and Soldiers* that
I received a letter. "Greetings," it began. I know that for some
young men, those greetings meant a welcome chance to serve
their country. But I must confess that for me, "Greetings"
meant more confusion and hysteria in what was already a confused and hysterical time.

I reported for my physical at Grand Central Station with hundreds of other young men. It was an assembly line affair, the fastest physical I've ever had. This doctor flashed a light in your ears, that one tapped your chest, the last one handed you a cup for a urine specimen. I remember standing in that men's room for an eternity, trying to fill that goddamn cup. Guys were coming in and going out and I was still standing there. Nothing. I guess my body, like my mind, just shut down at the thought of going into the army. But I finally produced a few drops. That was all they needed. You had to roll into Grand Central in a wheelchair to be rejected.

It was like the old joke. "Doc, it hurts when I move my arm like this."

"So, don't move your arm like that."

Some guys were pointing out that they needed thick glasses to see. "So, wear your glasses." There was no getting out. I knew enough not to even try.

After that physical, I returned home to our crummy little apartment. Mona was waiting, anxious, terrified really. I looked her in the eye and saluted . . . then watched the color drain from her face.

A few weeks later I packed up my little bag with my shaving equipment, not much more, and kissed Mona good-bye. The bus was going to be picking me up, along with about twenty other men, at the corner of Twenty-fifth and Broadway at seven-fifteen A.M. I arrived around six-thirty only to discover that I was standing in front of a Serbian Orthodox church. It had recently been converted from an Episcopalian church and I had never known it was there until that morning. I tried to get in, but it was all locked up, so I just got on the bus and headed upstate to Camp Upton.

Just when I thought I was beginning to get some kind of handle on life in New York, I found myself in a barracks with a bunch of fellas I didn't know. Fortunately, an actor called Ezra Stone was running a theater up there to entertain the troops while they were being held awaiting classification. Ezra knew me slightly because he had played the very popular Henry Aldrich on the long-running radio show of the same name and I had guested as his sister's boyfriend once. He kindly asked me to stay there and be part of his company. But I already had a plan.

I had heard that Moss Hart was putting together a show that would be for the air corps what *This Is the Army* had been to the army. I turned down Ezra's offer, explaining that I was trying to get assigned to the Air Corps so I could audition for that show and be back in New York with Mona. Ezra understood.

A few days later I marched off to the briefing site with everyone else where our assignments awaited us. It was a room full of lines of young men. I got put into one of those lines. I was moving up slowly when Ezra Stone came over to me and told me to move to another line. I did as he said. When I got to the head of that line and gave my name, the officer said, "Malden? You're a friend of Ezra's?"

"Yes, sir."

"Air corps."

Okay. Big deep breath. The first hurdle was over. But I was still taking a gamble. Even in the air corps, I could have been assigned to air traffic control or the weather bureau. I could have ended up a mechanic. I was banking on one thing and one thing only: getting that audition for the Moss Hart show.

Within two days we were shipped to Greensboro, North Carolina. My group contained a bunch of young hotdogs who, as civilians, had been taking flying lessons so they could land in the Corps. As it happened, they were all from Texas. So not only was I the only one who had never flown a plane, I was from the wrong side of the Mason-Dixon Line. That didn't matter to the brass. They wanted to teach these Texan hotshots a thing or two and I was guilty by association. They really made it tough. KP, latrine, loading garbage trucks, cleaning out garbage cans. I suppose it was the usual army grunt work but that didn't make it any more fun. Pushing thirty by now, I just kept thinking, "I'm too old for this." But I was competitive enough to push to keep up with kids ten and twelve years younger.

I was so depressed, that if any germ came along I was sure to catch it. I had no resistance to anything. I began to think something might be wrong with me one day when we set out for a ten-mile hike with full pack to the outskirts of town. The drill was two men to a pup tent for two days and then hike back to camp. On our way there, a terrific pain in my chest nearly crippled me. I could hardly breathe. I finished the trek bringing up the rear, doubled over. But I didn't tell anyone. Just set up my tent and crawled under my blanket.

It poured rain that night, so that all the tents were soaked and mud was seeping in everywhere. I sat up all night on my pack. In the morning we set about making a mound of mud to serve as a retaining wall for the coming night, but it did little good. More rain all day and all the second night. Nothing but wet.

From that time on whenever I exercised even the slightest bit I got that pain in my chest, but I never said a word. I waited for time, the great healer, to work its magic. It didn't.

I made it back to camp and life got back to normal, what was normal for boot camp. I was so relieved when Millard Lampell, the guy in charge of broadcasting radio shows for the camp, came to my barracks and asked if I wanted to do shows for him. Millard tried to get me off duty during the day but no dice, so from then on I'd go through basic training all day and spend my evenings rehearsing until about ten o'clock. I'd get show day— Friday—off.

Working on the shows, I met a couple of guys who were also actors or dancers. Like me, they had all filled out request forms to try out for the Moss Hart show now called *Winged Victory.* One by one they began getting calls to go to New York. One day, one guy would be packing up and out; the next day it was someone else. But I was still hanging around. I went to the commanding officer and asked if he had sent in my audition request forms. He assured me he had, but still—nothing.

A week went by and I called Mona. She already knew what was going on because our Goodman friend Ralph Alswang had an inside track, helping the wonderful designer, Harry Horner, design the sets for *Winged Victory.* I told Mona to ask Ralph to check on the status of my request.

One night Ralph was working late and wandered into the production office after hours. He went into the office of Captain Irving Lazar who would later become the legendary literary agent known as "Swifty." (Lazar had been the one to approach Moss Hart about creating the show because, like many of us, he was looking for a soft spot that would keep him from going overseas. If he could get himself attached to a show, that would do it.) Ralph rifled through the "in"- and "out"-going mail on Lazar's desk. There was a lot of "out"-going mail calling people back to New York to audition. Ralph later told me he was about to leave when he spotted a couple of forms sticking out from under the desk blotter. He pulled them out. My request was among them. I don't know if mine was accidentally stuck under there, or if it was just in a holding section because Lazar was really after bigger Hollywood names, but if it hadn't been for Ralph Alswang, my form might very well still be shoved under that blotter and my whole life might have been dramatically different, if not cut short entirely.

So I finally got called to come in. A lot of my old friends were there, a lot of the guys I'd been knocking around with over the last five years. It was a producer's dream come true. Call in a thousand young men from all over the country to audition for three hundred spots.

I was happy to be back in New York, but I was forced to spend my first week back in a crummy hotel the Army was putting us up in. Meanwhile, Mona was still on Sixth Avenue. At first she had gotten a job in a trendy furniture design store called Artek-Pascoe, but soon after Jimmy Russo happened to call her about a play he had tried out for. Before she knew it, Mona had a job in a play called *I'll Take the High Ground* starring Jeanne Cagney, James Cagney's sister. Mona was briefly out of retirement, but the play only lasted two weeks.

Meanwhile, it took Moss Hart about a week to audition all the guys; every day about a hundred guys were sent back to boot camps all over the country. I came at the end of that week along with George Petrie, Peter Lind Hayes, Marty Ritt, and Alfred Rider. Hart, a dapper young man, had already made a name for himself. This play, *Winged Victory*, he was writing and directing himself with the intention of raising money for the Emergency Relief. (Years later I found out that he donated his own percentage, amounting to one million dollars, to the fund as well.) The play included a fifty man choir as it followed five boys through the various phases of their training up to the point when they shipped out overseas in the "Winged Victory." The four of us auditioned with the scene in which the plane was christened the "Winged Victory." We got the jobs and ended up playing that one scene in the production.

Moss had spent four or five months traveling around the country from camp to camp seeing how the boys are carried from the day they're inducted to the day they ship out and go to war. It was an Everyman story and we played to sold-out houses at the 44th Street Theater every night for one year. The show was a big hit because of the times. Civilians thrilled to the sight of three hundred young men in uniform. The show fed into the rah-rah temperament of the war years with just enough humor to take the sting out of the reality that for every boy on stage there were thousands of others across the ocean.

Being in *Winged Victory* allowed me to meet people I probably would never have met otherwise. Ray Middleton, the Slate Brothers, and a guy who was actually in his thirties but looked sixteen years old, Red Buttons. But my favorite part of rehearsals was listening to the chorus. They were all professional singers, including one Mario Cocosa.

Whenever the Red Cross or some other organization wanted to throw a fundraiser, they'd call on the *Winged Victory* company and we would send out a group of about ten guys to entertain. Claude Stroud and Peter Lind Hayes would do a little comedy routine. Marty Ritt and I did a little something. We would also help set up a little piano and the makeshift P.A. system with a couple of other guys. Another fella would play that piano, then we'd pack it back up and start to carry it off to the truck. Part of the shtick was that Hayes would say, "Wait a minute. Ladies and gentlemen, this guy is just moving the piano, but if we could get him to sing for us, it would be great." Then Mario Cocosa would take the stage and sing "Pagliacci." He brought the house down every time. Later, after the war, he became Mario Lanza.

During the year at the 44th Street Theater, we were actors at night and soldiers during the day. We all had the feeling that the Army was making it doubly hard on us. They didn't want people to be able to say, "My son has gone off to war and these boys are goofing off on stage." So after finishing the long show at eleven at night, we had to report bright and early to the New York YMHA (Young Men's Hebrew Association) or, if the weather was nice, Central Park. We'd run through the drill, all the usual calisthenics, then they'd lay blankets out on the floor of the basketball court and we'd have to take our rifles apart and put them back together blindfolded. Then over to the rifle range for target practice. Then back to the theater by curtain time.

Winged Victory did the grand old 44th Street Theater in. When we closed, they tore the place down.

The minute we knew *Winged Victory* would be going on the road, I started lobbying to get Mona into the show so we wouldn't have to be separated again. She hadn't been able to try out originally because of her stint in the short-lived Jeanne Cagney play. Wouldn't you know it? She finally got a job on Broadway just long enough to prohibit her from getting a really, good long-running job. That's showbiz in a nutshell.

This time around it worked out better. Some of the women in the company didn't want to go on the road, so they started replacing them with the wives of the men in the cast and Mona nabbed a spot. We hit the road. Chicago, Kansas City, Denver. Then we landed in Los Angeles to make the movie.

The single guys had to live in a sort of tent village slapped together in Santa Monica, but married couples were allowed to live off the base. Mona and I moved in with my former mentor, Robert Ardrey, who had gotten married and transplanted himself to L.A. to write movies. He offered us a room for seventy-five dollars a month in a house he had on Fremont Place with his wife, Helen. The place looked like a mansion to us. We jumped at the chance. We bought an old rattletrap Ford with a sawed-off roof for two hundred and fifty dollars. (Four or five months later I sold the damn thing for the same amount.) The car was falling apart; I never changed the oil, just kept pouring it in, but we were ready to tackle southern California.

I had to be in Santa Monica every morning by eight o'clock

and my route included picking up another soldier, Ray Middleton, at Wilshire and Rossmore. Middleton had been a singer and would go on to be in *Annie Get Your Gun*. He and I would sing Shubert musicals all the way to the beach while Mona went to work as an extra at Fox.

But we only stayed with the Ardreys for two months. Bob's wife, Helen, proved to be more than Mona could bear. We were more than happy to share food costs right down the middle, but Helen's habits were too frugal even for us. She would buy the rotten vegetables off the produce truck—really rotten, not just day old. She stood watch over Mona when Mona was peeling potatoes to make sure she didn't scrape off too much peel. If I reached for a second piece of bread or got up for a second glass of milk at dinner, she would shoot me a look that nailed me to the floor. She would stand outside the bathroom and listen to make sure we didn't run more than about six inches of bathwater. After a while, I gave up and started taking showers at the base, but Mona was left with Helen, the water monitor—shades of Mona's miserable childhood where she had always felt like the unwanted cousin in some relative's home.

If the Ardreys ever entertained, Helen would pass a tin of cookies, permit each guest one cookie and return the tin to the kitchen. Then, after an hour or so, she would take out her darning to signal that it was time for her company to go home.

Despite this pathetic example of hospitality, after a while, Mona and I decided we should invite some of the *Winged Victory* company over. We informed Helen that this was going to be our party; we would pay for everything. Believe me, it wasn't anything elaborate, just dessert and coffee. That night, it wasn't very late, Mona and I were sitting in the dining room with our six or seven guests when Helen came padding down in her flannel wrapper and slippers. Absolutely silently, she circled the

table to see if we were eating anything from her half of the re-
frigerator, then she disappeared back upstairs.

That sent Mona over the edge. After the company left, she dis-
solved into complete hysterics. We found a rooming house near
the Ambassador Hotel the next morning and stayed there for
the rest of the summer of '44.

Shooting the picture *Winged Victory* meant a lot of free time.
On any given day maybe some fifty to a hundred people were
working. The rest of us were at the camp. Although I felt so
lucky to be in the play and then the movie, my two year stint in
the service was basically a miserable period because I could
never make peace with the routine. I couldn't enjoy the downtime. I didn't play poker. I had a hard time being one of the
guys. I guess my dad's nightly lesson—you must account for
your day—was too strong and too well learned. I knew *Winged
Victory* was never going to be a career move; I was just one of a
hundred guys with a line or two. So I felt I was just marking
time and that was a feeling I could never adjust to.

Even so, there were a lot of laughs. Our unit was put together
with spit and glue. In many ways we were the original *MASH*
type of unit. We had the usual duties at the camp, but when we
had completed our assignments we could request a walk down to
the beach. One day about forty guys signed up to go. So off they
went, down to the blue Pacific, in formation. They were headed
downhill when a car parked on the other side of the street started
to roll. It rolled up against the rear of the squad but no one was
hurt. Of course by the time a couple of guys ran back to camp to
report what had happened and we all went running down to see,
guys were lying all over the road. I ran up to one fella. He pushed
me away, "Leave me alone, I'm hurt. Don't touch me." I hurried
over to another guy. Same routine, "Goddammit, get away from
me." By then an ambulance was there. The works. No one was

really hurt; they were all just looking for a way out of the Army. The medics declared them all unscratched, let alone seriously injured, and they all picked themselves up and went traipsing the rest of the way down to the beach.

Red Buttons, enlisted as Aaron Schwat, used to disappear every afternoon around three o'clock along with a bunch of other guys. He would take a shower, get all dressed up, and just take off with a group—the majority of the unit actually—who would head for Hollywood and a good time. The rules said we had to stay on base until five or six but these guys didn't care a whit about rules.

At that time we had a colonel who had been an organist in a church in Texas. That distinction, his vast musical background, entitled him to head up a showbiz unit. We had been going through colonels one after the other, nearly one a week, but this guy dug his heels in and decided he was going to do something about this group who played hookey every afternoon.

Word filtered down from the guys in the office, "Don't leave tomorrow. We're going to have retreat and roll call." Retreat meant the ceremony for taking down the flag and this colonel wanted everyone present, accounted for, and saluting.

At the end of the next day, about a hundred guys were left instead of the usual twenty or thirty. The colonel started calling roll, not by squad, but alphabetically, individual man by man.

When he reached the *s*'s he called, "Schwat, Aaron Schwat." No answer.

"Is Schwat working?" he asked.

"No, sir."

"Anyone know where Schwat is?"

From the middle of camp, we heard, "Here!"

That didn't make it. The colonel bellowed, "Aaron Schwat, front and center!"

"As is?"

"As is."

Red Buttons came running out from the direction of the showers, stark naked. He stood in front of this officer and offered his sharpest salute.

One of the Slate Brothers (we had two of the three) called out, "Hey, Red! I didn't know you were Jewish!"

I can't remember if the colonel finished roll after that. He may have quit on the spot.

There was simply no controlling this group. When we were still in New York, the non-com officers would drill us and half the time when they said, "Column right," everyone just kept on marching straight ahead. It was understood that the first four guys, whoever they were, would not follow directions and the rest of us would just keep following them. The brass had us all taking turns to see if there was any one of us whom the rest of the fellas would listen to. I had my shot once, but I was no good. Kevin McCarthy was pretty good; he had a certain quality to his voice and he had been in the M.P.'s before joining *Winged Victory*, but, ultimately, it didn't matter. Nobody listened. Nobody cared.

This general attitude, anything for a joke, sometimes took the form of cruelty. Before we left for Hollywood, one of our unit, George Petrie, had his teeth fixed, believing like half the guys that this was going to be his crack at stardom. He spent a lot of money and was thrilled with his dazzling new smile.

He had one scene in which to make stardom happen. The director, George Cukor, had the shot lined up so the non-com soldiers would introduce themselves to the commissioned officers. We'd walk right up to the camera, salute, and give our name. I was, "Adams, radio operator, gunner." That kind of thing.

It came time for George Petrie's turn. He walked right up,

saluted, and stated his name and position. The cameraman said, "Hold it a minute." He turned to Cukor and said something. Then Cukor said, "George, your teeth are awfully shiny. Makeup!" Makeup came over and smeared some brown stuff on George's five thousand dollar teeth.

Take two. Same thing. "Again, sorry." It seems the brown stuff had rubbed off, so the makeup man started applying calodium, which is stinky, foul stuff like spirit gum. By then, the whole place was breaking up. Eddie O'Brien had put them up to it. Poor George Petrie blew his top. He took it all out on Cukor. "You call yourself a big man. Big Hollywood director. I'm nobody trying to make my way and you're giving me a hard time..." Cukor apologized, but it was really too late.

That kind of thing went on a hundred times during the picture.

Even when we had to go for psychiatric evaluations (I can't imagine why), everyone was doing shtick. The Slate Brothers came in together on their knees. Red Buttons walked in backwards saying, "Is anyone here? Where is everybody?" Only dear sweet Ralph Alswang, the designer, didn't try to psych himself into a discharge. He was his usual quiet self. And only Ralph ended up with a recommendation that he be checked out further in the hospital for a couple of days. They thought there was something peculiar about him and only him. That's what it was like. Crazy times deserved crazy behavior. It was a situation where only nonsense made sense.

After a year and a half playing *Winged Victory* in New York, around the country and making the movie, I began to realize I hadn't felt well for about six months. I wondered if I hadn't really felt a hundred percent since I'd gotten that pain in my chest during the hike. Not so much ill as chronically exhausted. I fell asleep every time I sat down. One day while we had the show in San Francisco, I simply couldn't go on feeling this way any longer. I checked myself into Letterman Hospital. The doctor examined me, ran the usual tests, and came back a few hours later. I had TB.

In those days, TB didn't necessarily mean a long course of antibiotics after which that would be that. My first thought was of a beautiful young girl in Gary, the daughter of a lovely Serbian family with whom I had grown up, who contracted the disease and was sent to the tuberculosis hospital on the outskirts of town. She died a few years later. I wondered, too, if I'd been incubating it for years, if the Gary steel dust had damaged my lungs irreparably. I thought about how when the wind blew off Lake Michigan from the north, you could feel the dust, smell it, see it—how many times when you would blow your nose, the handkerchief would be black.

An officer with the show who was originally from Denver told me that the army had a great hospital there that specialized in the sort of illness I seemed to have. If I could hang on until the company moved to Denver in a few days, I should go there. So I went to Denver with them and checked myself into Fitzsimmons Army Hospital the minute I could. The day I checked in, I had no idea I would end up staying there for six months.

In many ways it was like being sentenced to six months in hell. They kept changing the diagnosis every other day. Pneumonitis. Desert fever (which was spreading through California at the time). Then they'd decide once again that I had TB because the shadows on the X rays were above the third rib. That's the way the Army doctors classified things. Any shadow above the third rib meant tuberculosis. They showed me the X rays. It looked like snowflakes flecked an entire area of my lung. After a while the next series of X rays revealed the snowflakes converging into one clump. They swore that meant it couldn't be TB. Of course, they had no idea what that did mean.

In the beginning they put me in a ward of maybe twenty beds, like a barracks. But it was a part of the ward that wasn't occupied yet. I was all alone in there. I thought I was lucky to have some peace and quiet, but now I wonder if they just weren't sure what was wrong with me and wanted to keep me away from other patients in case I was contagious with something especially terrible.

It was the usual miserable and frustrating routine of constant blood tests, being poked and prodded. The test I learned to dread the most was one they called the "spaghetti" test in which I had to swallow a little knob at the end of a long tube. They put the whole contraption on ice over night to make it go down more easily, but you just had to keep swallowing and swallowing to push it down and by the end, all the ice in the world wouldn't have helped.

I remember another test, too, where they lay me on a table and tilted my head back over the edge. Then they inserted a rod down my throat into the lung area. This was the forties and plastics had not evolved very far, I guess, so the rod was stiff, not pliable. Then they'd manipulate it around so they could see how things were down there. It was like the old joke. Things down there were a lot better until you stuck that stick down me.

After three months, they said I still wasn't well enough to be released, but that I could, at least, get out of bed for short stretches. They assigned me to do a radio show broadcast within the hospital interviewing soldiers and reading the news. I wasn't very good at it, but it was something to keep me occupied.

To add insult to injury, my confinement meant I had to worry about Mona, too. In many ways the ordeal was much harder on her. She came with me to Denver and got a job at Neuststetter's department store wrapping packages. Then in the cold and snow, like something out of a forties movie, she would travel an hour and a half taking a bus and a streetcar and another bus to the hospital. She made the trip three or four times a week.

Needless to say, I looked forward to her visits more than any-thing; they were all that kept me going. I think I was amazed that she was hanging in there with me, but I still had an awful lot of time with nothing to do but think. I didn't realize it at the time, but in many ways those six months changed my life. I felt as though I couldn't sink any lower. The whole time I had been looking for work in New York, I had tried to avoid feeling like I was just a piece of meat selling myself. Now, here I was lying in bed, truly reduced to little more than a piece of meat, just a body and one that wasn't working very well at that. I guess I'd spent all that time in New York fighting to keep hold of my hu-manity and it wasn't until I was stripped of everything that I was really forced to confront it head on.

I realized for the first time that there is more to life than your career. I was forced to say to myself, "Where do I go from here? What if they tell me I can't live the life I've been leading any-more?" I had to make peace with the idea that I might have to quit my profession and get a regular job. My body simply might not take the stress anymore. I promised myself that I would make more time for the people I loved and try to be less self-absorbed. By the end of six months in bed, I figured I would have had enough self-absorption for a lifetime.

No doubt, there were times over the years when I temporarily forgot the lessons I'd learned during those long six months. But something deep within me did change during that time; some-thing fundamental about who I was being more than what I was doing.

When the time came for me to be released, standard procedure called for me to be sent back to my outfit. But there was no outfit. *Winged Victory* had been over for a couple of months by then and the fellas in the company had been sent all over the world. The captain, a doctor, told me it was crucial that I take it easy, while the administration kept talking about which camp I should go to. I kept saying, "How can I take it easy when I'm only a corporal? I have to do what every sergeant tells me or get in trouble." By now I was terrified of having a relapse, so I asked them to put it on my record that I had to take it easy; but they said they couldn't. I asked to be sent to someone who could.

They sent me to a general who gave me the same runaround. I kept saying, "If I don't feel well I'm going to be a bad soldier." He said he could send me to a veterans' hospital but that would mean I'd be a civilian since veterans' facilities are for people who are no longer actively in the service. That sounded good to me.

When I was finally transferred from Fitzsimmons to Livermore Veterans Hospital outside San Francisco, I thought the worst was going to be over. But my stay there ended up being the longest nine days of my life. I was in the TB ward with a lot of World War I vets who spent their days making those little red paper poppies to sell for a penny apiece. Cigarette money, they said. Fashioning paper flowers makes for long days, but the nights were even longer; these old men spent their nights coughing. Coughing and dying. In the middle of one night, I heard a little rustling. In the morning an empty bed told the story. Death was closer than it had ever been and all I wanted to do was get out of there.

I called Mona who spoke to her uncle who was a doctor in Los Angeles. He advised me to come there as soon as possible. The hospital administration insisted I would never get insurance and never be hired if I left, but I had to get out.

I made it to L.A. where Mona's Uncle Charlie put me in touch with a doctor who examined me more thoroughly in the first twenty minutes in his office than I think I had been examined during my whole stint in the army hospitals. He told me to go to bed and stay there for two weeks without moving. I was sick of bedrest, but still exhausted (if loathe to admit it), so that's what I did. During the second week I woke up spitting blood. I got myself dressed and made it back to the doctor's. He took another X ray. As he held it up to the light, he smiled. It was the first smile I'd seen on a doctor's face in a very long time. He explained that I had had an abscess on my lung, probably for a very long time. It had begun to drain of its own accord and that accounted for the blood. That's what he had hoped would happen; otherwise he would have had to operate.

To this day my chest X rays always reveal scar tissue there. That's my war wound.

My brother, Milo, was not so lucky. He had been in the army for about five years before he got sent overseas as part of Patton's Third Army in an outfit they called the "Tough Hombres." I knew he was on the front lines, but I didn't know exactly where.

One night when I was at Fitzsimmons, I had what, in retrospect, must have been a feverish vision. I was sure I was awake, but the next day I decided I must have really been asleep. Whatever—it was one of those altered states you can fall into when you are gravely ill. But to this day I can recall the bright light that kept moving toward me and then receding into a corner, over and over again. I kept moving my head, but wherever I looked there was the light, a light so blinding I couldn't look at it for more than an instant, and at its center, the Virgin Mary and child.

Shortly thereafter I received word that Milo was missing in

action. I thought, "That's it. He's dead." Months went by before we learned that he had been taken prisoner of war.

He finally returned home after five months of being a P.O.W. with two wounds in his leg that would never really heal for the rest of his life. I was released from the hospital, too, and we shared a joyous homecoming in Gary. I told Milo about my dream and when we compared dates, we figured out that I'd had this dream within a day or two of his being captured. Milo asked me if I remembered a tiny icon that had always been in our home, an icon depicting the Virgin Mary and child. I remembered it. It was probably tin, but I recalled it being encrusted silver with distinct little patches of enamel or paint. It was only about two inches by three inches. As Milo reminded me of it, I realized the picture on that icon was the image that had come to me that night.

Milo told me that Pa had given it to him when he left for overseas, just as Pa's mother had given it to him to keep him safe many years before when he set out for America.

It was the first thing the Germans took from Milo when he was captured.

facing page:
**One of my first stabs at radio. I never
did get the hang of it.**

Chapter 6

As grateful as I was to spend the war on American soil, even if a big chunk of that time was in a hospital, I tortured myself by thinking that those two years away from New York were going to put me back at square one. By now, I had replaced my father's voice in my head with my own. "What did you do today?" I felt that I had accumulated two years' worth of "Nothing." To make matters worse, I was certain that the two years had wiped out any small progress I had made in New York up to that time. Who would remember me?

Amazingly, someone did. After I had been at my folks' for about a week, a telegram came. It was from a producer by the name of Carly Wharton. "I am doing a play by Irwin Shaw. There is a part for you. When will you be back in New York?" That one wire wiped out all thoughts of staying in Gary and taking a stab at a normal life. I wired back, "Immediately."

Mona and I were back in New York within the week. We moved into a little midtown hotel called The Laurelton. We were barely unpacked before I was out the door and in Carly Wharton's office. I nearly died when she offered me two hundred and fifty dollars a week. I had no idea how salaries had skyrocketed while I was in the army. The law of supply and demand had jacked salaries way up; there just weren't many actors left so they could demand more money. I tried to play it cool but I felt like I'd won the lottery.

The next day I signed the contract and met with Irwin Shaw. I had been in *Gentle People* and *Sons and Soldiers* for him, so he told me he had actually had me in mind when he was writing this new play entitled *The Assassin*. This was a first and I was enormously flattered. The play was a political melodrama based on a true incident. Like nearly every other new play on Broadway at the time, the play dealt with the national obsession—trying to make sense out of what the country had just been through. I was to play the head of the French underground. I couldn't wait to get back to work.

Martin Gabel, a successful radio actor, was directing. Consequently, he hired a lot of his radio cronies. They all had magnificent voices, the kind of instrument I simply have never had and will never have, but they also had a completely different style of working. These were actors who could pick up a script and give you a great performance right there on the spot. A performance that sounded magnificent. However, that was still the performance you got after three weeks' rehearsal. I always thought of it as acting from the neck up. I admired the skill involved, the particular craft, but knew it would never work for me.

The clash of the two styles became clear during rehearsals for *The Assassin*. I had a big scene with a long speech that ran about a page. This speech really voiced Shaw's theme of the play: "What is man? Why do we do what we do? What makes us human?" I worked on it and worked on it. What works for me with a long speech is to deliver it so that half the speech is over before the audience even realizes you're doing a speech. Since I don't have one of those melifluous, resonating voices, I have to make up for it by keeping a good pace. The audience can't languish in the sound; I figure I have to hold them with sheer energy. So that's the way I did this speech in *The Assassin*.

Toward the latter part of rehearsals, Gabel, the director, kept saying he wanted me to take more time. I knew that wouldn't work for me so I kind of ignored him and kept at it my way. Finally, we went out of town for tryouts. I don't remember where. But in those days out of town always meant Boston, Philadelphia, Baltimore or New Haven. Wherever we were, Gabel kept urging me to slow it down, play with it. He became more and more insistent and, since, after all, he was the director, one night I did the speech his way.

The next morning, Irwin Shaw came up to me and said, "What the hell were you doing last night?" I told him that Martin Gabel had wanted me to do it that way. Shaw said, "Fuck Martin Gabel. Do it the way you used to."

That night, I went back to my old way. The minute the curtain came down, Gabel was on me. I said, "Talk to Irwin Shaw. You two figure out how you want it done and I'll do it." I never heard another word about it.

It ended up not mattering how I did the speech. The play got fair notices (to me, "fair" always meant just being kind) but closed in a couple of weeks.

Back to the old pattern. Out of work. But my experience with all those radio actors had reminded me about radio as a source of work. I began to do a few bits and pieces here and there. A couple of those cops and robbers shows like *Gangbusters*. Morning soap operas. I loathed it, mostly because I knew I was so bad at it, but it meant a paycheck.

Then I got a call from my old friends at the Group about a new play called *Truckline Cafe*. It was an especially sweet offer for me because Clurman and Kazan knew me by now, which meant I didn't have to read. I asked my one and only question: "When do I start?"

Kazan told me and added that I would be making a hundred dollars a week. For the first time in my life, I decided I'd better take a stand about money. I was embarrassed as hell and I wanted to do the play desperately, but I told Gadge I didn't think I could work for that money since I had just made two hundred and fifty a week.

I said, "I've never done this before but I'm going to say no this time."

Gadge took me out in the hallway of the Group offices and said, "Listen, we'll pay you a hundred and twenty-five dollars. I'm telling you that's all the budget can take. But I promise you when I do a film, you'll be in it and you'll make up the difference there." Kazan can be an exceedingly convincing man and he knew he had something extra going for him: I wanted to believe him. Kazan was one of the first people I had met in New York. What's more, he had given me work. Sometimes you have to trust people, so I said okay and signed the contract.

I was thrilled the minute I had. This was a different type of part for me. Since coming to New York, I had done nothing but heavy, dramatic parts. This was a drunken sailor and I was determined to make him the drunkest sailor you ever saw. It was a part to have a great time with. And I was ready. What a relief it was to be called so quickly a second time after getting out of the army. I began to believe that all my worries about my two years out of the loop really were unfounded.

In a way, this marked the beginning of a new phase for me. Instead of looking for work all the time, I felt that maybe I was turning a corner, maybe producers really were going to remember me. It's a moment every young actor dreams about. At least it was a moment I had dreamt about. Not stardom. Not the biggest part. Certainly not millions of dollars. Just getting called for work on a regular basis. Above all else, reputation earns you the chance to work, and I was beginning to feel like I had built some sort of reputation. Even if they had nothing for me, producers were beginning to sit and chat with me for a few minutes. My days sweating it out in the outer office, forcing a smile for some disinterested secretary, were finally over. I was happy to kiss them good-bye.

Kazan and Clurman were taking a leap of faith with me in the part, and I think they breathed a sigh of relief when they discovered how willing I was to throw myself into this wacky drunken sailor. In fact, as rehearsals progressed I began to worry about exactly how far I was going. Was it too far? As I have said, Clurman was great with theory but couldn't move an actor across the stage. Here I was working up a character who bordered on slapstick without a director letting me know when

I was going overboard. In comedy more than anything you rely on the reaction of the audience. When you're rehearsing, the director is your audience. I felt like I was working without a net.

I worried more and more that I was going to make a fool of myself. I had a little drunken song in the part, and I used to walk around the apartment singing it day and night. One afternoon, in the middle of that crazy song, I turned to Mona and said, "You know, I'm going to make an ass of myself. Harold isn't telling me anything." Mona assured me that the part was coming along beautifully, but I grew increasingly uncomfortable.

Finally, I was so scared of humiliating myself I decided I was going to quit the play. I labored over a letter of resignation and appeared at rehearsal one morning with the finished product— on the stationery from the Laurelton Hotel—in my pocket. I walked up to Gadge and handed it to him. He opened it and read it silently. Then he tore it up.

He said, "I don't accept this. You never wrote it." And he walked away.

I just kept plugging along, working on my own, and ended up having great fun with the part. Little did I know I had been having a little too much fun rehearsing at home. It turned out that a neighbor went to see the play, not knowing I was in it, or even that I was an actor. The next day he stopped Mona in the hall of the Laurelton and said, "I saw that *Truckline Cafe* last night. All this time I'd been thinking your husband was a no-good drunk."

Not only did *Truckline* turn out to be a wonderful experience, but for the first time, reviews consistently singled me out. No matter what anyone says, that feels pretty good. It was ironic actually, because everyone else in the play was beating their brains out, and the notices mentioned me and one other kid who also had a small part.

This kid had made us all sit up and take notice at the very first "table reading." Generally, no one really goes for a full-out per-formance at that first reading, but at least they project enough to be heard around the table. Not him. We got to his scene and no one could hear a word out of his mouth. Everyone looked at one another. What is this kid doing? He just sat there, looking down, mumbling into his script. He never spoke up throughout the entire rehearsal period. Little did we know that his mum-bling would make him world famous. Of course, that wasn't all that set Marlon Brando apart.

I remember one day when the director, Harold Clurman, kept Marlon on stage while the rest of us broke for lunch. As usual I grabbed a quick bite and came back to the theater early. I hap-pened to come back in through the front rather than the stage door and I heard wild shouting from on stage. I snuck in and took the last seat in the last row of the theater. Clurman was putting Marlon through his paces like a gym teacher.

He was blasting him. "Louder!" Harold would shout. "I can't hear you!" Marlon was livid, but he never fought back. He just did as Clurman instructed him: climbing ropes, shouting, run-ning around, anything to energize him. Anything to get what was all internal out. Harold had a really tough job and one that his temperament was not particularly suited for, but whenever he succeeded in lighting a spark in Marlon, the spark burst into fireworks.

After we had played a couple of performances out of town, Clurman and Kazan came to me to ask a favor. They believed that playing in front of an audience had proven something about the structure of the play. I had one scene in each of the three acts and they had decided that my third act scene needed to be cut. They felt its humor distracted from the tragic melo-drama of the scene that followed it—Marlon's scene. I didn't put up a fight. Naturally, I wasn't thrilled, but I had to put my money where my mouth had always been. You're there to serve the good of the play; that had to come first.

I just steeled my determination to score a couple of good moments in the first two acts.

In the first, I entered with each arm draped around a girl, and approached the counter.

"Do you have a vacant cabin for three people all very much in love?" Big laugh.

By the time we opened, I had grown comfortable with playing this character as broadly as possible. I did everything you're not supposed to do as a serious actor. Burlesque double takes. All kinds of shtick, but the character needed it. I have always felt that the audience's first impression of a character is fifty percent of the battle. If you can nail that, you're halfway home.

In the second act, I entered, suffering from a whopper hangover. Clurman told me, "You have the biggest hangover in the world." Of course, he was talking to a guy who doesn't drink. I racked my brain for something to use and finally decided to make it visual for myself. When I started to analyze a hangover, the main thing I could grab onto was fear of movement. I thought, "I don't want to move any part of my body, no matter how tiny." When I came out, I moved as little as possible. I visualized a basket on top of my head containing two dozen eggs. I crossed to the table, sat down, and delivered my line: "Coffee. Black . . . Very black." Another big laugh.

Marlon's scene was in the third act. Having discovered his wife had cheated on him when he was away at war, he takes her out on the dock and, off stage, drowns her. He staggers back into the cafe wringing wet and had his big scene. It was clear why Clurman didn't want another laugh before Marlon entered. Marlon sat at the table in the cafe and had this one scene that lasted about five minutes.

But first he had to get into the scene. I remember that Clurman had a devil of a time persuading Marlon to enter far enough center stage so that the audience could actually see him. Marlon tended to enter a few feet, then pause behind a post that blocked him from most of the audience's view. After much cajoling, Clurman managed to get Marlon to make his entrance farther into the set. At least during rehearsals. Come opening night, Marlon paused behind that post again. Even in something as mechanical as blocking, Marlon relied so completely on his instincts that he simply couldn't do anything that didn't feel absolutely right to him. Or did his instincts tell him to make the audience strain to see him? Who knows?

It didn't matter one bit. Once he was into the scene, he owned the stage one hundred and ten percent—every table, chair, and even that damn post. He absolutely stopped the show. When he finished his scene and left the stage, the audience started to clap. Then they whistled. Then they stomped their feet. This went on for a minute and a half, two minutes. Each of the eight nights we ran. Two minutes is a long time to wait on stage to carry on with the play, but the audiences wouldn't stop.

Even after witnessing that reaction, I still wasn't sure Marlon would be a big star. Clearly he had something unique, but it took so much energy from the director to bring it out of him. Could he deliver it reliably? *Truckline Cafe* only ran eight performances but the buzz on Marlon Brando had started. Little did we know it would last a lifetime.

In spite of Marlon's show-stopping scene, the critics absolutely blasted the play, so belligerently, in fact, that the management (Clurman, Kazan, and Maxwell Anderson) took out an ad in *The New York Times* blasting the critics. But the damage was done. The play closed.

The company had a little farewell midnight supper in a

restaurant close to the Belasco Theater. I was doing the usual closing-night wallowing in self-pity when Maxwell Anderson came over to me.

"You did something with that part that I didn't know was there."

I thanked him, but I already had the out-of-work blues. I said, "I'm getting older. I'm not sure it's worth it anymore. To work and prepare for four or five weeks and then, a couple of nights later, it's all over."

He said, "When you choose to be in the theater, that's what you have to accept. You just stick to it. It'll come."

I'm sure he never thought twice about what he said to me, but his words meant a lot, enough that I still remember his kindness. Everyone needs to hear those things from time to time and most people don't take the time to say them.

Fortunately, I didn't know ahead of time that I was going to have to stick to it for nearly another full year, one of the longest dry stretches of my career. I couldn't believe it was happening again.

Much as I hated to, I looked for work in radio again. I tried even harder this time to understand this different style of acting, but radio never came easily to me. I still hadn't perfected the cold read (and never would). I felt like a jerk standing there at the microphone, throwing my whole body into a performance; but I couldn't help myself.

Our friend Augusta Dabney (who was married to Kevin McCarthy in those days) reminded me recently of exactly how miserable radio made me. She remembered visiting with Mona in our apartment one afternoon when I came rushing in, white as a ghost, and made a beeline for the bathroom.

She asked Mona, "What's wrong with Karl? Is he sick?"

Mona replied, "Oh no, it's just radio."

My folks' wedding picture, 1910.

Me, age 4, preparing for a future role in
Jack and the Beanstalk.

Emerson School Varsity Basketball team, my junior year. I'm fourth from the left with a pretty good Slavic nose even before it was broken.

Mona, my future bride, the most beautiful girl at the Goodman.

My high school yearbook picture—the last time I had a full head of hair.

With Mona, as the Giant and Mrs. Giant, in *Jack and the Beanstalk* at the Goodman.

Mr. Pim Passes By.

[Above left] *The Late Christopher Bean.*
[Above right] Doc Gnesin—the man who took a gamble on me.

[Below] *Counterattack.* Struggling in New York.
(Photo courtesy of Eileen Darby.)

The early days in New York, newly married.

Arthur Miller's *All My Sons*—one of my first big breaks. (Photo from the private collection of Karl Malden.)

The first film I was ever in, *They Knew What They Wanted.* (Photo RKO, ©1940 Turner Entertainment Co.)

Publicity still from the film version of *A Streetcar Named Desire* with Vivien Leigh, Marlon Brando, and Kim Hunter. (Photo © 1951 Charles Feldman Group Productions.)

Oscar night, 1952.

[Above] With Monty Clift and Alfred Hitchcock on *I Confess*. (Photo © 1953 Warner Bros. Pictures, Inc.). [Below] The three Sekulovich boys— Milo, Dan, and me—at my parents' fiftieth wedding anniversary.

[Left] *Desire Under the Elms.* I thought I could sneak onto Broadway without Warners finding out. (Photo courtesy of Vic Shifreen.)

[Center] With Anthony Perkins in *Fear Strikes Out.* I didn't know how much I was playing my own father until I saw myself on screen. (Photo courtesy of the Academy of Motion Picture Arts and Sciences and Paramount Pictures, © 1957 Paramount Pictures. All rights reserved.)

[Bottom] With Gary Cooper in *The Hanging Tree.* When Mona went to see this movie, she couldn't believe she was married to this slob. (Photo courtesy of the Academy of Motion Picture Arts and Sciences, © 1959 Baroda Productions Inc.)

[Top] I treasure this photo from *One-Eyed Jacks* inscribed by Marlon: "In remembrance of things that will never be past. We had the very best of one another, that's a lot for one life. With love and respect, Marlon." (Photo courtesy of Para- mount Pictures, © 1961 Paramount Pictures. All rights reserved.)

[Center] My family makes their first visit to the studio.

[Bottom] *One-Eyed Jacks.* (Photo courtesy of Paramount Pictures, © 1961 Paramount Pic- tures. All rights reserved.)

[Left] The pioneer father in *How the West Was Won*. (Photo © 1962 Turner Entertainment Co.)

[Center] *All Fall Down*—quite the group: Angela Lansbury, Brandon de Wilde, Bill Inge, John Frankenheimer, Warren Beatty, and Eva Marie Saint. (Photo © 1962 Turner Entertainment Co.)

[Bottom] *Gypsy*—a big Hollywood musical that was a joy from start to finish, mostly because of these two wonderful women, Rosalind Russell and Natalie Wood, (Photo courtesy of the Acadamy of Motion Picture Arts and Sciences, © 1962 Warner Bros. Pictures, Inc.)

[Right] The Chinese restaurant scene from *Gypsy.* This number was one of my favorites, but it got cut. (Photo © 1962 Warner Bros. Pictures, Inc.)

[Center] *Cheyenne Autumn*—one of John Ford's brilliant Western tableaus. (Photo courtesy of the Acadamy of Motion Picture Arts and Sciences, © 1964 Ford-Smith Productions.)

[Bottom] *Dead Ringer*—with Bette Davis, a real pro and a pleasure to act with, even in a movie that didn't make it. (Photo courtesy of the Academy of Motion Picture Arts and Sciences, © 1964 Warner Bros. Pictures, Inc.)

Sitting between two different schools of acting in *Cincinnati Kid*—Steve McQueen and Eddie G. Robinson. (Photo courtesy of the Acadamy of Motion Picture Arts and Sciences, © 1965 Turner Entertainment Co.)

Playing Keycase in *Hotel*. I never said so little on screen, or had so much fun. (Photo courtesy of the Academy of Motion Picture Arts and Sciences, © 1967 Warner Bros. Pictures, Inc.)

Facing Page
[Top] A boy from Gary meets the Queen of England. [Center] It was a pleasure to act with George C. Scott in *Patton*. [Bottom] The real Bradley and the ersatz Bradley. The inscription reads: "For Mr. Karl Malden with warm regards, good wishes, and my thanks for a job well done. Omar N. Bradley."

Streets was a training ground for a lot of young stars, including this kid with a name as long as Mladen Sekulovich. (Photo © Thomas Seiles.)

Returning to my roots. I finally got to play a steelworker in the limited TV series, *Skag*.

Facing Page
[Center] *Fatal Vision,* with Eva Marie Saint and Gary Cole.
[Bottom] Barbra assembled a great bunch of actors for *Nuts.*

I signed on for a year. Who knew that twenty-one years later
I'd still be saying, "Don't leave home without them."

Johnny had gotten so much mileage out of my hat and
my nose that I thought he should have a set of his own.

My family today. (Photo courtesy of Leslie Barton.)

I still hated it even when I landed a steady job on the radio soap opera *Our Gal Sunday*. I'd be studying my script and sweating out a performance while the real radio pros would show up five minutes before air and read their parts letter perfect. Some of these people were so proficient at their craft that they had several shows lined up per day. I remember one fellow, Carl Svensen, whose schedule was so heavy he would slip the elevator man a few bucks to hold the elevator for him so he wouldn't waste even a minute waiting for the elevator. He even had an assistant who would attend the dress rehearsal, mark his script for him, and hand it over as Svensen would step up to the mike. He had a whole smooth-running machine going. Not me. It was torture.

During this time, I also began to work for the "Theater Guild on the Air," which was a radio program that did abbreviated, sort of "Reader's Digest" versions of plays. We would rehearse the play for four or five days and then broadcast in front of a live audience in a theater instead of behind a mike in a radio station. To this day people often believe I played the Gentleman Caller in *The Glass Menagerie* because I did it so many times on radio—with Helen Hayes, Shirley Booth, and Mildred Dunnock.

I was much more comfortable with this format, but I was never completely at home with the rhythms of radio. In radio, tempo means so much, everything really. You must paint a picture with your voice, take your time, draw the audience in, let them travel into your imagination. It was very difficult for me to do all that without the visual component.

I suppose that's why the transition to films was an easier one for me. My first movie was years earlier in 1940. When I was on the road with *Key Largo*, Garson Kanin had come backstage to visit with my dressing room mate, Tom Ewell. In the course of conversation, Garson, then the boy wonder of the movies, asked us both if we would like to be in the film he was making. It was called *They Knew What They Wanted* and it turned out that my first bit of screen business was to kiss the star, Carole Lombard.

The scene called for Tom and me to be celebrating at Carole's wedding. I turn to Tom and say, "I'm going to kiss the bride," then walk over and kiss her. We rehearsed once, twice, and each time Lombard pushed my face to the side. Finally I cornered Tom and asked him if I had halitosis. He assured me I didn't and I tried again. This time, Lombard pushed my face away again and whispered in my ear, "Get your puss in the camera." She knew this was my one moment and she was a big enough star and a gracious enough human being to force me to take it.

My next film job didn't come until seven years and nine plays later, after *Truckline Cafe* had closed.

After the play closed, I got a call from the movie director, Henry Hathaway, saying he was casting a movie called *13 Rue Madeleine*, starring James Cagney, Sam Jaffe, and Nick Conte. True to his word, Kazan had asked Hathaway to put me in the picture. It was to shoot in Quebec, so I hopped on the train and headed north. Who should be on the train with me but my old army buddy, Red Buttons. I asked him where he was headed.

"Quebec."

"Me too."

"I'm making a movie."

"Me too."

It turned out we were both headed for the same picture so we traveled together, checked into the hotel, and waited for our audience with Henry Hathaway. At eight in the evening, after he had wrapped that day's shooting, Hathaway summoned us.

"I got two parts. One part has one word. The other part has a couple of lines. Which one do you each want?"

Always the smart comedian, Red said, "You mean you brought me all the way up here for a couple of lines?"

Hathaway looked at him and said, "No, I brought you up here for one word." Then he pointed to me. "Him I brought here for a couple of lines."

Kazan lived up to his promise again when he used me in the next film he himself was directing. This time, it was a full six weeks of work. The picture was called *Boomerang*. It starred Arthur Kennedy and Dana Andrews. Dana was a lovely man, but it is no secret that he had a drinking problem at the time. Though it did not appear to be interfering with his work, Kazan worried about the possibility that one of his actors might not be giving a hundred percent. He thought that Dana could not possibly be in top form after a night of boozing it up. Rightly or wrongly, Gadge decided to teach him a lesson.

Dana had a long speech, a courtroom summation, at least a full page of dialogue. Kazan thought, "Here's my opportunity." He told the writer to rewrite the whole speech. When Dana showed up for work Kazan explained that he hadn't liked the speech and had had the whole thing rewritten. Kazan figured, I guess, that this would throw Dana who could not possibly be up to the task of memorizing this hefty block of dialogue with a hangover.

Dana just said, "Give me about twenty minutes."

Then he retreated into his dressing room and came out letter perfect. I was stunned. Mostly, Kazan was stunned. He had been waiting for fireworks, probably choreographing them intentionally to elicit a specific reaction that would work on film. Instead, he got a perfect recitation of the new speech.

Dana was one of the few actors I have ever seen who was able to pull off that kind of memorization, sober or otherwise. As much as I loved and respected Kazan, I must admit it was fun to see someone turn the tables on him, because in almost all situations Kazan was the master of subtle control.

Kazan had the gift of being able to see through to an actor's unique vulnerability. With me, I always felt that he knew how basically insecure I was. What's more, we had come from similar ethnic upbringing, he being of Anatolian Greek descent; so on some level he knew how important my father's approval was to me. As my director, Kazan often became like a father.

The opening night of the next play we did together, I remember him stopping by my dressing room with the author, Arthur Miller. Arthur shook my hand and said something, I don't remember what. Then Gadge grabbed me in a great bear hug and said, "You're wonderful in this part." And he walked away. As a director, he knew what you needed to hear to shape your performance, but then he also knew what you needed to hear as a human being.

That play was *All My Sons* and would end up running over a year.

facing page:
Being directed by Elia Kazan in
***A Streetcar Named Desire.* (Photo © 1951**
Charles Feldman Group Productions.)

Chapter 7

Popular opinion holds that good, old-fashioned movies are the great American art form. I agree. But for a time, the Golden Age of the American theater offered an actor the chance to forge new ground. From the midforties through the fifties, Broadway plays were exploring the human condition in ways that theater never had before.

Luckily, my timing was just right. You didn't have to have the face of a leading man to be in a play about some ordinary guy just trying to make a living who finds himself caught in a moral dilemma; or about a woman too sensitive to maintain her sanity in this brutal world; or a family struggling to know one another. These were plays that rivaled any other theatrical tradition. British, Russian, you name it. When playwrights like Arthur Miller and Tennessee Williams were at their prime, an actor couldn't help but be proud to be working in the theater. Broadway was the place to be.

Three years of straight work is a great run for any actor, but when I got to spend three years in the late forties segueing from Miller's *All My Sons* to Williams' *A Streetcar Named Desire*, I really felt like I'd made it. Success meant something different then. At least it did to me. These days, success is measured in money—millions of dollars for snarling some catch phrase and dodging explosions. Working in the best plays by the world's best playwrights surrounded by the best actors guided by the best directors was all the success I could ever have imagined.

All My Sons centers around a man who profits by making faulty parts for war planes. His partner takes the fall and goes to jail. Kazan knew me and my work quite well by then so I didn't have to read. I was lucky that Kazan thought of me to play George, the partner's son.

Ed Begley played the crooked father. Begley had been a hugely successful radio actor, but this was his first play on Broadway and he was terrified. He was a wonderful man who naturally exuded the qualities of the father. He was a blustery kind of a guy, always jovial, always with a joke and a great big laugh. But not before going on stage.

When we first opened out of town, Begley lost all his bravura. He stayed in his dressing room until the last possible moment, summoning his courage, then he simply stood backstage, panicstricken. He'd pull out a hanky and start mopping his face; he was already drenched with nervous sweat just standing there. But once onstage, he was perfect as Joe Keller, the man who could talk his way out of anything.

Kazan's direction of *All My Sons* strived for a break-neck pace, incredible speed. During rehearsals, we could barely catch our breath between lines. Kazan was constantly admonishing us to pick up our cues. He wanted the play to move like a runaway train. But out of town, he started to slow it down in certain key places. He would study the audience's reaction and decide, based on that, where to alter the pace to make his points.

I was in the second act and I was to enter at a fevered pitch and build from there. I would stand in the wings working myself up. I'd do anything physical: pace, shadowbox, jump up and down. At the same time, I'd be working myself into an emotional lather. My character's whole action was to avenge my father. So in my mind, I would pick on different actors in the scene and think, "I'm going to show him how to act tonight. I'm going to go out there and get my due. I'm going to get what's coming to me. This moment belongs to me." That's what the character was thinking, but I needed to make it personal. That's what worked for me. Then I would burst on, ready to do my scene.

One day during rehearsal, my entrance arrived and I exploded onto the stage as usual. But I had worked myself up into such a frenzy backstage that I hyperventilated. The stage, the entire theater, started spinning.

There stood Kazan, laughing. He said he knew this was going to happen sooner or later. He advised me to prepare in the same way, but then to give myself a few minutes of downtime before my entrance. That seemed to work from then on and I learned that controlling the artistic process is as important as freeing it.

During the run of *All My Sons*, Darryl Zanuck saw me in the rushes of the film, *Boomerang*, which Kazan had directed. He wanted me to be in a new movie he was mounting called *Kiss of Death* to be directed by Henry Hathaway. A little-known actor with whom I had worked in radio had a part in it as well: Richard Widmark. He would be considerably better known after he made this particular movie where he pushed an old lady in a wheelchair down a flight of stairs, cackling all the while.

I explained to the movie team that I was appearing in a play, but they promised me that shooting the film would not interfere with the play. I knew that it would be tough to be performing eight performances a week of *Sons* on stage and also shoot the film, but it was an opportunity I could not pass up.

I knew I'd end up exhausted and delivering less than my best on stage and on the set, so I borrowed a folding cot from a friend, traipsed across town with it in a taxi, and set it up in my dressing room. My plan was to finish on the movie set around six o'clock, grab a sandwich, and sleep for an hour before my entrance in the second act. Fortunately, I was not in the first act at all so I had a good hour and a half before I even needed to start getting into makeup.

My first day shooting the movie was a Tuesday. I went to work and made it to the theater on time. The next day was Wednesday, an afternoon performance. I told the director and producer I would have to leave early. I guess they hadn't thought about matinee days because they blew their tops. They demanded I call the theater and have my understudy put on. I called Kazan and explained the problem. He said, "You come do the play. That was your first commitment." He called Zanuck and had a little talk with him. I felt like a kid who had gotten himself in a jam and had to get a note from the teacher. I'd been there before—way back in high school when my basketball commitment conflicted with play rehearsal.

The next day, I was excused—permanently—from the picture. Much to my delight, they still had to make good on my four week guarantee. I thought I'd hit the big time. I made four thousand dollars for one day's work. It was the best deal I'd make for a long time.

During the run of *All My Sons*, Kazan gave me another play to read. He told me that the producer, Irene Selznick, didn't know it yet, but as far as he, Kazan, was concerned I was going to be in this new play.

I brought the play home and read it on a Saturday morning before the matinee of *Sons*. At that time, Mona and I had rented a one room furnished apartment. She stood, ironing, a few feet from where I sat reading. Suddenly she looked over at me and asked, "Why are you crying?"

I'm not even sure I knew that I was crying. All I could answer was, "You read it when I finish."

Finally, I finished. The tears were still streaming down my cheeks. I handed Mona the play. She handed me the iron. The last line was still echoing in my head as I took over ironing the shirts. "I have always depended on the kindness of strangers."

When Mona finished reading, she was crying, too.

For my money, *A Streetcar Named Desire* was then and remains today the best play I have ever read. Hands down. I knew instantly that *Streetcar* was a better play than *All My Sons*. *Sons* was a good, solid play, but *Streetcar* was a work of art. It was as though *Sons* was a rough canvas made of sail cloth. *Streetcar* was fine, delicate lace. Miller was steeped in reality, raw to the bone; Tennessee wanted to escape reality. Streetcar was poetry.

Kazan had wanted to know what I thought about playing the part of Mitch. That was easy. I had to be in that play. I had been in New York almost ten years. I knew that if I was in this play it would be a long time before I had to look for work again.

When we began rehearsals, Kazan spent a few minutes with the usual get-acquainted introductions. Then he looked at us all gathered around the table and said, "There will be no changes. Not one word. Let's go to work."

He remained true to his word. I don't recall any changes being made during the rehearsal period. Some changes are usually routine during that phase of a production, whether just a word here and there that doesn't feel right or a whole scene that needs to be added, restructured or deleted. But the only glitch I remember in *Streetcar* was a minor technical one.

A couple of times during the course of the play, a musical piece called "The Vesuviana" echoes in Blanche's mind. The music had to have a slightly eerie, dreamlike quality. What instrument could achieve that?

The pianist laid a couple of sheets of newspaper on top of his keyboard, but that only produced a rattly sound. It did not evoke the ethereal sense of distorted memory the play called for. We all had a sense that every little detail had to be absolutely perfect for this play; there would be no settling. Finally, the pianist tinkered with a Hammond organ and achieved the proper sound.

I'm sure that other petty logistical problems must have cropped up, but that is the only little stumbling block I remember. As for the play itself, it was perfect as Tennessee had written it.

Tennessee himself appeared briefly during the first week of rehearsals. He was a short, slightly stocky man who chain-smoked cigarette after cigarette, which he inserted, one after another, into a special little holder. His voice seemed to crackle in the back of his throat. He laughed at the lines; he seemed to really enjoy what he had written. I recall him as someone who was always running away; he would hang around rehearsals for a few days, then disappear for a couple of weeks.

I regret now that I did not try to get to know Tennessee better.

Certainly, part of me felt intimidated to be meeting the man who had written this remarkable play, as well as *The Glass Menagerie*, which had already had its successful run on Broadway. But it was more than that. I never extended myself. I was not good at holding a conversation, worse at initiating one. I could never just walk up to someone—especially someone I so admired—and strike up a conversation. Small talk still escapes me to this day.

Besides, in the case of Tennessee, what words could I use to talk to a man who could work such magic with words? I was horribly self-conscious about the way I expressed myself. Looking back on it all now, I realize I wasted an awful lot of years, terrified that I would embarrass myself by making some horrible faux pas. It has always been easier just to keep quiet. I'm sure that over the years, many co-workers must have thought I was removed, even aloof.

I was lucky that I found a common ground with Kazan where we could become friendly. That was the basketball court at the gym, an arena where I felt comfortable. Though we had our immigrant backgrounds in common, I always felt that he was in a different category from me. He had gone to college and I viewed him as a true intellectual while I was nurturing a king-sized inferiority complex.

I like to think that one of the reasons Gadge and I became friends was because he felt that I had some talent to offer. As a director, he sought out people who could deliver. If you didn't come through for him, he didn't use you a second time. Since he kept using me, I began to realize that he must have seen something in me and that realization put me more at ease with him. As I grew more at ease, we became better friends. Otherwise, we might never have had anything more than a working relationship, instead of the lifelong friendship I am so grateful for.

It was also during rehearsals for *Streetcar* that I really began to know the kid playing Stanley Kowalski. I had been in those paltry eight performances of *Truckline Cafe* with this kid in his early twenties—Marlon Brando—and had come away from that experience wondering if he would prove to be the force he obviously could be, or if his promise would evaporate.

Streetcar would tell.

We opened out of town in New Haven, Connecticut. Kazan had invited Harold Clurman, Wally Freed (a theatrical business manager), and Arthur Miller to attend opening night there. During intermission, Kazan came to the dressing room I was sharing with Marlon and invited us to come to his hotel suite later for a round-table discussion about the play.

It took me about a half an hour to get dressed and get myself over there after the performance. Everyone was there except Arthur Miller. I asked Gadge, "Where's Miller?" No one knew.

Finally, Arthur Miller arrived, some time later.

Gadge asked him, "Where were you?"

"I had to take a walk," Miller replied, clearly distraught. "That damn Tennessee Williams."

"What do you mean?" Gadge pressed.

"Space and time don't mean anything to him," Miller explained. "Indoors, outdoors, nothing makes a difference to him."

Gadge asked, "What's wrong with that?"

"I can't do it," Miller said. "When I write I say to myself, 'Is that going to be an act change? Does that need to be a scene change?'"

Gadge told him, "Don't worry about that. Just write it the way you want it. Let the director and the scenic designer worry about how to pull it off."

The footnote to the story is that the next year Arthur Miller appeared with a new play: *Death of a Salesman*. The uncle comes from Africa. Willy Loman is in his house, in his office, everywhere. The brothers are talking in their bedroom in their pajamas one moment, and the next moment they are in the backyard. It doesn't matter. Miller had forced himself to plumb the depths of his soul because he had been so challenged, so inspired by another playwright. That was the beauty of the theater at that time. Greatness inspired greatness, no matter how different the styles.

Opening night of *Streetcar* in New York left no doubt about the impact of Williams' achievement on the theatrical world. What I had suspected in rehearsals proved true. Marlon Brando was a genius (a word I do not use loosely and one I don't think I have ever applied to any other actor I have worked with). There was no doubt that he was an actor the world would talk about.

Years later in his autobiography, Kazan would call the phenomenon of Brando as Kowalski a "performance miracle." I believe that watching Marlon be Stanley Kowalski gave Kazan a vicarious thrill, not only as a one-time actor but also as a man. It was a performance of force, power, and undeniable sexuality, but also of breathtaking reality, the quality that Kazan was striving for philosophically and practically.

Kazan's genius was in casting Marlon. Kazan had a gift for casting; he could match the character to the emotional core of the actor. He knew that Marlon would instinctively find the emotional center of Stanley. All Kazan had to do was let him go. After that, Marlon simply could not do anything phony on stage.

Oddly enough, that did not necessarily hold true backstage. Marlon and I shared a dressing room for the two years that *Streetcar* ran. Many nights, I watched him court backstage sycophants with his devastating charm. The minute they would leave the dressing room, he would turn to me and pronounce them "a stupid prick." On the other hand, he could be the softest touch in town. I couldn't believe it when he would lend money—

money he often didn't have—for the second or third time, to every down-and-out wannabe with an outstretched palm.

Or even to any oddball character. For about six weeks during the *Streetcar* run, Marlon invited a new friend—Igor, I think—to our dressing room to play the violin for us while we dressed and put on our makeup. This fellow played the violin in the gypsy manner; he could really make that fiddle weep. One night I couldn't find an important prop, the silver cigarette case from which Mitch reads the inscription to Blanche. I looked high and low, but no cigarette case. The prop man couldn't find it either, but fortunately had a backup. We never could find the damn thing.

About a month later, one afternoon between the matinee and evening performances, I grabbed a quick sandwich at a nearby deli and went back to the dressing room to take a nap. I lay down on the sofa in the corner behind a wardrobe rack. As I was dozing, in came Igor who began rummaging through the pockets in our wardrobe. I kept my mouth shut until he took something from one of Marlon's pockets.

I said, "Put it back."

He panicked and started to say something.

I just said, "Put it back and never come back into this room again."

Igor must have run crying to Marlon because about a half an hour before that evening's curtain, Marlon came in and really let me have it. He told me he had been trying to help Igor change his thieving ways. Marlon had known all along that our violin-playing friend had swiped the cigarette case and never said a word.

Ironically, when he was onstage "acting," Marlon was incapable of the secrecy he perfected backstage. Marlon brought a reality to the stage that the theater had never witnessed before, a sense of immediacy and passion that would change the style of acting in America.

The Stanislavski influence on the Group Theater dictated that acting on stage should be as real as possible. The Group brought a real sensibility to the theater that far surpassed anything happening on Broadway at the time. However, even the Group productions possessed a certain theatricality about them, about their style, that permeated everything from the makeup to the acting.

Marlon challenged that. He took the concept of reality to a totally new level. He *was* Stanley Kowalski. To this day, I cannot think of a marriage of character and actor to rival that of Marlon and Stanley. I cannot imagine why any other actor would ever want to attempt that part, so profound and absolute was the connection. To use a "Method" acting term, he instinctively lived "in the moment" in a way that no other actor ever had before. Not only was he in the moment, you felt that he had never been there before. Every breath brought a new sense of discovery, with no censor between raw emotion and action. He was a revelation.

Watching this marvel in action—not to mention having to act with him—challenged me to make the character of Mitch more real than anything I had ever done before. Marlon made me work harder, dig deeper than any other actor I have ever worked with.

Marlon himself had Kazan to bring out the best in him. Kazan's gift was that he was somehow able to see into Marlon's soul and set him free. Marlon also had Stella Adler, the acclaimed acting teacher, who took the time to probe him, to coax. She really made a pet project of him, instructing him to read certain books, listen to certain music, study certain paintings. She fancied that exposure to the arts would help turn this raw talent into a cultivated artist.

In *Streetcar,* the combination of working with Marlon and Kazan was unbeatable for me. Kazan was the great psychological mind of the theater. In subtle ways, he got to know the people he was working with so well that he knew more about what made them tick than they did themselves. Often, he manipulated actors and their off-stage relationships for the good of the play. Of course, you weren't aware of this when it was happening to you. You never knew what he had told other people about you, or if what he had told you about the other people was true. He just presided over the production like some magic puppeteer jerking the strings of his actors, the marionettes. But it turns out to be a wonderful, freeing experience for the actor because you feel safe and in good hands, and he makes you feel as though you have thought up all the good ideas yourself.

I remember an episode during *Streetcar* rehearsals, which, to this day, I do not know if Kazan masterminded. There was a moment in the play when I came out of the bathroom and bumped into Blanche. My line was, "Excuse me, excuse me." As she and I were dodging each other, Marlon would call, "Hey, Mitch!" and then a second time, "Mitch!" I was to yell back, "Coming!"

Some days, Marlon took the longest pauses I have ever sweated through. Other days, he would come in too soon. Sometimes, he just said the line flatly, giving me nothing to scream back at.

After a few weeks of this, I hit the ceiling. "Who the hell can get anything done around here? There's no rhythm to the scene. One day you're too early, the next day you don't come in at all!"

Kazan played the peacemaker, but for all I know he had directed Marlon to deliver that line differently every time to keep me on edge and uncertain.

I have always differed from Marlon in that regard. I like to be cooperative in a scene, to help someone deliver in any way I can. Marlon's attitude was very much, "This is how I'm going to play this scene today. I may play it differently tomorrow. You have to figure out what you're doing yourself." It's an attitude that can make playing a scene with him pure hell. Especially because of those damn pauses of his. I firmly believe that he was never trying to steal a scene. He just had a tempo all his own.

Other actors (usually young ones trying to find their style) often try to imitate him, but their pauses are flat. Just so much dead air. Marlon could fill a pause because he had a fire inside him that kept everything he did interesting. Later, he perfected this on screen. You could look at his face for two minutes and stay fascinated. I knew that if you stayed on my face that long, the audience would be pleading, "Say something, do something already." Not necessarily because I'm not "full," but because there is something about beauty on screen that captivates us. Marlon knew how to work that.

Ultimately I grew to look forward to the challenge of playing with Marlon. I am competitive enough to flatter myself into believing I could keep up with him. And that is why I say I believe playing with Marlon consistently brought out the best in me. I guess, in the final analysis, it is impossible to beat genius, but it can be great fun to try to match it.

In *Streetcar*, it worked for the character I was playing, Mitch, to let Marlon's Stanley take the lead. Mitch would have loved to have been Stanley, so I just did a lot of watching him in the beginning, practically the whole first act. Once again, I had to make it personal. Mitch was in awe of Stanley, so I was in awe of Marlon.

That wasn't hard.

Marlon's instincts took him to places on stage that no one had ever gone before. One day when Jessica Tandy, Kim Hunter, and he were rehearsing the famous birthday party scene around the dinner table, he stood up from the table, gave one of those pauses that only he could, slammed his hand down on the plate in front of him and smashed it to smithereens. The shards flew all over. It scared the hell out of Jessica and Kim. He delivered his line, "I cleaned up my plate. You want me to clean up yours?" Then he played the rest of the scene picking pieces of china from his bloody hand.

Kazan had created an atmosphere in which that could happen spontaneously. If that's what Marlon wanted to do, that's what Marlon would do. Kazan simply instructed the prop man to order some plates that would break without leaving sharp edges. So that's what Marlon did every single night. And that moment took every single audience's breath away.

Of course, just laying eyes on Marlon had that effect. In *Streetcar*, the first time Marlon appeared was when he and I ran across the back of the stage on our way to go bowling. On opening night—and every night after that for two years—you could hear the audience gasp when he crossed that stage for those few seconds. You could feel the electricity of their reaction to him. It was one of the joys of my career to share that moment.

And, as I have said, it was one of the great honors of my career to be able to create Mitch. I wish that I could say I have a distinct way of going about creating a character. But I can't. Because I was around on the ground floor of the Actors Studio, people might assume that I would call myself a Method actor. But I don't. I do have a method, of course. That is, any method that works.

Sometimes I start from the outside in, sometimes from the inside out. With some parts, they solve themselves. You read the script two or three times and the character becomes clear. He just opens up to you. Why beat your brains out thinking, "I must use the Method." But even in those parts, there might be a moment that presents a hurdle. Then it's wonderful to have something, some little approach to solving the problem, to fall back on. To be able to ask yourself, "Who am I playing with?" "What's the problem?" "What's the opposition?" If I can use the Method at these moments to make my job easier, great. If not, I have to use something else.

I take a little from this school of thought, a little from that. Whatever works for the particular character I'm working on. Because every character has a life of his own, I feel I have had to create each one in a different and unique way. I think of it as finding the hook. Every character has his own key that allows you to discover all his colors and dimensions. Like pushing at a small drop of water with your finger. You push it this way and that way until another droplet breaks off, and then another, and another. Before you know it, you have a whole array of drops, of personality traits that might make up an individual. That's a good start, but all those facets do not become a fully realized character until they are connected, preferably in a way that is unique to that character. So you begin to connect the water spots, attaching them to one another carefully to become one big pool of water. That's the way you create a part—grabbing onto something here, something there, and pulling it all together into a whole. A whole human being.

Damn near every time it's starting from scratch. From a different angle, a different attack, a different source. It's not necessarily in the lines, though you must know the lines inside out to free yourself enough to be comfortable with the character. It is what happens to you, inside you, as you're developing the character that counts. It is the truth you find that counts most.

The process is like growing a good, strong tree. You have to have a solid trunk—the basic truth of the character—before you can add the branches, the personality traits. And that trunk has to be straight, its roots extending deep into the ground, before you can add the leaves, the flourishes that can give the trunk (the character, the performance) its color and beauty.

For me, that doesn't happen when I'm in rehearsal with the other actors. If I wait until I'm on the set, I'm in big trouble. It has to happen when I'm all alone in my room. That's where it comes true. A door opens and you're through it to the other side. A glow envelops you that is unmistakable. It is an unparalleled thrill. That's what keeps you coming back for more misery through all those agonizing attempts when you think you've cracked a character, but his spine just isn't strong and straight yet so that tree starts snapping in the wind.

And almost every time, it means finding something within yourself. At least it does for me. You can always access something in your own life to help you. As different as my upbringing was from Mitch's in *Streetcar*, it was enormously helpful to me in finding the key to that character.

I knew from the start that the key to Mitch's character lay in his attachment to his mother. That was fascinating to me in itself. That is to say, the fact that his key lies in a character we never meet. The fact that we feel her influence so strongly, but only through him, could make that influence all the more powerful.

When the poker buddies are drinking beer, Mitch doesn't drink. When Mitch gets up to leave the game, Stanley says to him, "You're ahead, you can't go now." Mitch answers, "My Mother." That's all he has to say and that says it all.

If he could just be rid of his mother, he'd be free. My task became to keep my mother's voice in my head. Mitch had to hear a running question in the back of his mind all the time. "What would my mother think about this situation?" "What would my mother think about Blanche?" "What would my mother think of what I just did?" "What would my mother think about every single thing I say and do all day long?" The constant questions suffocate him.

When I began to think along those lines, my high school years came flooding back to me. I could remember countless times when I would become involved in some activity and I would say to myself, "Be careful. Don't disgrace the Sekulovich name. What would people think? What would Pa think?" Maybe that's not unusual. Maybe that's what every kid thinks when he is trying to find his own way. It didn't matter to me. That was something I could draw on without ever really articulating it to myself.

It was also easy for me to recall the desperate need to break away. So that became the essence of Mitch for me. To break away from his mother. To be free of that voice inside his head. I remembered the pressure to do the Serbian community—and my father—proud. Mitch felt the same pressure to be the best for his mother. He wore his "lightweight alpaca" sport coat in stunning contrast to Stanley in his torn T-shirt two sizes too small. A T-shirt that spelled sexuality like nothing on the stage ever had before. Stanley was free. He had no voices going on in his head. He operated from a region way below the brain. But it was my job to make the audience hear Mitch's mother saying to him, "Put on that coat and tie," even though it was a hundred degrees and a hundred percent New Orleans humidity.

Mitch's mother has not only kept him under her thumb, she has kept him different from everyone around him. That became another key to Mitch for me. He is different. I knew what that was like, too. After all, I could barely understand English when I went to kindergarten. Although I was an American, I was a foreigner, too. I knew about different. And I knew how it felt to hate being different.

That opened another door to Mitch for me. A big moment in the play comes in the scene between Blanche and Mitch when she asks him, "You love your mother very much, don't you?"

"Yes," Mitch says. "I love her very much."

I know that most actors who have played Mitch since then have played that answer honestly, literally. I decided to do the opposite. I decided that deep in his soul, Mitch hates his mother. He hates her for making him different and crippling him. But he knows that he can never admit this to anyone, most of the time not even to himself. That became the critical moment for me. I remember that when Jessica as Blanche asked me that question, I looked away and struggled to find the courage to say, "No, I hate her. I wish she were dead." I went through the process in my mind, but just couldn't say it. For the one time in my life, I took a pause as long as any of Marlon's. So that when I finally did answer, "Yes . . . I love her very much," it became a moment of great defeat for Mitch.

Blanche becomes his last hope. From the perspective of my character, that was the great tragedy of the play. Blanche took Mitch down with her. She took so many people down with her.

I'm so sorry that it was not common practice in 1948 to film stage productions. There is no record of Jessica Tandy's performance as Blanche and that is a great loss. She brought a unique quality to the role that no other actress ever has. I believe she understood the character better than any other actress who has ever played her. Most of the other actresses latched onto the undercurrent of sexuality that defines Blanche.

What Jessica was able to convey that the others ignored was equally important—the schoolteacher in Blanche. For example, you totally believed the scene with the newspaper boy. You could see in that scene how Blanche behaved with her high school students. You could even see it in her first scene with Stanley. Unlike with Vivien Leigh, if there was any attraction to him with Jessica's Blanche, it was buried so deep you couldn't see it. She treated him like he was one of her errant students. Jessica had that mother hen element about her.

That was true even in terms of the *Streetcar* company. Jessica was the real seasoned pro of the group. She kept the company together during our long run and every now and then she would have to nudge someone back into line—especially Marlon—but thank God for the mother hen.

Jessica acted the mother not only to the company, but to the entire crew at the beautiful Ethel Barrymore Theater. Every holiday, it was Jessica who threw the party for everyone from the cast to the stagehands and ushers. I believe everyone who worked in that theater for those two years had the sense, albeit unspoken, that we were uniquely privileged to be a part—any part—of that production. We enjoyed coming together for special occasions as a family and Jessica made sure that happened.

Jessica Tandy was a consummate professional. I remember one day during the first year of the run when she received a phone call informing her that if she went on that night, she would be shot on stage. This was nearly fifty years ago when no one had ever heard of celebrity stalking. When Jessica stepped on stage that night, two detectives were covering the house. She gave her usual dazzling performance without missing a beat. We all breathed an enormous sigh of relief as she delivered her final line, suddenly possessed of an added resonance. "I have always depended on the kindness of strangers."

Recently, since reading Marlon's autobiography, I couldn't help but wonder if Marlon made that call. He loved to play practical jokes, even cruel ones, and he locked horns with Jessica regularly. I wouldn't have put it past him. The only thing he loved more than a prank was pulling off a prank in absolute and eternal secrecy.

I'll never know and I could be way off base about the call, but there was no getting around it; Jessica had a hard time with Marlon. Basically, they simply didn't get along very well, which, of course, Kazan worked to the play's advantage. Jessica's training ground had been the British theater. At the age of eighteen, she had played Ophelia to Gielgud's Hamlet. She placed a premium on consistency, reliability, being able to deliver one hundred percent one hundred percent of the time.

Jacob Adler, father of Marlon's coach, Stella Adler, and renowned actor in the Yiddish theater, had imparted a very different philosophy to Marlon. Don't push. If you arrive at the theater feeling ninety percent, give eighty. If you feel fifty, give forty. Make the audience feel that you've got more, that there is more there that they are not seeing. I suppose he felt that a certain longing kept the audience engaged. It was an attitude that appealed to Marlon's basically undisciplined nature and to his sense of mystery.

It was hard to argue with Jessica that sometimes Marlon did things that made him seem like a "damn fool" as she would put it. During the second year of *Streetcar*, Marlon bought a set of boxing gloves. He figured that boxing for twenty minutes or so down in the basement would help him stay in shape and keep his energy up for the end of the play while the two women, Kim and Jessica, were having their big scene. He made the rounds in search of sparring partners. One of the poker players, Nick Dennis, had been a boxer, even fought at Madison Square Garden, but he refused. I traded a few jabs with him for a couple of nights, but then I decided I'd had it, too.

Finally, Marlon convinced a young stagehand to go a few rounds with him. Marlon kept prodding him, "Come on, come on. Don't hold back." The kid hauled off. His left fist made contact with Marlon's nose. They could probably hear the crack all the way up on stage.

Marlon stumbled back upstairs and asked the prop man for a towel. He played the last scene of the play pressing the blood-soaked towel to his face. After Jessica said, "I've always depended on the kindness of strangers," she made her exit and muttered under her breath to him, "You stupid ass." I put my head down on the table as I did every time she exited. The audience must have thought I was really giving it everything I had as my head shook with sobs. That particular night, I was actually shaking with laughter.

In fact, I think I had originally begun putting my head down on the table at that moment because Marlon often broke me up. As the doctor and nurse were taking Blanche away, Marlon would be muttering under his breath, "It's about time they got that lunatic out of here . . ." or "Thank God, now we can pull the damn curtain and we can go home." As far as Marlon was concerned, the play was over. But it was still an emotional moment for my character, and he was making it tough for me.

Finally, I said, to him, "Marlon, you know you've got all these sides. You're on every page of the play. I've only got fourteen sides. You can throw half of yours away and still register. I've got to register on every page." He understood and he never did it again. If your argument made sense to him, Marlon would listen and stop giving you a hard time.

I must admit I got him once. When summer arrived, the old Barrymore Theater got very hot. After the opening where Marlon and I would run across the stage, he and I would sneak out the stage door and cool off in the breezeway at the side of the theater. There would always be a policeman on horseback there and we'd feed the horse and chat with the cop to kill the ten or fifteen minutes before Marlon's next entrance.

One night, we stayed out there a few minutes and then I went back inside. I came running back out. "Marlon, we missed your cue! Hurry up!" Marlon ran on stage . . . about ten minutes early. Jessica and Kim were in the middle of their scene. They stared at him. He stared at them.

After an interminable moment, Kim said, "What are you doing here?" Then Jessica, ever the professional, jumped ahead about five pages and picked up the scene where his entrance should have been. The play was about ten minutes shorter that night.

When Marlon came off, he said to me, "I'll never listen to you again." But he thought it was funny. I'd gotten him at his own game.

As *Streetcar* began its second year, I started to feel like my life was finally falling into place. I was in the middle of a good, long run and Mona and I were about to have our first child.

We did not own a car so we had arranged with our friend and neighbor, Kevin McCarthy, to drive us to the hospital when the time came. In classic movie fashion, the time came at three in the morning. The father was relegated to the waiting room in those days; so when they told me it was going to be quite a long while before the baby was born, I walked to the nearby apartment of an old army buddy, Gary Merrill, and woke him up. I hung around there for a few hours, then went back to the hospital.

Late that afternoon Mona gave birth to a baby girl. I had to run to the theater, so I didn't get to see the baby until the next morning. I stood gazing through the nursery window for a long time in disbelief. Next to me, looking at his baby, stood the publisher of a popular newspaper of the day called "PM."

After a while, I said to him, "We're very lucky."

He could barely look at me. "I'm not so lucky," he said. "My wife died."

I didn't know what to say. I managed to sputter, "I'm sorry." I spent another minute looking through the glass and then I walked away. As I headed down the corridor to Mona's room, I said a prayer for how lucky I was. I think I even crossed myself in the Serbian Orthodox manner without realizing what I was doing.

It took us a few days to name the baby. We were closing in on "Deborah," which was fashionable at the time, but it didn't quite speak to us. In the cab on the way to the theater, I started racking my brain for a Serbian name. A lot of them were real mouthfuls like Mladen and I didn't want my daughter to have to go through grammar school having to correct every teacher's pronunciation of her name as I had. Suddenly I hit on Mila. The name means "dearest," "lovable," words that definitely applied to my brother, Milo. I knew in my heart that that was what the baby's name should be. Happily, Mona was enchanted by it immediately. So, while I had thought Milo Malden was a little too melifluous for me when I was in the process of changing my own name, I now had Mila Malden. It suited her just perfectly; she was a lot prettier than I was.

After about two years, my three fellow principals in *Streetcar* announced they would be leaving the play. The management came to me and asked if I, too, would leave since they believed it would be an easier and smoother transition to bring in a whole company that had already been playing together as a unit in another city.

I don't remember exactly how or why, but I ended up staying on to play with the Chicago company for about a month. Actually, it was only part of the Chicago company. Anthony Quinn bowed out of New York so Marlon was replaced by Ralph Meeker, but Uta Hagen came from Chicago to replace Jessica as Blanche.

That ended up being a unique and fascinating experience for me. My style of working depends a great deal on the people I am playing with, even so far as how I deliver a line. I was eager to see if I could adjust to a new group after evolving into such a strong team with the originals. After so long, I wasn't sure I was capable of changing to mesh with different actors. In many ways it was like starting all over again to get to know Mitch; if there was going to be a different Blanche, there would have to be a different Mitch.

There was an added challenge in that I was playing with the "old" company at night and rehearsing with the "new" company during the day. Harold Clurman had directed the Chicago company and he had implemented a different concept of what the play should be.

Our rehearsals were going along fairly well; everything blended . . . until we came to the big confrontation scene where Mitch holds Blanche under the light and tells her off. It just wasn't working. It didn't pull together. I was used to chasing Jessica around like a delicate moth flitting from flame to flame. Uta was a sturdy, Germanic woman with two feet planted firmly on the ground. We kept trying, but the clash of interpretations only escalated.

I stepped down to the footlights and begged our producer, Irene Selznick, to call in either Harold Clurman or Kazan to help us. I didn't care who, but Irene insisted we just keep trying ourselves. One more time, one more time. She tried to make us listen to each other—as the characters and as actors. We kept going and we both gave in a little and finally got through the scene, but that was about it—just getting through. To this day I believe Uta Hagen holds a grudge against me, but I still think it was just a case of two different interpretations. It wasn't her fault and I hope it wasn't mine. It was nobody's fault at all. That incident was a revelation to me that such a pure, clear piece of work could still be open to such diverse interpretations.

I played with the new cast for about a month and then I, too, left *Streetcar*. It ended up being my longest run with any play—nearly two years.

Recently, I had the interesting experience of meeting with a new generation of actors who were doing *Streetcar* as a television special. My agents at that time also represented John Goodman who was playing Mitch, and they told me he was interested in meeting me. I stopped by the set one afternoon. It ended up that Goodman and I really didn't discuss the part much. At first, we didn't even discuss the play. But when they broke for a few minutes, we sat around and started swapping stories.

Alec Baldwin and Jessica Lange, who had done the play on Broadway together, joined us. Baldwin asked me how long I had played *Streetcar*.

I told him, "Two years."

Their jaws dropped. They were floored.

"We did it for six months and we were exhausted."

Ever since this meeting, I have been thinking about this difference in our experiences, trying to figure out what accounts for this generation gap in actors. How is it that one group of actors can play the same thing every night for two years and love

every minute of it while another group feels utterly drained after six months? Have techniques changed? Did we have a different type of training? Or is it purely economical? Were we—a
bunch of hungry, young actors—just so thrilled to have a job,
while they came to the play as movie stars eager for the experience only, not the employment? Is it because we were doing a
new play, an unknown quantity? Does that same play, no matter
how magnificent, become a burden after the initial excitement
wears off because the ghosts of other actors haunt every line? I
don't pretend to know the answers to these questions. I do believe that a certain energy begins to crackle in the theater when
you are discovering a new play that you really think is a special
piece of work, and also later when that play becomes a hit, the
talk of the town. Surely it is a very different experience when
you are rediscovering a classic. Or is it just the difference between being dazzling sprinters versus long distance runners?

I only know that every night we found our two-plus hours on
stage stimulating and exhilarating. Granted, the routine
changed. After six months or so I started needing to arrive at
the theater a little earlier; after another six months, a little earlier than that. It becomes harder and harder to throw off the
problems of the day because you no longer require such complete focus on the lines. But you do it, you make the adjustment.

Even after I left *Streetcar*, I was destined to have another
Blanche in my future. About a year later, we were all called together again to shoot the film. All except Jessica.

I know that it broke Jessica's heart when she was not hired to
do the film version of *Streetcar*. There was, of course, no question that Marlon would be in the film, but at that time, he had
no screen recognition.

(Marlon had recently completed a picture called *The Men* directed by Fred Zinnemann. I remember being in Kazan's office

one day when he received a phone call from Zinnemann. I could hear Kazan advising him, "Let him go. Give him the reins," and I knew instantly that Zinnemann was wondering how to handle Marlon. Kazan was offering the only advice he could: Just let him do what comes naturally.)

Despite *The Men*, Marlon did not yet have what they call "marquee value." Vivien Leigh, however, was a major star, still so powerful because of *Gone With the Wind* that she could carry all of us nobodies, including Marlon Brando.

It was a wonderful experience for me to be able to come back to the role of Mitch after two years, having done other things in between, with a fresh perspective. After the play had closed, I was plagued by the usual ideas about things I could have done differently with Mitch. Thoughts like that (often in the middle of the night) come with the territory. Doing the film presented me with a unique opportunity to try all those ideas out. Some worked. Some didn't.

Oddly enough, I believe the truer interpretation of the play ended up being the movie's. Marlon was so powerful on stage, so compelling, that through nothing other than his own presence, he distorted the play. When Marlon stepped onto that stage, it became a play about Stanley Kowalski. You held your breath until he came back. It was no longer a play about Blanche DuBois. No matter what Jessica did on stage, or what any actress could have done, she could not overcome his force. The movie gave Kazan the chance to keep the focus where Tennessee Williams intended it, on Blanche. He could manipulate the focus in the editing room.

Vivien Leigh had played Blanche in the London production, which her husband, Laurence Olivier, had directed. She had a very different take on the play.

I recall the moment when Mitch lifts Blanche to see if he can guess how much she weighs. I had always raised Jessica straight into the air like a ballerina and then brought her down, vertically, close to my body. That worked for me, because the next moment Mitch is trying to kiss her. That move helped to make a smooth transition from a playful impulse to a sexual one. Vivien wanted me to pick her up as though I were lifting her over a threshold. That's the way Olivier had directed that action in London, but it made the moment awkward for me because I had to put her down on the ground, then bend down to try to kiss her. It didn't seem to flow as well, but we did it her way. Kazan made a point of wanting us to try to accommodate Vivien since she was the outsider.

Unlike Jessica who was as gracious and well-grounded a human being as you could hope to meet, Vivien was more like Blanche herself. She had a more tenuous relationship with reality.

I remember that when we had finished shooting, Vivien and Olivier invited Mona and me to a party. Although Mona and I are chronically early, we happened to arrive late because we were unfamiliar with Los Angeles and had gotten lost. Everyone was already seated around their tables. I was called over to a table and left Mona stranded for a moment. She finally ended up sitting on a swing by the pool all by herself. Who should come along but John Buckmaster, an English actor, and Vivien Leigh. They sat down on either side of Mona. Mona told me later about how they literally, and figuratively, talked over her head. Vivien and Buckmaster traded bizarre non sequiturs as Mona sat there, utterly baffled. Never once did they acknowledge that another person was even there, let alone sitting between them. Vivien didn't have to be polite, or even civil; after all, she was Scarlett O'Hara.

Several months later, we read in the paper that Buckmaster

had been spotted running down Fifth Avenue stark naked, brandishing a knife. Mona was actually relieved by the news; it assured her she had not been the crazy one sitting on that swing after all.

By then, I was wading through my first real experience with the press. Warner Brothers sent me to the Beverly Hills Hotel on a junket. I pulled up, handed my rented Chevy over to the valet, and started toward the hotel entrance. All of a sudden I heard someone calling my name. I turned around but didn't see anyone. Finally, I spotted a hand waving from inside a car. I peered in. There, behind the wheel, sat Spencer Tracy.

"Hey, I saw that *Streetcar Named Desire* last night at a screening. You were terrific."

"Thank you," I managed.

"Okay, kid," said Tracy.

With that, he drove off, leaving me to pick my jaw up off the pavement and stumble into the hotel.

I have no idea what any reporters asked me that afternoon. All I knew was that I had found myself face-to-face with Spencer Tracy. I was awestruck.

A year after wrapping *Streetcar,* I was working on a stinker of a movie called *Operation Secret* with Cornel Wilde when word came that I had been nominated for an Academy Award. It never occurred to me that I would have a shot at winning. Nor did I even think about attending the ceremony, which, at that time, was more like an industry party, not the worldwide media event it is today.

But when the night arrived, Steve Trilling, a Warners executive, asked me if I was going.

I told him, "No, I'm not a part of that crowd. I live in New York."

Trilling said, "You should go."

"I haven't got a tux." That had been a crisis in high school; now I just hoped it would work as an excuse.

Trilling instructed me to go to wardrobe and get myself one. "You've got to go."

That night, I put on my Warners wardrobe tux and drove to the Pantages Theater in my same old rented green Chevy. As I turned onto Hollywood Boulevard, I spotted searchlights in the distance. When I realized they were illuminating lines and lines of limousines, I began to get a sense of what I was in for. Embarrassed by my old rented rattletrap, I parked two blocks away and walked to the theater, happily unnoticed, wearing my brown overcoat over my tux. I was, as I had said, still very much the New Yorker and couldn't go anywhere without a topcoat.

Once inside, I took my seat. I had the third seat in from the aisle. Actually, I had a ticket for the fourth seat, too. But Mona and I had agreed she should stay in New York with Mila while I shot the film and I saw no reason why she should fly out for this one evening. I threw my overcoat over her seat.

Humphrey Bogart and Lauren Bacall took their seats, the aisle seats, right next to me. I knew Bogart from the Warners lot at least enough to say, "Hello, how are you?" He introduced me to his wife, we all smiled at each other, then I faced the stage and waited for the evening to begin.

Danny Kaye was the master of ceremonies. I was enjoying the show in the way that you can when you are sure you're not going to have to get up there. I sat there, pretty calm, as they announced my category. Best Supporting Actor.

Then, suddenly, I heard my name. I jumped up and bolted into the aisle. I took a few steps, paused, and turned back to Bogey.

"Look after my coat, will you?"

Bogart looked at me like I was crazy. "Just get up there."

I have no recollection of what I said on stage. The usual thanks, I'm sure. They didn't have television cameras recording the event then, so I can forever hope that I didn't make too big a fool of myself.

Then I was ushered backstage to meet the press. I was there for about a half an hour, when who should appear but Humphrey Bogart. He had just won the Best Actor award for *The African Queen.*

He stepped up to join me at the podium. And what did I have to say to him?

"What did you do with my coat?"

Bogey shot me that same look. Then he said, "Screw your coat. You've got an Oscar."

facing page:
Warners ran me through the publicity
mill, but they never could make a leading man
out of me, despite the yachting cap.

Chapter 8

Back in the early fifties when I won the Oscar, the Academy Awards were not quite the big deal they are today. Of course, the show wasn't on televison and that made a difference. When the whole world wasn't in on it, the ramifications of winning were not so great. The hype machine didn't shift into high gear with promises that you would have your pick of scripts and that your next picture would earn you ten times as much as the one that won you the award. Even so, getting that stamp of approval meant a lot to me.

I wonder if it actually meant more to me because there wasn't so much hoopla. All it meant was what it meant. Respect from my peers. A phrase that has almost become a cliché because we've heard it so many times by now, though I know it is always delivered honestly and genuinely. But for me—that Serbian little boy who couldn't spell, the young man who spent his free time in the boiler room at the Goodman Theater—winning really did sow the seeds of a sense of belonging. At least, I finally knew I'd made the right choices.

What I didn't know was that becoming more a part of the film community would mean having to make another big choice, a choice that I really didn't want to have to make. These were still the days of the studio system. Every studio held contracts with actors who formed their "stable" of players—not only actors, but writers and directors.

After winning the Oscar, Warners approached me to sign a contract, a straight seven-year deal. Agent Sam Weisbord at the William Morris Agency explained to me that Warners would have the right to exercise their option to drop me or keep me under contract at the end of every year. If they chose to keep me as a contract player, that would mean I would have to be in whatever picture the studio told me to be in. That part of the idea didn't appeal to me even though the security of the deal was enormously tempting. So I said, "How about just two pictures a year?" I figured that would leave me some time to work in the theater. Warners agreed. But I still needed some time to think it over.

Two pictures a year for seven years. That sounded pretty good. Guaranteed work, guaranteed income, no more pounding the pavement, no more begging for a job. At least for a year at a time. It almost seemed too good to be true. I was being offered security in a profession that defied the term. What's more, I felt like my turn had finally come.

The big "but" was how to make it all work.

It didn't occur to me right away that still living in New York would present a problem. And it certainly didn't occur to me to move to L.A. I had, by now, become a true New Yorker, even taking a real Easterner's holiday, the first real, true vacation of my life. After finishing the Broadway run of *Streetcar,* I decided that Mona, Mila, and I needed a vacation. I guess I finally felt maybe I had earned one. Mona and I packed us all up to Monhegan Island off the coast of Maine. I decompressed from the two-year run of the show by wheeling Mila, then a toddler, around the island in a little cart I built from an old box, some wheels I found behind the general store, and a handle I fashioned out of an old two-by-four that I nailed under the box. Mila and I became quite a conversation piece as we wandered the tiny island, which was only about a mile and a half long and a half mile wide.

We'd stop at the tip of the island and buy a couple of lobsters and a few pounds of hake from the old fisherman out there. Our haul would cost me about a buck and a half. Then we'd come back to the house we had rented and throw the lobsters in a pot. We spent a wonderful month there, just enjoying the long summer days.

It was the first time I ever really allowed myself to do nothing. Luckily, there was nothing to do. No communication with the mainland—and the rest of the world. If you needed to send a message, you'd take it to the general store and they'd send it out on the boat that made its daily trip to the mainland. Otherwise, there was no rest of the world. It was like going back in time.

At the end of the summer we returned to the city where we were now living in Peter Cooper Village. A few years earlier when Mona had become pregnant, we were still living in a fourth floor walk-up between Park Avenue and Lexington. It was a nice address for once, but it was just the usual one room with a kitchen in a closet. The big plus was that our friend, a young actor named Montgomery Clift, lived right next door. Instead of walking down three flights, then up four, he used to walk up the fire escape the one flight, cross the roof, and knock on our window to join us for dinner or just a good talk. We spent a lot of evenings together absorbed in conversation. Monty was in his prime, excited about acting and hungry for conversation about his craft.

We became good friends, even spending Christmases at his family's plush apartment on Park Avenue. Mona and I were wowed by this glimpse of Monty's background. Clearly, his father had done extremely well as a stockbroker on Wall Street and the apartment proved it. The holidays in the Clift home were like nothing I had ever seen before. An enormous tree exquisitely decorated, Czech silver, beaded ornaments. All very uptown. Everything perfect.

Monty's mother was in the habit of inviting her son's close friends to lunch to check up on him. I remember once she invited Mona. Mona was terrified of this elegant lady, but she went ahead and met her at some classy hotel. When Mona returned home she burst into tears. Through her sobbing, she managed to explain that Mrs. Clift had talked about the "Jews" all through the meal, never realizing she was sitting across from Mona Greenberg. Mona became hysterical not so much because of what Mrs. Clift had said, but because she was so furious with herself for not saying anything in response.

That evening, Mona told me a story of an incident that had happened to her in the eighth grade. One day her teacher opened up a discussion about different types of people. After a

WHEN DO I START?

while, the discussion got around to Jews. There were only three Jewish families in Emporia, Kansas at the time and most of the kids in the class figured they didn't know any. The kids started spouting the usual stereotypes—Jews are this and Jews are that—as Mona sat there silently, fighting back tears, just as she had at lunch with Mrs. Clift. As it so happened, after this discussion the class held elections. They elected Mona class president.

The teacher smiled at the class and said, "You have just elected a Jewish president. Class dismissed."

It was a moment Mona would remember forever and she could only hope that the rest of the kids in the class remembered it as well. All those kids' comments came rushing back as Mona had sat across the table from Mrs. Clift trying to choke down her expensive lunch.

Of course, Monty was nothing like his mother. He was sweet and sensitive, ultimately maybe too sensitive for his own good. When I was working, he and Mona would take in a play or a movie, and the two of them became dear friends. Leaving Monty behind was the hard part of moving, but before long we were happily ensconced in Peter Cooper Village.

We had moved to Peter Cooper when Mona was pregnant with Mila. Peter Cooper Village was a new apartment complex, New York's answer to all the returning G.I.'s and their young families. It was going up one monolithic brick building at a time, and as each building went up, it would be rented out immediately. Young couples couldn't snatch up those apartments fast enough. Mona and I put in our application eagerly, though we were sure one had to pull strings to get in and we had none to pull. All we could do was wait.

Finally, a couple of months before Mila was born, we walked back into the office and pleaded desperation. The sight of tiny Mona who looked ten months pregnant must have gotten to the powers that be because shortly thereafter we moved in. Apartment 6F.

Peter Cooper was a godsend. It was clean and new and had elevators! To us it seemed like Buckingham Palace. For the first time we had an apartment, with two bedrooms no less. We combed the antique stores along Second and Third Avenues and bought our first piece of real furniture, an eight-foot pine table that we still use today as our dining room table.

Peter Cooper offered an instant community for people just starting out: Howard Cosell, Tony Randall, John Forsythe. It was a place tailor-made for young families, complete with trees and grass and playgrounds. I used to play basketball on the courts with Walter Wriston while our babies slept in their carriages. (Walt was a young bank teller at Chase Manhattan who, a few decades later, would become the head of Citibank.) Walt and I would take our daughters trick-or-treating on Halloween, ringing countless doorbells, without ever leaving the building. Peter Cooper had a real neighborhood feel right there in the heart of Manhattan.

Between our dear friends and our own apartment, which really felt like our first true home, a big-time studio contract was not enough to entice us to leave all that behind and move out west. I don't think the term "bi-coastal" had been coined yet. Basically, as an actor, you were expected to choose. But I figured I could do it all—live in New York, continue to work in the theater, and do films in Hollywood. It would just take a little effort.

And some sacrifice, almost entirely on Mona's part. By then we had two daughters and we decided early on that we were not going to drag our children across the country during the school year. Mona would stay home with Mila and Carla when I went to L.A. or wherever else a picture would take me.

When word got out that I had signed the contract with

WHEN DO I START?

Warner Brothers, I felt like Benedict Arnold. When I discussed the matter with dear friends like Kazan and Eli Wallach, they made me feel like I was quitting, turning my back on what was really important as an artist.

They told me, "You're an actor, not a personality." But the more I thought about it, the more that Warners contract came to represent the best of both worlds. A secure livelihood *and* working as an actor.

My colleagues at the Actors Studio didn't see it that way. The first day I walked into the Studio for a session, everyone hit me: "You've sold out." "How can you go to that wasteland?" "There's no art there, just commercialism." The young kids who had just gotten into the Studio didn't say anything, but I could feel their disdain.

I think the reason their reaction made me particularly uncomfortable was because I understood it so well. I had felt the same way myself. When I had left the Goodman, there had been a choice to make. Hollywood or New York. I thought Hollywood was all glamour, all superficial, a wonderland where talent doesn't count for much, so I chose New York. Now, suddenly, I found myself having to defend the other choice. I wasn't a hundred percent sure I could, but I had to try. How quickly things change when the chance is yours!

My dear friend, Mike Strong, came up to me with a twinkle in his eye. "Karl, how could you do it? You sold out for money. You signed a contract."

I didn't know what to say.

But Mike wasn't through. "Karl, do you think they might have another contract for me?"

The flack I got from my friends at the Studio steeled my determination. There must be a way to do it all. They do it in England and France. Why can't we make it work in America? I decided, "I'll show them." I thought it was just a matter of simple math. Films only take twelve or fourteen weeks to make; two films a year mean twenty-eight weeks. That would leave me half a year to do theater, I thought.

It was a noble idea. What I hadn't realized is that when you are under contract and they call you to come to work, you go to work. You're an employee. Fitting the theater into that "on call" schedule was tough, nearly impossible really. But I tried for as long as I could.

Seven years turned into nine. It was all of the fifties really, a period that narrowed the gap between theater and film not just for actors but for everyone, the entire culture. At the beginning of the decade we were still coming out of the Golden Age of the theater. By the end of that decade, movies would rule in the American consciousness. By then, many of the kids who arrived at the door of the Actors Studio began to have their sights set on the silver screen as much as the stage.

The Studio had begun in the late forties as a place for actors to come and flex their muscles. Obviously, it provided a place for those actors who were out of work to practice their craft, but it also afforded a wonderful opportunity for those actors who were in long-running plays, delivering the same lines every night, to work on other parts—to expand their capabilities, to stretch their creative muscles and keep limber.

When the Group Theatre disbanded in '42, Kazan, Bobby Lewis, and Cheryl Crawford—the troika—gradually began to talk about starting a new group. By '48, they had launched the Actors Studio. I became one of the original members. We had a tough time that first year; many days we would stand on street corners, ten or fifteen of us, trying to figure out where we could go that day to hold class. You never knew who would show up on any given day: Maureen Stapleton, Marlon Brando, Michael

Strong, Eli Wallach, Montgomery Clift, David Wayne, Tom Ewell, Mildred Dunnock, Kevin McCarthy. We would each pitch in a couple of bucks and rent studio space for a couple of hours, often ending up at a place called the Malin Studio. Before long, though, the Studio found a permanent home, semipermanent anyway.

As I recall, Cheryl Crawford got to know a woman who was related to the International Harvester Company in Chicago. This woman happened to be a theater lover so Cheryl convinced her to put some money into the Studio. We took over half of the fourteenth floor of the Ed Sullivan Building where we remodeled a couple of suites into a small theater with a little stage and an office up front. We used the closets for storing props and wardrobe. Having a home base really helped to pull the Studio together and a lot was accomplished during that period. We really began to feel like a group.

The Studio even produced a television show for a very little while, just a couple of months probably. They were original live shows but the schedule turned out to be too demanding, especially for those of us working in plays.

We stayed there in the Ed Sullivan Building for a few years until our Chicago patronness decided she could no longer foot the bill. Two Studio actresses, Thelma Schnee and Mildred Dunnock, took it upon themselves to find a place we could buy. They started hawking bricks. Actually, they sold little brick-shaped coupons. Buy a brick for a dollar. I remember these two dedicated women standing outside Sardi's, peddling their brick coupons.

People bought as many as their financial situation would allow until, finally, after Thelma and Millie had worked incredibly hard, they collected enough to buy a place. At first they found a space above a Hungarian restaurant on Second or Third Avenue, but that didn't work out. Finally, we ended up in some old run-down church on Forty-fourth Street. A lot of the members did backbreaking work to transform this crumbling structure into a functional theater. That old church is where the Actors Studio still exists today.

Whatever the address, the Studio was a place where you could come and go as you pleased, doors open at both ends. For actors constantly running to auditions, that was essential. Kazan took the beginners' class; Bobby Lewis the advanced. I was in Bobby's class during most of the run of *Streetcar.* So was Marlon. But Marlon never did a scene.

I remember we'd been in class for about a year when Bobby Lewis said to Marlon, "You better get a scene prepared. Otherwise, you're out of this class." Marlon picked a play called *Reunion in Vienna* in which he would play a count or a prince, I forget which, who has come to this country and is now driving a taxi. Marlon and I were in *Streetcar* at the time, sharing that dressing room, so he discussed the scene with me at great length.

"There's a problem. In the play we know he's driving a taxi. He doesn't have a dime for a pack of cigarettes. But when he comes into this scene, this big reunion party, he's all dressed up in his prince's uniform. How will the audience know?" We threw some ideas around, but Marlon never settled on anything as far as I knew. Then the afternoon came for him to perform the scene. He asked me to introduce it, which I did.

Then Marlon stepped out in full royal regalia and sat down. What he did next was pure Brando. He sat down in a chair and took off one boot . . . revealing a big hole in his sock. He tried to stretch the sock over his toes this way and that to cover the hole, then he pulled the gleaming patent leather boot back on. That was Marlon. Very simple, absolutely brilliant, communicating everything we needed to know about his character in the most economical way.

Of course, the punchline is that the poor girl who did the scene with him swore she would never work with him again. He made her life miserable. She said that the day they performed the scene for the class he did things she'd never once seen in rehearsal. She had no idea what was going to happen next and was a nervous wreck by the time the scene was over.

I remember that the scene involved drinking champagne. At one point Marlon suddenly poured his entire glass down her blouse. She was stunned, but the audience went wild. The incident caused great debate about whether what he did to her was fair. Did the audience reaction justify humiliating a fellow actor? Were we laughing with her or at her, with the scene or at what Marlon was doing to this poor girl personally?

Emotions always ran high at the Studio, a hothouse full of people who cared passionately about what they were doing. After about a year, Bobby Lewis decided it was time to put on a production, or at least some sort of recital of scenes, so that the public could find out what the Studio was all about. Kazan disagreed; this was supposed to be a workshop. So Lewis left. Kazan kept the Studio going, believing that if he, too, dropped out, the Studio (which was still getting its sea legs) would fall apart.

Kazan still taught the beginners, but Bobby had taught the advanced group, so a period of floundering followed his departure. Marty Ritt would take one of his sessions one day; then Danny Mann the next. I'd take a session; then Eli Wallach. Josh Logan stepped in for a while, then Clifford Odets.

I remember one day when Odets came in brandishing a couple of pages. He said he had been working on this scene and asked Rudy Bond and Maureen Stapleton to read it. They did, and when they had finished, he said, "Now you know what the scene is, give it some life this time." They read it again, still simply, but with greater depth. After that second reading, Odets turned on a tape recorder. We listened. It was the same scene word for word. When the tape finished he explained that he had visited his aunt and uncle in Philadelphia over the weekend and recorded their conversation. The "scene" had been a word-for-word transcription of his relatives' conversation, but the "interpretation" and the "real thing" were as different as night and day. The reading was simple yet honest. The real aunt and uncle were boisterous, seemingly bigger than life, definitely what an audience would consider hammy and "unrealistic."

It was a wonderful lesson in what is real and whether art should strive to recreate "reality" or to create an emotional reality—honesty.

Sometimes the line between reality and the scene really blurred. Once David Wayne did an improv with about ten other members of the class. The setting was a gas chamber. The ten extras were corpses and Wayne was a Nazi soldier combing through the bodies for gold teeth. The ten actors got together without Wayne knowing and decided that when he reached a certain point they would gradually begin to stir until they came to life and surrounded him. They all arose from the dead beautifully, like ballet in slow motion. At first Wayne didn't know what was happening. When they started to come at him he went for the door, but one of the corpses blocked his exit. It wasn't play acting anymore. Wayne really became terrified as the corpses closed in on him until he finally thought, "To hell with this!" and he leapt right over the footlights and ran out to his seat.

All the while the Studio was "entertaining" various guest leaders, I think Kazan was trying to seduce Lee Strasberg into coming on board, but Strasberg resisted. In his autobiography, Kazan writes that it was the failure of Strasberg's production of

Ibsen's *Peer Gynt* that ultimately brought Strasberg to the Studio. Whatever, it wasn't long before it was Lee Strasberg's Actors Studio.

Lee's production of *Peer Gynt* was my first play after *Streetcar*. The rumors about this innovative production had been flying for weeks by the time I got a call from producer Cheryl Crawford asking if I would be in the play. She invited me to her office the next day to discuss it. Lee was there and they asked me if I would read for the part of the Buttonmolder. I was secretly offended to be asked to read. I knew that Lee had been in and out of the Studio watching me do scenes. He had been associated with the Group in some way and must have seen me in the Group productions, not to mention *Streetcar*. Frankly, I was insulted. I grappled with how to handle the situation, embarrassed to point out all the times Lee had seen my work. Should I just tell them I didn't want to read? Was I willing to refuse to audition even if it meant walking away from a good part in a fascinating production? Was this just Lee's way of making me squirm?

I decided I had to at least try to explain that I had never gotten a part from a cold read, so I came right out and told them I just wasn't any good at it. Lee sat there, stone silent. Thankfully, Cheryl finally said that they knew my work; I could have the part. In a way, I hoped that moment would be a small turning point for me. Maybe it meant I really would never have to audition again.

John Garfield was set to play Peer Gynt and Mildred Dunnock had the part of Peer's mother. Millie and I were old friends and I knew that her sweet, level-headed approach was always a good influence on any project. And this was bound to be an enormous undertaking. So much so, in fact, Cheryl Crawford went to Actors' Equity to request a one week extension of the usual four week rehearsal period.

The reading started in the usual way. Three days around a table with Lee's input. We listened as he talked about the style of what he intended to do. He would mention particular paintings when he referred to the troll scene or the asylum scene. It was exciting to hear his theories, but there wasn't a lot of rehearsing going on that first week. I think that maybe I did my first scene once.

By the beginning of the third week, I had also done my second scene once. Millie had done her scene once as well. Lee was preoccupied with the big scenes, so Millie spent most of her time in a corner going through her lines alone while I was in another corner doing the same thing. Every now and then, Millie and I would look up at each other, shrug, and look back at our scripts.

Finally, Millie and I decided to go to work on our scenes together, to help each other as best we could. It wouldn't be ideal, but at least we'd know our lines. That's what we started to do, and still no direction from Lee.

Sometime during the fourth week, I arrived at the ANTA Theater for rehearsal one afternoon. Millie rushed over to me.

"Who are all those people?" she asked.

I looked out into the audience and saw about fifty people. I didn't have a clue who they were.

Lee arrived and called the whole cast together. "I want a complete run-through. Don't stop for anything."

Millie looked at me and I looked at her. We were both thinking the same thought. We had only rehearsed once, if you could call it that. But we did what we were told. We just kept going. I just said the lines. Thank God I knew them. John Garfield was struggling with Peer, managing what amounted to a good improvisation of the scenes.

When it was all over, Lee came on stage and started giving

notes . . . in front of the fifty strangers. Personally, I felt he was putting on an act for these fifty people, whoever they were. Before long he got to me. He really started in.

"What were you doing?"

"Nothing."

"It looked it," he said. He raised his voice for that jab.

I could take direction; I raised my voice, too. "Lee, how many times did I rehearse this scene?"

He didn't know.

"Once," I told him.

That started it. I guess I embarrassed him in front of his guests and before I knew it, we were in a shouting match.

A few minutes—and a lot of harsh words—later, that lovely, sweet, gracious lady, Millie Dunnock put her hand on my knee. She understood how I felt; she felt exactly the same way, but she knew this wasn't going to solve anything so she stopped me before too much damage was done.

That was it. The afternoon was over. No more notes. No more rehearsing.

My call for the next day was for eight A.M. and Lee had me rehearsing all day. Over and over and over. Just John Garfield and me. What a day! But I didn't care. Lee wanted to prove that he was the boss, and I wanted to crack the scenes and get a sense of how to play with Garfield. I guess we both got what we wanted.

Many years later, people would stop me on the street or come up to me at various occasions and say, "I was there the day you and Lee had it out." I'm not proud of that distinction, but I still believe no one has the right to criticize an actor—especially in front of strangers—when that actor hasn't had the chance to try anything out yet. I don't mind someone saying what I did was bad, that the choices I made didn't work, if I have had the chance to work.

My admiration for Garfield grew immensely during the short run of that play. He plowed through one of the most difficult parts ever written, a part that involves aging from a boy in his teens to a man in his nineties. And, to my mind, he had very little real help. Lee could talk for hours, but for me, there was ultimately very little you could use in all his words.

I know that not everyone feels this way—I am definitely in the minority—but I did not come away from my experiences with Lee Strasberg as a fan of his. My personal opinion about criticizing actors is that the first element of that criticism must include recognition of how awfully hard the actor has worked, even if it's just for a five minute scene. My approach is always to begin, "How would it work if . . . ?" Lee often started out with, "What were you doing?" As an opener, that question immediately puts you on the defensive. I suppose it could mean, "Explain to me what you were striving for." But when Lee said it, it always sounded like, "What did you think you were doing anyway? Why are you wasting my time?" Then Lee would often work his way all the way to, "How could you do that? It's all wrong." Time and again, I saw him leave actors stripped of their spirit and enthusiasm, totally demoralized. I never understood what good could come of that. How were they supposed to dredge up the energy to continue after a session like that?

When Bobby Lewis ran the class everyone always volunteered. No one could wait to get up on stage for the smallest scene. But when Lee arrived, it wasn't long before everyone grew much more hesitant to get up there. The joy of performing was replaced with a horrible, crippling fear of exposure, a tension that grew out of Lee's personality. He even sat in a special chair and basically allowed himself to become a god, a god whose every word was being taped for posterity.

Lee's methods never worked for me, plain and simple. Once,

Maureen Stapleton suggested she and I do a scene from *Macbeth* together. We chose the scene where Macbeth comes out after committing the murder. We worked on it long and hard. Then the day came for us to do it for the class and Lee. To this day, I can't tell you what he said. I only know he definitely didn't like it. He gave us long notes, all convoluted and full of psychological terminology, then he sent us away to work on it for another week. I was relieved to learn that Maureen hadn't really understood a word he'd said either. She decided, "Let's just play the scene quietly between the two of us. Let's do nothing."

That's exactly what we did. We just looked at each other and said the words.

Lee loved it. "Now that's what I mean!"

Maureen and I looked at each other and thought, "Either something's wrong with us or something's wrong with him."

Lee Strasberg was only one of the larger-than-life personalities in the theater world at that time. Acting teacher Stella Adler had her own following who worshipped her as the key to unlocking their talent. (In essence, Lee touted reflective memory while Stella believed more in tapping the imagination.) And of course, there was still Kazan along with various other members of the original Group Theatre. Their arguments about the theater and acting could cause great animosities, but then, in the early fifties, a much more insidious force entered all our lives. Politics. Specifically in the person of Senator Joseph McCarthy.

At that time I was, as I had always been, completely apolitical. Even so, I missed the blacklist by the skin of my teeth.

When I was in *Golden Boy* (a Group production) in '37, I had no idea that many members of the Group were card-carrying members of the Communist Party. Frankly, I barely knew what a communist was. When I was in high school singing in the Karageorge Choir, there had been a choir member who worked in the mills and would show up with a "Daily Worker" every now and then. Everyone would kid him about it, saying, "Here he is, our leader." But no one took it seriously. Before World War II Yugoslavia still had a king; the Serbs in Indiana didn't much care about anything else.

When I arrived at the Group, every other day somebody would shove a petition of some kind under your nose, but I didn't think much of it. I just figured, "Everyone else is signing, I'll sign." When they asked for a contribution, I'd throw in a dollar, feeling that maybe that would help me to belong. Suddenly it dawned on me that I should look at these things I was signing, so I started looking at the list of sponsors' names: Albert Einstein, Eleanor Roosevelt, Mayor La Guardia. That was good enough for me, so I kept on signing.

It didn't occur to me until years later that I had possibly been "assigned" to a particular Group member. To this day, I don't know whether or not this man was a member of the party, but he kept on me to come with him to meetings to hear different people speak. I always begged off and he never pushed it, just kept inviting. I did go to his apartment a few times with some other Group members to listen to records and have a little party. Sometimes I would do a little bit with Leif Ericson who had been singing professionally with a band (and was married to Frances Farmer during the Group production of *Golden Boy*). We would imitate Russian singers, singing in gibberish. That was always worth a couple of laughs. But I always declined the hard-core meetings.

About a year later during the next Group show, *Gentle People*, this one fellow was still after me. I finally agreed to go.

One night after a performance we went to the Unity Church,

on Forty-sixth Street I think, which we often used for rehearsing. We went down a few flights of steps to the basement and he knocked on the door. No one answered. Instead someone slid the silver dollar–sized metal plate from a peephole and checked us out, like a speakeasy. Finally the door opened. Instantly I thought, "What the hell am I doing here?"

We passed by a table that was set up with some literature for sale and a little wicker basket with some money in it. I grabbed a couple of pamphlets and I threw a dollar into the kitty just because I thought it was expected of me. Then we sat down with some twenty-five people (I recognized maybe four or five of them), and listened to a lecture. Typical left-wing politics from a professional recruiter. I listened, but it didn't really penetrate. I kept thinking, "I shouldn't have come. I want no part of this." Besides, I couldn't quite concentrate because something was bothering me. It was that stupid peephole. It made me queasy. Of course the irony was heavy; my father was a laborer and I had worked in the mills myself. I felt like I personally knew more about being a laborer—about what it does to the human spirit to do detestable, backbreaking work, about how it feels to hustle for a buck in front of a raging furnace—than any of these professional speakers.

After that evening I stopped signing petitions. Some of the Group ridiculed me when I claimed I didn't understand what all this was about. I knew that the Group was trying to help the country out of the Depression and champion the common man. Something had to be done, it was clear. Men in camel hair coats and alligator shoes were standing on corners trying to sell apples for a nickel. I admired that the Group priced their tickets low, fifty cents for a balcony seat, so that students could see their productions. Who could argue with that? But beyond that, I wasn't interested.

It turned out my disinterest and ignorance were enormously lucky, a blessing really. That, and the fact that I just wasn't a joiner. I never even joined the Boy Scouts; why would I join the Communist Party? I've always been wary of adding my name to any organization because what if that organization takes a twist? You're still part of it even if you don't agree with the new platform. But that night in the church basement I felt like my presence there might have been all that was needed to join me up in spite of myself. A few years later, any number of people could have said I was there, and they would have been telling the truth. By then, with Senator McCarthy presiding over the witch hunt, guilt by association would be all it would take. And I had been associated, no doubt about it.

Every May Day, the workers of New York marched in a parade. During *Golden Boy* they asked me if I wanted to march with them. I said no, but they must have thought I was a good mark because of my background so they kept at it. Finally, when an actor dropped out of a play called *Transit* being produced by the Theater of Action, a young leftist company, I was hired to step in. We rehearsed this one-act after performances of *Gentle People* from eleven-thirty to three o'clock in the morning and then we'd perform it on Sundays. *Transit* was an Americanized version of Gorky's *Lower Depths* about bums in the bowery. I guess an interesting part got me involved where lectures never could.

Later, during *Gentle People* I was invited along with Sam Jaffe and a couple of other people to actor Phil Bouerneff's house for a bite to eat and to meet someone. I remember how this special guest introduced himself. "My name is Paul." That was all he said. Sam asked what his last name was, but he refused to say. Another red light went on for me. Again I thought, "I want no part of this."

But the bottom line is that it was sheer luck that kept me out of the fray. As the House Committee on Unamerican Activities began to call all my friends, one by one, I thought, "Okay, here goes. It's got to be my turn sooner or later." I was absolutely terrified.

My friends were dropping by the wayside one after another. Those who refused to name names, like Marty Ritt, were really suffering. Phil Loeb, a great actor, killed himself. And then there were the friends who talked. They were all people I admired: Lee J. Cobb, Clifford Odets and, most notably, Kazan. The question, "Are you now or have you ever been a member of the Communist Party?" rippled through the circle I lived in like an earthquake. You couldn't remain untouched.

I was in California working on one of my Warner's assignments when I read that Kazan was going to appear before the Committee. Rumor had it that he was going to name names. They were using him like they had Fredric March, plastering his name all over the papers to get publicity for the Committee's activities. I wrote to Gadge and told him that no matter which way he decided to go—and I honestly had no idea which way that would be—I would still be his friend. I was just holding my breath, temporarily relieved not to be sitting at that desk in front of that microphone with those questions coming at me. For a long time, a couple of years maybe, I honestly believed it was just a matter of time until I got the call. After all, my signature was all over the place. Also known as Mladen Sekulovich, no less; how much more Bolshevik could you get? It took a long while before I realized the call was never going to come.

But the trauma didn't stop there. I was still worried that even if they didn't call me personally I would end up on the blacklist. Even when that didn't happen and I began to breathe a little easier, my life was not quite back to normal. After Kazan made his

217

appearance and named names, and mutual friends realized that I was not dropping him, many of those friends refused to speak to me. Zero Mostel didn't talk to me for years because I maintained my friendship with Gadge. Somehow Gadge became the lightning rod; people were crossing the street to avoid him while I was trying so hard not to judge, not to take a stand, that I was kidding myself. During those horrible times, it was impossible not to take a stand. Every action, every friend you had—every friend you kept or dropped—carried enormous moral implications. Everything you did meant loyalty or betrayal.

I remembered back to the incident with Bud Bohnen at Lake Grove during the Group Theatre retreat. What had seemed like a question of employment, taking a job in Hollywood, had been more than that. Obviously, it was a question of loyalty to the Group, but it was more than that as well. It had really been a question of politics.

I remembered, too, that when I had been in the army I had gone to see a revival of *Our Town* starring Monty Clift. He was magnificent and the evening reconfirmed my belief that it is one of the most beautiful plays ever written. An army buddy of mine, Alfred Ryder, disagreed with me.

He said, "It's a terrible play."

"What makes you say that?" I asked him.

"Because it deals with death."

I argued, "It deals with life. The girl comes back to show her family how to really live."

Before long, Ryder and I got so hot and heavy into this argument that we darn near came to blows over sweet, gentle *Our Town*. Suddenly I realized that he had more invested in this conversation than met the eye. The line at that time was to blast Thornton Wilder because of his politics. I was talking art; Ryder was talking politics.

I never believed that politics had a place in art, that is to say, not in artistic relationships. It might inspire great works of art, great plays, but it can destroy creative partnerships. The two great talents of Kazan and Arthur Miller, which came together for *All My Sons* and *Death of a Salesman,* should have had so much more greatness in them. But the McCarthy era severed their partnership. Neither of them really suffered in terms of their own careers. Not Miller. Not Kazan. What suffered was the American theater. Many years later Kazan directed Miller's *After the Fall,* but it wasn't the same; the chemistry was gone. Politics had spoiled it.

❧

My first few pictures under contract all had something in common. They were uniformly forgettable. A bunch of bad pictures.

I was shooting *Operation Secret* with Cornel Wilde when I won the Oscar. I remember that the next day, they took a typical corny publicity shot of me on the set knocking on the door of the underground headquarters, holding the statuette. They just don't take photographs like that any more! They just don't make directors like that any more either. He was an old-timer named Lewis Seiler who would show up to work, pull three pages of script out of his back pocket, and start shooting. He would refer to those pages all day, then toss them in the trash at the end of the day and show up the next morning with three more. No matter what time it was, when we finished those three pages we wrapped for the day. I don't think he ever read the script from cover to cover.

But that was a pleasure compared with my experience on *Where the Sidewalk Ends* directed by Otto Preminger. The picture had already begun shooting when I arrived in L.A. from New York. The wardrobe man waltzed me in to meet Preminger. He was a typical Prussian character; it wasn't hard to see why he had been cast as a Nazi in New York. He looked me up and down and said, "Ah, you have arrived," then sent me off to wardrobe.

I was pleased to meet two old pals on the set: Dana Andrews whom I knew from *Boomerang* and Gary Merrill who'd been in *Winged Victory* with me. They took me aside like concerned big brothers and told me, "Don't let him throw you. He's mean when he's behind the camera. He likes to put people on the defensive."

I was cocky. "I know my lines. I know what I'm going to do. Everything will be fine. Don't you worry about me." I figured I was a Broadway actor. Nothing could throw me.

My call came a couple of days later. I was a detective and I had a long speech about how the victim could have been killed, the logistics of the murder. "He came through here, walked over there . . . ," that kind of thing. The shot called for the camera to be tracking me the whole time. And there was Otto, stationed high above it all with the camera on the boom. I delivered all of two lines when he shouted, "Cut! Karl, you are wrong!"

He started out full steam, shouting at me, I don't even remember what. Do this and that, look here and there! We did it again. I thought I did it exactly as he said. Again, it came from on high with that thick German accent, "Cut! Karl, what happened?"

"Nothing happened," I managed.

"Well, you are not doing it." Always good and loud so everyone anywhere on the soundstage could hear.

We did it again. And again.

Finally, "You know, Karl, I brought you all the way from New York. A good actor. What happened to you? Did you lose it on the way here?"

After five or six takes with Preminger berating me after each one, he had me so confused I didn't know whether I was in New York or Los Angeles, let alone how to play the scene. I didn't know what hit me. All I wanted to do was get out of there. Humiliation has never been the way to a great performance as far as I'm concerned, and it didn't work that time. Finally, after another three or four takes, he hollered, "Print!" and that was that. He had done his job on me, initiated me into the Preminger school of filmmaking.

To top it off, Dana and Gary were grinning from ear to ear. They bit their tongues, but their "I told you so's" came across loud and clear.

I did another turkey called *Diplomatic Courier* with Tyrone Power directed by Henry Hathaway. Power never really did anything exciting as an actor. His looks kept you watching the screen, but he knew how to do just enough to keep you interested.

Working with Ty was one of my first experiences with a really big star. He used to invite ten or fifteen people to his dressing room for drinks and hors d'oeuvres every Friday after work. I remember the first time I stepped into that dressing room, my eyes fell on his open closet. On the floor of the closet and extending out into the room must have been a hundred pairs of shoes. Every style and color. I thought, "These are just in his dressing room, never mind what he has at home. Boy, that's a star."

He also had a sense of humor. In one scene he was to rush out of a building, jump into my car, and we were to drive away. We were supposed to be in Europe but they couldn't find a European car. This was the olden days of the movies and audiences weren't so sophisticated. The crew simply rigged an American car to look like a right side drive by removing the steering wheel from the left and adding a full set of controls to the right.

On "Action!" Ty came running out and jumped into the car. I stepped on the gas but the car barely moved. This is supposed to be our great getaway. I floored it, but nothing happened. "Cut!" We did it again. Same thing. My foot hit the gas and the car just barely inched along.

Finally Henry yelled, "Jesus, Karl, don't you New Yorkers know how to drive?"

"What's the difference? New York, California, you step on the gas, the car should go. And it's just not going."

Suddenly, I heard Ty giggling. He had been pressing his foot on the second brake, the original one on the left, the whole time. The more Henry (a renowned screamer) yelled at me, the more Ty thought the whole thing was hysterical.

Another scene called for us to make yet another escape. Once again we were riding in a jeep, this time in front of a process screen. That's where they project footage on a screen behind you, in this case to make it appear that we were actually driving outside (the kind of thing you could never get away with today). We just couldn't make Henry happy. After several takes, Ty looked at me and said, "Henry's used to Westerns. What do you say we whip the jeep like a horse?" And that's exactly what we did. Ty was pounding the back of the jeep while I beat the dashboard like we were on horseback. Henry was thrilled. "Cut! Print!" and on to the next shot.

That same year, 1952, I also did *Ruby Gentry* with Charlton Heston (this was maybe his second part) and Jennifer Jones. This was the first of a very few films where I got the girl. She married me for my money and it didn't last for long, but who cares? I got her.

Jennifer had an acting technique all her own. Before starting a scene it was as though she was hypnotizing herself, actually putting herself in a trance. You would be doing a scene with her, but you felt like she really wasn't there. We shot one scene in a boat out on the Pacific. Jennifer was at the helm. I was down in the hold. The director, King Vidor, called out the blocking to Jennifer from the barge parallel to the boat.

"The boom will swing around at this point."

She said, "Okay."

Sure enough, the boom swung around and hit her in the head. She didn't duck.

We did it again. Same thing. Whacked her in the side of the head.

King shouted, "Did you hear?"

I called up from the hold, asking her the same thing.

She nodded yes.

Again. It hit her in the head.

Finally, we had to do it without recording the dialogue, talking her through it by the numbers. From down in the hold of the ship I waited until I heard "Action!" then started counting; I yelled to her to duck when I hit ten. I wondered what Stanislavski would have thought about that.

Jennifer was simply in her own world.

All of these pictures were pretty bad at best, downright rotten at worst. But I was learning how to work for the camera so they were a good training ground.

After about two weeks on *Ruby Gentry* King Vidor said to me, "Let me talk to you."

He took me aside. "You know, you play every scene you're in with a beginning, middle, and an end."

"What's wrong with that?" I wondered.

"This is a movie; not a play. When you leave a scene it's like you're pulling the curtain down with you. Boom. Every time you make an exit it's like the end of the entire movie."

It took me a while to figure how that approach might work in a play that runs for two continuous hours, but not in a movie that takes twelve weeks to shoot. I had to remember that the scene might continue the next day when you come to work and that a full day of shooting might amount to just a minute and a half or two minutes of screen time. I learned that I could still come in with a purpose, an action, but that I didn't need to play every action to its climax within that scene. I was turning every scene into a one act play, an aria, playing every scene as though my character knew the end to the whole movie. In part, I think I was struggling with learning how to shoot out of sequence when I was so used to moving straight through a play. It was a valuable lesson from a wonderful director.

I was shooting *Ruby Gentry* when I got a call from Harold Clurman and Bob Whitehead, a producer, saying they were mounting a production of Eugene O'Neill's *Desire Under the Elms*. They wanted to know if I was interested in playing the part of the father. I read it and told them I'd love to.

After I accepted the part, I panicked. I was close to forty and this was a man in his late seventies. Everyone warned me not to do it, that it would be a very bad career move. But I had fallen in love with the part (which Walter Huston had originated). The play is about an old pioneer farmer who wants to leave a legacy but feels that his three grown sons are no good. In order to produce another heir, he marries a young girl. Another son is all he wants of her, but the young wife ends up having an affair with the youngest son and bearing him a child, which the old man believes to be his own. The baby ends up killed and the old man is left with nothing. Greek tragedy, Eugene O'Neill style.

The depth of longing and loss experienced by this old man was an actor's dream. I had to gamble that I could bridge the gap in our ages. I enjoyed working on this part all the more because I had the time to really do it right. While I was shooting

Ruby Gentry I spent all my free time doing research into the play's period. I read and reread the play almost every night after shooting. I worked on my makeup. I had the luxury of time to really explore this old man from the inside and out.

I thought this old man, Efram, needed to be as tall as he could be. Tall and thin, yet with the heaviness of age. There were many moments in the play where the character talked to God and I wanted to be as high as I could, as though I could really reach Him if I tried, yet still look slumped with age. I knew there had to be a way for wardrobe to help. The wardrobe man came up with a pair of wonderful old workman's pants that I suggested he line with linen to pucker them up in back. This made the knees always appear bent like an old man's, but still allowed me to stand at my full height inside them.

Then I went to the makeup man, Bob Jiras. I told him about the makeup I'd devised for Rip Van Winkle way back when— lots of powder blended into the makeup and applied while I crinkled up my face so that it gave me wrinkles that had wrinkles. But he told me about the wonders of something new: latex. He built my look with this new material and gave me a wild hairpiece and a mole like Abraham Lincoln.

The one scene that worried me was the little dance that Efram does in a rare moment of joy. It had to have abandon and spontaneity but I also had to deliver some important lines while doing it. With the help of the female lead, Carol Stone, who had been a dancer, I ended up really breaking that scene down into the smallest possible beats. Do these steps, deliver this line, do that step, deliver that line. All very pat. I remember this particularly because of Lee Strasberg's reaction. He came to see the play and although he never came backstage to say hello, the next time I saw him at the Studio he remarked, "I loved when you did that dance." I chuckled to myself because the way I had approached it was a hundred and eighty degrees opposed to Lee's teaching, against everything he ever preached about the psychological moment. It was absolutely and completely technically crafted, choreographed second by second. It just goes to show—whatever works. It's the product, not the process that counts in the end.

There was just one hitch to doing this play. My studio contract. I thought Warners didn't have anything for me at the moment so I went back to New York and snuck back onto Broadway. That was my original plan anyway. I can't believe I was so stupid to think the studio would never find out I was doing a play! The play got great notices and was a big hit . . . and Warners tacked another year onto my contract.

While I was in *Desire Under the Elms,* the Yugoslav consulate contacted me about being part of a cultural exchange program. They wanted me to go to Yugoslavia and do something there, a play or a movie, since they knew that I was first-generation American. I met with various members of the consulate about three times in New York, discussing what we could do. Mona and I kept throwing around titles of plays. We thought *Life With Father* might work until we began to worry that a comedy about a stingy father might not go over so well in a noncapitalist country.

One night a famous Greek actress came to see *Desire Under the Elms.* She came backstage to chat after the performance and I told her I was trying to come up with something to do in Yugoslavia. She said, "Do what you're doing. They'll understand this play."

She was right. The terrain there is similar to New England in many respects, rocky and mountainous, and it was basically a universal story about a farmer having a hard time. I let that idea percolate for a few days only to arrive home one night to

226

have Mona inform me that I had received a call from the FBI. I returned the call the next morning. They said they wanted to talk to me and set up a lunch date for the next day. Feeling like I was straight out of a cheap spy picture, I asked how I would know them.

"We'll know you."

After a sleepless night, I met them at a fish house on Twenty-third Street. I was early, as always, and waited a few minutes before two men walked in and led me to an isolated corner booth. When they introduced themselves, one name ended in the classic Serbian "vich."

I said to him, in Serbian, "You're one of us."

"Yes, I am."

One of them asked me what was going on between me and the Yugoslavian consulate.

I told him.

"We know you have had three lunches with them."

I explained that I was very interested in participating in the cultural exchange.

It was just like in the movies; one of them did the talking and the other one just sat there stonefaced. "Our advice is don't go. Because of who you are."

"Why?" I wondered. "We have an exchange with Russia."

"But you are first generation. Our advice is don't go. We cannot stop you, but that is our advice."

I told them that I wasn't planning to go until I got a letter from the State Department backing me.

"Next year's State Department may be different from this year's. You never know when some politician five years from now, looking to get his name on the front page, will ask what the hell Karl Malden (born Mladen Sekulovich) was doing in Tito's Communist Yugoslavia."

227

I listened hard. Then I said, "That's all I need to know."

I decided not to go and notified the Yugoslavian consulate accordingly. End of story. But it always nagged at me. Why did they look out for me? Were they really looking out for me or just trying to squelch the exchange program? To this day I can only guess. The whole experience left me even less inclined to get involved in politics than before . . . if that was possible. I've driven Mona crazy ever since because she is passionate about politics and has been a hard worker for many candidates and causes over the years. But that's something she does without me. The McCarthy era clinched that for me, I suppose. My name doesn't go on anything even remotely political anymore.

Meanwhile, I just kept showing up for work under my contract. As I have said, most of these first pictures were just assignments. This was before the antitrust laws that prohibited studios from owning theaters, and Warners required product to fill the theaters they owned. That was the business we were in: creating product. You just hoped that every once in a while a good one would come along.

For me, the advantages of being under contract outweighed the disadvantages. Sure, the studio owned me; I was their property. But that meant they wanted to turn me into a marketable commodity. Fine with me. I was a press agent's nightmare in many ways—married forever, in my pajamas by eight—but that became Warner's headache, not mine. I never hired a publicist. Warner's did all that for me. They were in the business of developing talent and making sure that the public got to know that talent.

Everyone was so pleased when Warner, Mayer, Cohn, and Zanuck sold their businesses. People thought, "Now the film industry is really going to sparkle. Now people will be able to have some creative freedom." And, of course, that was true. Well, I never thought I'd say it, but I miss those guys. When they said yes, you had a deal. You didn't even need a handshake, just their word. These men loved the business and loved being competitive with one another. They were the hub of the business. Now it's the banks and the agents. I'm afraid that these days, all too often the creative energy goes into making the deal, not the picture. I'm not kidding myself. I know that it has always been a business and business is about money. But today, it's nearly impossible to sustain a personal vision when the business is run by a conglomerate, not by an individual. These old-time producers had power; sure, they abused it, but they often used it for the good of a picture as well. Very few directors had that kind of power in the early fifties. Alfred Hitchcock was one of them.

I was back in New York between pictures when I ran into Monty Clift one day. He told me he was about to start a picture with Hitchcock and that there was a good part in it for me. Ever since Monty and I had become friends, I had been dying to work with him. I knew that Hitch was preparing something for Warner's, my studio, so I found myself in *I Confess*, the story of a priest (Monty) who hears the confession of a murderer and ends up indicted for the murder himself because his vows prohibit him from revealing the killer. Monty was perfect for the priest; he had the face of a saint but when you looked into his eyes you saw a tortured soul trying to make its way out of utter bewilderment. I played the detective on the case . . . again. But I was happy to be working with Monty in a picture that also happened to fulfill one of my contractual obligations.

I found Hitch to be the perfect British gentleman. He created a high-class atmosphere on the set just with his very presence. He always came to the set in a suit and tie. He was never ruffled, he never shouted. Everything was quiet with Hitch. He never seemed to direct anyone, never suggested how to play the scene.

229

He had a special table reserved for a party of eight every evening in the Chateau Frontenac in Quebec where we were shooting. Invitations to join him for dinner rotated.

I finally had the courage one evening at one of these dinners to say to him, "Hitch, you never tell actors what to do. You set up the scene, we know our blocking, we come in, we do the scene, and you never tell us what you expect from the scene."

He said, "Karl, I am a professional. And I hope that I have hired professionals. We all do our jobs and we go on from there."

After observing him further, I decided that Hitch was so confident about where to put his camera that if a scene wasn't going well he knew exactly how to protect himself. He always knew what he could do in the editing room. For Hitchcock making a movie was like putting together an elaborate jigsaw puzzle; everything had to be that precise.

As unflappable as Hitch was, Monty was, tragically, beginning to fall apart. He had hired as his coach and confidante Mira Rostova, a Russian exile who had been an actress in Europe. She served as a kind of sounding board, almost a buffer between him and the rest of the world. He relied on her heavily, sometimes, I felt, too much.

When the time was coming up for us to shoot our scenes together, Monty invited me to his room to rehearse. Mira was there. Fine, no problem. We kept at it for two or three days and everything was going great guns. I was comfortable; Monty was comfortable. It was a pleasure. We were ready to roll.

The day came for us to shoot the scene where I question him about where he was at the time of the murder. The usual detective bit. We did a take. Then another. Then another. And every time we finished a take, Monty would look over at Mira. She would give him a signal. "Okay" or "Do it again." I could tell that it bothered Hitch to have her on the set, but he was used to it by this point and never said a word. We just kept going, did the scene again. Cut. This time Monty walked over to Mira and started whispering. The whispering turned into a long discussion. I looked over at Hitch. Nothing. So I figured if they were talking about the scene I wanted to hear what they were saying. I got up from behind my detective's desk and walked over to where they were, but the minute I got within earshot, they stopped. I thought, "What is this?"

I asked Monty, "Do you want to do it again?"

He said nothing. I just walked back to my desk and sat down, thinking, "What is this all about? Is this what friends do to one another?"

From that time on, things changed between us. I felt betrayed and, at the same time, my competitive streak had been exposed like a raw nerve. I felt like, "I can play it your way. It's catch as catch can now. You're on your own, buddy."

The truth is I didn't care if Monty and Mira were talking about me. If Monty had told me what I was doing wrong, I would have been happy to work with him. It was the secrecy that irked me.

Fortunately for me, Hitch realized what was going on. When he put the picture together he called Ann Baxter, the female lead, and me in to see the first cut. (Ann, who had all her scenes with Monty, had also been terribly annoyed by his shenanigans with Mira.) I saw the rough cut and grabbed hold of Hitch in a great big bear hug.

"Thank you very much," I said to him.

He had been very kind to me in the editing process. In the very early days of motion pictures, the twenties and early thirties, big stars used to demand a close-up for every one that their co-star received. If the woman had twelve minutes of close-up time, so must the man. Clauses detailing demands like these were even written into contracts. As a supporting actor, particularly in the kinds of pictures I had been doing under contract up to this point, I was well used to having scenes end up on the screen that played entirely over my shoulder. I knew the star's face meant gold, not mine. But Hitchcock gave me a break. My scenes with Monty featured me every bit as much as Monty, if not more.

After I thanked Hitch, he smiled and said, "I thought you'd like it." I felt like it was his way of offering me a little prize for staying cool about Monty and Mira.

During the editing period back in L.A., Hitch invited me to dinner along with Monty and Mira. (By that time it seemed that Monty never went anywhere without her.) I picked them up and drove to Hitch's lovely home in Bel Air. Everything went along smoothly for a while, but it wasn't long before Monty got really drunk. I had heard about a little leather case full of prescription pills that he always carried around, but I had never seen it personally until that night. An hour or so into the evening the case appeared and Monty started popping pills. Between the pills and the booze, he was really out of it. I was terrified that some horrible scene was going to erupt, so I got a hold of Mira and suggested we excuse ourselves early.

Twenty years later, shortly before Hitch died, I was working on *The Streets of San Francisco* when I heard that Hitch was shooting in that city's beautiful Grace Cathedral, which happened to be right across the street from where I was staying. I dropped in on him and we sat and chatted for a good hour. He asked me, "What happened that night? Did you ever get him home?"

I told him we did. But not before Monty used the back seat of my rented car as a bathroom in every possible way. By the time I drove up to the Chateau Marmont, I had to scoop up his limp body. I got him walking, but he didn't know he was walking. It was a pathetic sight—this great talent, this man who could have been our country's Gielgud, who should have been playing Romeo, Hamlet, all those parts that require the class he had naturally. Instead, slowly, so slowly, he simply lost control.

I had been dying to work with Monty Clift for years. *I Confess* offered me that chance, though witnessing Monty's unraveling made the whole experience more bittersweet than joyful. Three years later Monty wrapped his car around a tree and basically broke every bone in his extraordinary face so that for the rest of his short life his face became, sadly, a truer mirror to the suffering he did so much to try to escape. But even when we were working together you could already sense that his life was an accident waiting to happen. And that broke my heart.

Chapter 9

By the late fifties, I was still trying to juggle movies and the theater while keeping home base in our two-bedroom apartment in Peter Cooper Village. By now Mila was ensconced in school and Carla was just starting kindergarten, so it was even harder to think about uprooting my family to join me in Hollywood and on other locations.

And there were beginning to be more and more "other" locations. I was still working with Kazan often (whenever possible as far as I was concerned), and he was at the forefront of the movement to shoot movies where the stories really took place. Film historians call it "neo-realism," but before this trend had a name, it was just an impulse to explore the humanity of the common man. How could you do that properly on a backlot or a soundstage? How could you tell the story of a broken man running a broken cotton gin in a broken little Mississippi town from Hollywood? How could you tell the story of hard-boiled longshoremen against a painted backdrop?

Baby Doll and *On the Waterfront* were pictures that helped define the gritty American film of the fifties and, I think, became two very different kinds of classics in the process.

It's hard to imagine *On the Waterfront* starring anyone besides Marlon Brando, but he almost wasn't in the picture. Kazan was still the brunt of a lot of criticism because of his naming names during the McCarthy era (as he remains even today in many circles). When he presented the script for *Waterfront* to Marlon, Marlon said no. It had nothing to do with the part; he said he just couldn't bring himself to work with a man who did what Kazan had done. Marlon simply refused. Kazan had told me about the picture and I was more than interested, but to all of us involved, it seemed increasingly clear that the picture would have to be made without Marlon. He had dug his heels in. But in that case, with whom?

Kazan asked me to start working with Paul Newman on a scene (not from the *Waterfront* script, just a sample) to show the producer of *Waterfront*, the formidable Sam Spiegel. Paul chose a scene from Molnar's *Lilliom* to do with a young actress with whom he felt he had good chemistry. Her name was Joanne Woodward. I worked on the scene with them until we all felt they were ready to show it to Spiegel. Paul was nervous, he knew there was a lot at stake, but I thought both he and Joanne were absolutely great. Regardless, after the scene, no decision. Spiegel remained characteristically unreadable.

It would turn out that Sam Spiegel secretly had his eye on Frank Sinatra to play the young fighter, Terry Malloy. Apparently, unbeknownst to anyone, including Kazan, while I was working with Paul Newman, Spiegel had actually promised Sinatra the part.

To add to the mix, I kept getting calls from Marlon's agent, Jay Kantor, asking me how we could convince Marlon to change his mind. He begged me to talk Marlon into taking the part.

I told him, "You're his agent. I'm not even in this picture yet." (Kazan had promised me the part of the priest, but by then I knew enough to never confuse a promise with a contract.) Besides, I knew you could never talk Marlon into anything he didn't want to do.

Who knows why, but Marlon finally did change his mind without anyone twisting his arm. You have to have a mighty wide competitive streak right down your back to make it as an actor and Marlon was no exception. I had to wonder if all this talk about Paul Newman or Frank Sinatra playing a part that Marlon knew in his heart belonged to him was all it took for him to put his political ideals aside and follow his actor's heart. It was simple really; how could he pass up that part?

I think there was a moment when Spiegel felt he could have gone with either Marlon or Sinatra. Spiegel was the consummate producer, almost a caricature of a producer, and both Marlon and Sinatra were big names. It was win-win; either one of them would have meant business for the picture, but he had already announced that Sinatra was playing the part when Marlon came on board. When Spiegel informed Sinatra's agent that he was going with Marlon after the official announcement that Sinatra would star in the picture, Sinatra understandably lost his cool. He threatened to show up for work anyway and sue the pants off of Spiegel and the studio if they made him leave. Sinatra's agents at William Morris eventually calmed him down, but only to a point. He came back to Spiegel with a request. (This was Frank Sinatra. I can only assume it was more of a demand.) "If I can't play the lead, I want to play the priest."

When I heard that, I figured I could kiss Father John goodbye. Fortunately for me, Kazan stuck by his promise and despite all his screaming and carrying on, even Sam Spiegel acquiesced to Elia Kazan. I heard, though I don't know if it's actually true, that in order to placate Sinatra, Spiegel made him a gift of a magnificent painting, museum quality, of course.

So, the inevitable tempest surrounding Marlon calmed down. Kazan and he reached an agreement that included giving Marlon Wednesday afternoons off for his weekly therapy sessions. However, suddenly, Darryl Zanuck decided he didn't like *Waterfront*. After all this hoopla, the cast was falling into place, but now Kazan and the writer, Budd Schulberg, had to launch a search for a new studio.

Kazan had already committed to doing a new play called *Tea and Sympathy* after *Waterfront*. Finding himself occupied with trying to get the film off the ground for a second time, he asked me if I would cast the play for him. This was a new experience for me. I was actually working out of an office (at the Playwrights' Company) with regular hours, involved in the casting process, but this time from the other side of the desk. I wound up sharing the office with a writer. He happened to live next door to Kazan and his apartment was being painted, so he needed a place to work. Kazan had offered him his office, the half I wasn't using to be exact, and so I sat there studying eight-by-ten glossies of actors while he wrote. His name was John Steinbeck.

I would usually arrive around eight-thirty and get to work. Steinbeck would come in some time later, hang up his coat, and sit down at his desk. Then, every single morning, he would do the exact same thing. He sharpened his pencils. There must have been eighty to a hundred of them in a round container on his desk and he sharpened each and every one. I'd hear the bzzzzz of the electric pencil sharpener and know that the day had officially begun. When he finished this ritual, he would take a ledger and start writing immediately. Sometimes he giggled; he mumbled to himself a lot. Occasionally he would say "Karl, listen to this . . ." and read me what he had just written, often little sketches about the taxi drive coming in to work or how he hated having the house filled with painters or even the weather. Just a paragraph or two. Then he would crumple them up and toss them into the wastebasket.

Finally, I asked him, "John, you write all this but you're working on something else."

"But Karl, those are my warm-ups."

For years, I have wished that I had retrieved those warm-ups from the wastebasket and kept them.

Meanwhile, as I was casting the play, Kazan and Schulberg found a home for *Waterfront* at Columbia. Now, everything was in place except an actress for the part of the girl. One afternoon Kazan and I were walking from The Playwrights' Company to the Actors Studio for an afternoon session when he mentioned to me that he was having a helluva time casting that part. I was already familiar with the script and knew that the essence of the part was that this girl be different from everyone else in that tough neighborhood. She has spent her life in Catholic schools distanced from the waterfront existence. I remembered a girl with whom I had done a scene at the Studio who had that quality. Even her name was perfect: Eva Marie Saint. I mentioned her to Gadge but he had never seen her.

About a week later he asked me to start working with two different girls on the script. One in the mornings, the other in the afternoons. Eva turned out to be one. Elizabeth Montgomery was the other.

I worked with them both no more than a week, maybe just three or four days, when out of the blue, Kazan told me to forget it. He had made up his mind. When I arrived at the first rehearsal, Eva was there. If fifty percent of a character (at least) is in the first impression, I understood and concurred with Kazan's choice. Eva looked like a girl raised by nuns, a girl who had been protected from the raw side of life. Liz Montgomery, also a fine actress, looked like exactly what she was: a girl from Beverly Hills with the confidence that came from the prep school education she had actually had.

I was set to play Father John Corredon, a real waterfront Jesuit priest. It was the first time I had ever played a living human being and that task presented all the challenges you might imagine. As an actor, I would now have to be true not only to the character as he related to the story we were telling, but also to a real individual. I now had both an artistic obligation and a moral one, to a real human being. The bonus, of course, was that I had magnificent new source material for working on the character, the man himself.

I ended up spending eleven days with Father John. I would arrive at his church near Hell's Kitchen on the Hudson River and he and I would set out for some tavern where we'd have a little lunch. Father John always liked to throw back a few beers with his meal. I knew immediately that I could not play this man as a sanctimonious, holier-than-thou type. He himself begged me, "Karl, don't play me like a priest. Play me like a man."

Here was a tough, hard-boiled individual who told me, "I was born in this neighborhood. When I was growing up there were two ways to go. Become a priest or a hood." He had become the one, although in many ways, he had the personality of the other, and he had stayed in the neighborhood to try to bring the two forces together by teaching.

Father John was a compelling character. In fact, a speech he had delivered on the docks of the waterfront had provided the core of the story that *Waterfront*'s screenwriter, Budd Schulberg, had set out to tell. When a longshoreman had been refused a chip (the little tag that permits you to go to work that day), Father John had advised him that this was a violation of the law and that he should go ahead and work anyway. The longshoreman did that and, within a day, was beaten up and thrown into the river for dead. Miraculously, the man survived, but that night, while Father John was waiting to learn of his condition, he stayed up all night walking through Central Park mulling over what his advice had caused to happen. The next morning he walked back, stood on a box on the docks, and delivered the sermon that became the inspiration for *On the Waterfront*.

I knew that this speech—now transported from the docks to the hold of a ship—could be one of the centerpieces of the movie. We were set to shoot that scene on a Monday and Kazan invited Marlon, Mona, and me to dinner the Sunday night before. He told me to come early. When Mona and I arrived he ushered me into his study.

"You've got that big speech tomorrow," he said. "I want to hear you do it."

I was a little caught off guard, but I said okay. I pointed to a rug and said, "Let's say that's the body." (In the film, the man who follows the priest's advice is not so lucky as his real-life counterpart and ends up dead.) And I did the speech.

"Fine," Gadge nodded. "Do it again."

I did.

"Fine, once more."

"How come?"

"I just want to get the sense of your pace."

I told him I intended to do it at a fast clip, without too many pauses so that the one or two pauses I'd allow myself would take on real importance. Kazan seemed to like my approach and finally, after the third time, we went down and joined the group for dinner.

Only later did I learn that Spiegel had wanted to cut at least half the speech, fearing that it was too long and that audiences would get bored. I'm awfully glad I wasn't aware that I was fighting for my big scene that night in Kazan's study. Convinced that the speech was not doomed to be ponderous, Kazan was able to go back to Spiegel and fight for keeping it. He also assured him he would keep it visually interesting by cutting to reaction shots.

He also came up with another way to up the ante of the scene. He instructed various longshoremen (who were playing themselves) to throw things at me when I really got going. Finally, Gadge decided he wanted someone to really haul off and hurl a beer can down at me. The propman rigged up a rubber beer can as quickly as he could and handed it to Charlie Maguire, our first A.D. and a good friend. Charlie gave it a good toss but it bounced. Clearly that would never do.

I was standing there thinking, "Uh-oh," but I didn't say anything.

Kazan decided to try a real empty beer can. Charlie tossed that down, but it sort of floated a little. Not the impact Gadge had in mind.

"All right," said Gadge, "fill it half full with water."

The propman came back hefting the can. Charlie said, "I'm not throwing that."

No one would volunteer. Finally Kazan himself said, "Give me that thing," and he climbed a ladder behind the camera where he'd have a clear shot at me.

I looked up at him. "You better throw it right." And he did. A perfect aim. He cut my forehead wide open. But what was a little blood to a waterfront priest who smoked and drank? I consider it one of my proudest battle scars.

The actual shoot for *Waterfront* was brutal. I don't think I ever made another picture where the cold was so bitter, so tough to take. Not just for a day or two, but for the entire duration. We just couldn't put on enough clothing. Father John and I were roughly the same size, and I had bought him a new hat and coat so that I could wear his throughout the shoot, but it hardly mattered what you had on. When it came time to do a take, we all hated to leave the salamanders, the big wood-burning stoves scattered here and there for heat.

I recall more than one occasion when Sam Spiegel, ever the grand producer, would arrive on the set to check on the picture's progress. He would drive up in his limousine and step out of the car wearing a camel hair coat and fine leather gloves. Kazan tried to explain to him that this was insulting to all the real longshoremen who were working on the film as extras. Some of these men could barely afford a flimsy jacket, but they were working their tails off to help us in every way they could. Sam just didn't get it. Finally, Kazan just shut down work. he told Spiegel, "I'm not shooting another frame of film until you

243

leave this set." That Spiegel understood; time meant money. He disappeared back into his warm limo and the cameras started rolling again.

The longshoremen turned out to be a wonderful group who were thrilled to get their faces on camera (unlike professional extras who try to hide so they won't be identifiable and therefore not called back for another scene). Working with these men changed my acting. You automatically absorbed some of their style, and you discovered very quickly that if you didn't, if you were "acting," you stood out like a sore thumb. Pictures like *Waterfront* taught me that I had to make my acting look simple, like nonacting, like anybody could do it. Again, I fall back on a sports metaphor. Sometimes you watch an athlete and you think, "I could do that." All the training has to disappear and the effort must be invisible in that one moment—the dive, the free throw, or the scene—when everything comes together.

The *Waterfront* shoot suffered enemies besides the weather. There were times when we would spend one day shooting in a park, for example, and arrive at that same park the next day only to discover we had to move. Suddenly our permits had been revoked overnight. Kazan and Charlie Maguire would have to scramble to find someplace else that would match the previous day's shooting. Word was already out that this picture was not going to do wonders for the mob and they could revoke a permit to film in a matter of minutes. We were fortunate to have hired massive Tony Galento and some other ex-boxers as extras. They became our front line.

Even the privately owned locations were tough. I remember that the crew had to carry all their equipment up five flights of stairs to get to the location of the rooftop where Terry, Marlon's character, kept his pigeons. This particular rooftop was toward

the middle of the block, three buildings from the corner. We discovered that the first building on the corner had a bar with an
elevator to the roof so we paid the guy for the use of the elevator and then walked across the second roof to the third rooftop.
A couple of days of shooting on the rooftop went by before the
owner of the second building, the middle one, stormed out.

"You can't cross my roof!"

Kazan tried fighting it the first day. Lunches went up by rope
to the crew and when the day's work was over, the crew carried
down all their cables and lighting just as before. That lasted one
day. We ended up paying the man off for the enormous privilege
of walking across his roof.

Of course, amidst all these logistical nightmares and hard-
ships, Marlon was once again putting his stamp on a character
that would define his genius. Everyone thinks of the scene in
the back of the cab with Rod Steiger. "You were my brother,
Charlie." But the example of Marlon's instinctive cleverness
that comes to my mind is his scene walking through the park
with Eva Marie.

I recall that Eva was having a difficult time justifying her
stopping to talk with him and understandably so. It just didn't
feel natural to her. As Kazan and she were discussing this, Marlon said to her, "Take off your gloves and while we're walking,
drop one." On the next take, she did as he suggested and he just
nonchalantly picked up the glove while carrying on with the dialogue. Most people who have seen the movie can recall how he
kept playing with the glove—fiddling with it, trying it on his
own hand—as they continued to walk and talk. This bit of business changed the whole complexion of the scene. It gave her a
reason to linger; she had to get her glove back. And the physical
act of playing with her gloves gave his character a certain vul-

nerability we hadn't seen up to that point. It was a bit that was pure Marlon. What amazed me was the speed with which this idea came to him. He didn't have to mull it over, it was just his instincts at work.

Today people wonder if we knew we were making a "classic." I never believe anyone who answers "yes" to that question. When you're making a film, you're working in two and three minute bits; how can you know what's going to happen when they're all put together? And then how can you predict how an audience will react?

None of us working on *Baby Doll* a few years later could ever have predicted how the world would react to that film. *Baby Doll* evolved out of two Tennessee Williams one-acts, *27 Wagons full of Cotton* and *The Unsatisfactory Supper*. Kazan thought combining these two stories would make a good movie. Tennessee agreed and set about merging them into a script.

I was set to play Archie Lee, the owner of a dilapidated old cotton gin in a small Mississippi town. Two Actors Studio actors making their film debuts, Eli Wallach and Carroll Baker, completed the triangle. The story revolves around the relationship between my character, Archie Lee, and his teenaged bride. Archie had promised Baby Doll's father on his deathbed that he would take good care of his daughter, so her father agreed to this unlikely marriage. But then Archie and Baby Doll formulated their own little agreement. They would not consummate the marriage until her twentieth birthday. We meet them on the eve of that birthday. Needless to say, Archie Lee is a mass of frustration and nerves. To add insult to injury, an outsider—a foreigner no less—one Silva Vaccaro, has swung into town and opened a new cotton gin. Vaccaro invades their house and their world, which is as small and pathetic as the crumbling Mississippi town they live in.

I accompanied Kazan to Benoit, Mississippi about two weeks before we started shooting to scout locations and soak up the flavor of the area. We'd walk up and down the main street, just checking things out, savoring the atmosphere. We chatted with the sheriff; we met the mayor who, fittingly, also happened to own the hardware store. It was that kind of town, the kind of town where people were called Big Mama and Big Daddy. It had that kind of feel. Of course, it also had the feel of deep-seated ignorance and prejudice. The people who lived in Benoit at that time were, for the most part, small-minded bigots, a thousand or so folks who had elevated poor white trash to a fine art. As Archie Lee, I'd practically be their poster boy.

It was the start of deer hunting season and that's all we heard about as Gadge and I explored the town. When some of the locals invited us along, I thought this would be a good chance to see how Archie Lee really lived.

There were about ten men, twenty-five dogs, twenty rifles, and a lot of all-night drinking as they waited for the season to open the next morning. I passed some time reading in a sport magazine exactly how to hunt, where to aim, when to fire.

Four A.M. arrived and they started passing out the guns. They gave me a shotgun, but when I tried to open it to put the shot in, I couldn't. One fella had a carbine, an army rifle, and I told him I could handle one of those. He loaded the chamber and gave me eight extra bullets to put in my pocket. I never really expected to shoot anything. I figured I was just along to soak up the atmosphere.

We walked and walked, this one fella and I, until we came to a tree. He said, "You stop here. I'm going to go another hundred yards. If you need anything just holler."

I stood there. The sun was just starting to come up by now. I began to hear dogs barking in the dense wood, but I didn't see anything. Another half hour passed when suddenly, I saw a doe leaping by. The sight took my breath away. It wasn't long before another deer, a four-pointer with enormous antlers, stopped about seventy-five yards away. It just stood there. And so did I. It didn't move. And neither did I. And then Archie Lee took over. I raised the carbine up to my eye and pulled the trigger. I did exactly what the magazine instructed, aimed for the back behind the legs to get the heart. His four legs flew out from under him in a flash. It took me a minute to catch my breath. I managed to call out, "I think I got one!" before a fierce nausea swept over me.

Congratulatory shouts filtered back. Someone sent a jeep to pick up the deer. But that was the end of my day. I felt too sick to do anything but head back to camp. As I got closer to the cabin, it occurred to me, "I could have shot into the ground and said I missed. Why didn't I do that?" It was Archie Lee's fault.

All I knew was I would never go hunting again. The whole episode just goes to show how an actor can get lost in a role. I really felt that I was getting deeper under Archie Lee's skin and that gave me the liberty to do something I would never have otherwise done.

The house Kazan wanted to shoot in dated from the Civil War and was completely falling apart. But Kazan had his heart set on this particular house. He wanted it because it was open at both ends; in other words, you could see straight from the front door through the back door. It was a look that worked for the story; this was a house whose inhabitants were vulnerable to an intruder in a town where everyone knew everyone else's business. It took a lot of work and about ten thousand dollars (a decent chunk of money for such a small picture at that time) to get the house in shape.

When Eli and Carroll joined us, we read the script aloud every day for a couple of hours just to get the feel of the dialogue. It had the rhythm and poetry of Tennessee Williams, but it also had to crackle with tension. I think *Baby Doll* contained some of the best dialogue I've ever had the chance to deliver. How can you beat interchanges like:

Baby Doll: "You told a mouthful of lies to my daddy to get me."
Archie Lee: "Get you? I ain't got you yet."

I cannot remember if Gadge suggested that we look at our characters as the classic stock archetypes in the Italian theatrical tradition of commedia dell'arte or if that was a theory we all arrived at together. Whatever, it certainly applied. My character, Archie Lee, was the pantalone, the buffoon, the clown in the baggy pants. To that end, I started eating like a pig the minute I got the part. I drank a milkshake with every meal. By the time we started shooting I was up to two hundred and twelve pounds. (Needless to say, losing the weight after we wrapped the picture was not quite as much fun.) After *Waterfront* and a string of detectives I was delighted with the chance to do something else. Archie Lee, this tragic, funny simpleton—the pantalone—was made to order.

Carroll was Pierrette, the delicate ballerina. And, to complete the commedia dell'arte triangle, Eli was the sergeant. Just like the sergeant always had his sword at his side, Tennessee had given Eli's character, Silva Vaccaro, a whip. Eli played with it magnificently.

I guess we expected it to be cold when we were making *Waterfront*, but none of us were quite prepared for the freezing cold that greeted us in November and December in Mississippi. At least in *Waterfront* we had our winter wardrobes; it wasn't supposed to look cold in *Baby Doll*. Poor Carroll spent half her time in a little summer dress, and the other half in a slip.

When Carroll and Eli were shooting a scene on an old wooden swing in the yard, they draped Carroll in an electric blanket from the waist down. To avoid having our breath show, we had to suck on ice cubes between takes to bring our breath down to air temperature.

When I wasn't in a scene, Gadge put me to work running lines with a lot of the locals. There were only five professional actors in the movie; the rest were townspeople. The part of the sheriff was "played" by the real sheriff, and when, in one scene, he called to a black waitress to sing a song in the pizza parlor, she was the real waitress who sang that same song every night in that pizza joint.

As in *Waterfront,* working with these people kept me honest as an actor. Beyond that, the townspeople, both black and white, who lived and breathed segregation, meant a lot to the reality of the character I was playing. Archie Lee was poor white trash and the only thing that fed his feeble ego was the fact that no matter what, he could always believe that he (through no accomplishment of his own other than the color of his skin) held a higher status than the blacks. This story had a lot to do with the small town South of the fifties and that was the South Kazan was determined to shoot.

It was also the South that came a little close for comfort one day. Our company had hired a black nightwatchman to guard the equipment. One afternoon when he was off duty he walked into town and was stopped by a judge who wanted to fine him on some trumped up charge. The sheriff (who, as I said, was in the film) hauled him into some kangaroo court in the back of the mayor's hardware store and pulled a gun on him. The poor guy panicked, grabbed the gun and ran . . . back to our set. Fortunately, we were just over the county line so they couldn't touch him. He stayed right there for the rest of the picture but we never knew what happened to him after we closed shop. He never would have survived being thrown into a white jail and they had no real black jail, just a six-by-six foot shed without windows.

That was the South that Tennessee Williams loathed and believed he had left behind. But he was struggling with the end of the script even after we began shooting, so Kazan cajoled him into coming down to our location a couple of times. Clearly, he hated it there. He ended up dashing off two or three quick rewrites, got fed up and left as quickly as he could. Kazan fashioned a compilation of Tennessee's endings, striving for a little more action and a little less talk, but it was seat-of-the-pants when it came time to shoot the end. When we wrapped, we weren't even sure whether the picture's title would be *Hide and Seek* or *Baby Doll*.

We may not have been one hundred percent satisfied with the ending, but we thought we had made a good little picture. As always, we hoped it would find an audience. Little did we know that Cardinal Spellman of the Catholic Church would be our P.R. man. One Sunday the Cardinal stood in the pulpit of Saint Patrick's Cathedral in New York and proclaimed the picture to be "a contemptuous defiance of the natural law," forbidding Catholics to see the film "under pain of sin." His reason? He declared that the film went against natural law since Archie Lee and Baby Doll's marriage was never consummated. In other words, it was the lack of sex that got the picture banned by the Catholic Church.

I believe that was just an excuse. I think Spellman took one look at the billboard for the film and felt he had to do something about it. The billboard covered damn near one full block over Broadway, between Forty-fifth and Forty-sixth as I recall. There was Carroll Baker, hair disheveled, lying in an antique

crib not big enough to contain her, sucking her thumb and staring out of vacant, somnambulistic eyes.

It's hard to believe that such a tame image caused such a
furor, but that was the year that saw the release of films like
Around the World in 80 Days, Carousel, and *High Society.* Even
the heavy dramas dealt with sanitary issues like a murderous
child (*The Bad Seed*) and a demented painter (*Lust for Life*).
Nothing like a nineteen-year-old seductress stretched out in a
wrought iron crib. These days all the "bad" publicity would
probably bring audiences into the theaters in droves, but in
1956 ticket-buyers listened to authority figures, at least Catholic
ones did. The film had one great week and then business fell off.
What's more, the Church was so powerful that it even frightened Jack Warner "the Unintimidatable." He pulled the picture
and that was that.

The happy ending is that the film has achieved cult status.
Every few months I turn on the American Movie Classics chan-
nel and come upon Archie Lee, Silva, and Baby Doll playing out
their funny, tragic little human drama.

The bad news was that shooting *Baby Doll* kept me away
from home for Christmas. Mona had tried to compensate, so
presents for Mila and Carla had spread from under the tree
across the entire living room. Mona told me how it took the
girls hours and hours to open them all, until they were punchy,
drunk on wrapping paper and ribbon. I saw snapshots of Mila
hugging a new stuffed animal and Carla trying on a bright red
petticoat over her Doctor Dentons. But I hadn't been there.
Carla was still young enough so that several months were a big
chunk of her life, and there was a horrible moment when I
didn't think she recognized me as I stepped into the apartment.

Clearly, my plan for doing it all was beginning to unravel.

Somebody had to get the raw end of the deal and it was turning out to be my family.

Whereas making movies had once just paid the rent while I waited for a good play to come my way, all that was changing rapidly. Making *Baby Doll* had been a total pleasure from start to finish and two years went by after *Desperate Hours* before I was back on Broadway. Little did I know that my next play would be my last.

One day I got a call from Abe Lastfogel of William Morris. "Karl, there's a play you're going to do."

"What's that, Abe?"

"*The Egghead.*"

The Egghead was the new play that Molly Kazan, Gadge's wife, had just finished. I told Abe that I had already read it, and while I thought it was well written, I felt it wasn't exciting. It was a thesis, not a drama.

Abe said to me, "There are times you must do things for a friend and she is a friend of yours."

He had to say no more. He was absolutely right and I committed to the play right then and there.

My dear friend, the brilliant actor Hume Cronyn, found himself in a similar position when he signed on to direct the play. We met before rehearsals began and he said, "I don't think it's going to be a hit, but she asked us to do it so we're doing it."

Molly Kazan meant that much to a lot of people; I knew she did to me. I had even heard that my name had become a running gag in the Kazan household. Molly was such a champion of mine that it had gotten to the point where Gadge would get a new project and say to her, "No, there's nothing for Karl," before she even had a chance to start bugging him to give me a part. When she believed in a person or an idea for that matter, she believed in it without reservation. In a way, her play suffered for that unswerving commitment.

The Egghead was an intellectual exercise about how a professor could be duped by a student. It was no wonder that Molly fashioned her one and only play in the academic arena. That was where she felt comfortable; her grandfather had been the president of Yale. It was also no wonder that the meat of the play had to do with communism. The professor defends his student against accusations of communism, but then it turns out the student really is a communist. Ultimately, Molly was asking, "What difference does it make?" Of course, it made a great deal of difference to Molly's life because varying answers to that question had haunted her husband for several years by then.

When I accepted the part I was less concerned with the play's politics than with my own personal challenge, fear really. The idea of playing a college professor terrified me, drawing all my old insecurities about academics to the surface like a magnet. I confided my fear in Molly. She told me, "Don't worry about it. They're just human beings like anyone else." To prove her point, she drove me up to a college in Massachusetts where we spent a long weekend hobnobbing with the ivory tower set.

On the way home Molly asked me, "Didn't I tell you? They're people like anyone else."

I couldn't admit to her that I still felt there was a difference between me and these men who spent their whole lives in the world of ideas and words, a difference I wasn't sure I could overcome, even as an actor in a role.

As I continued to work on the part I decided that all I could do to span the gap between this professor and me was to play him as an Everyman, make him more ordinary for myself so that I would not feel so intimidated by him. I got closer to the character when I realized that his entrance could help me unlock something unexpected about him. The play calls for him to enter having just come from playing squash. I realized that meant he was a physical man; he enjoyed sports. Ah-ha! Something I could relate to. I decided that whatever I did, I would do it with athleticism so that this cerebral man would take on another color that was against type and therefore, I hoped, more interesting.

Because of Molly's style of writing there were other problems to overcome as well. She was a great critic; she could nail other people's work with enormous insight, but she probably had too great a critic running in her own head the whole time she was writing. Her writing was very much like herself. She was a tall, thin woman with an elegant reserve about her. So in her writing, she stopped herself short of emotion in favor of taking a stand. Hume, as director, had his work cut out for him. (Gadge was not involved in the production at all. He may have dropped in on a few rehearsals, but said nothing. Hume was the boss.)

I remember there was one moment in particular that was like jumping over a hurdle for me. My character, the professor, is talking to his family and quotes Roosevelt's "Nothing to fear but fear itself." I couldn't make the line flow naturally in the conversation no matter how I tried. Everything just stopped dead, and this had to be a man whose existence was bound up in his ease with words.

One day I complained bitterly about the speech in front of the whole cast. Hume immediately called, "Lunch!" Then he grabbed me by the arm—all five foot five of him—and said, "Wait."

He pulled me aside and really bawled me out. "You set the example here. If this is how you feel, come to me quietly. Otherwise the rest of the cast will take it upon themselves to belly-ache about everything in the play."

This was a first for me, I think, to have my name above the ti-tle on a marquee, and I hadn't learned all the lessons that go along with that. Hume taught me an important one that after-noon. I knew at once that he was right. But then, Hume is al-ways right.

After the first two or three performances on the road, Molly finally realized the quote had to go, but only after countless hours of discussion during which she defended the line ar-dently. Molly Kazan never let go easily. The line was cut, but my admiration for Molly as a human being had only deepened. I ended up telling her, "Molly, if there's ever a new pioneer period and we have to travel long distances by covered wagon, I want to go with you."

Quote or no quote, the play lasted only nine performances. I was disappointed—you're always disappointed—if not sur-prised. However, it's not the play's closing I choose to remem-ber. It's opening night.

I was in my dressing room at the Ethel Barrymore Theater (my personal favorite since I'd always had hits there) when Molly walked in, placed a tiny box on my dressing table, turned around and walked out. Gadge came in five minutes later and said, "I know Molly brought you something. What was it?"

I was preoccupied and said, "I don't know. I'll open it later."

"No," he insisted. "Open it now."

I opened the box and there inside was her Phi Beta Kappa key. Gadge was amazed; apparently she had never bothered to even order it before. The key was inscribed: TO KARL, EGGHEAD 1957. It was the kind of simple, classy gesture that came naturally to Molly and I only hope she knew how much it meant to me.

Six years later Molly would be dead. By then I was living in Los Angeles and when the call came informing me that she had died, I made immediate arrangements to fly back for her funeral. Dick Widmark offered me his apartment in New York and when I arrived there I discovered that Walt Wriston, my old neighbor from Peter Cooper, was now living in the same building.

A lot had changed. I was living in California and Walt had moved to Beekman Place, a New York address that is symbolic of having "made it." I was struck with how all of us, the old Peter Cooper group, had suddenly grown up. Walt, who had been a bank teller when we were pushing baby carriages together, was now well on his way to becoming the president of Citibank. And I supposed that I, too, must have chosen the right profession after all. I, who had struggled through school, had managed to acquire a Phi Beta Kappa key.

facing page:

The whipping scene in *One-Eyed Jacks*.

Marlon was always full of surprises, and when we

shot this scene, he worried that I might be, too.

Chapter 10

Up until I signed my contract with Warners I had never had an agent. Once or twice an agent stepped in and took care of the deal-making for me, usually someone already affiliated with that particular production. Then, when that play or film was over, I went on my merry way. Molly Kazan, who, as I mentioned, was the type of person who took it upon herself to right all wrongs, was the one who changed all that for me. She called

Abe Lastfogel (the head of William Morris) and informed him that something had to be done about the fact that I didn't have an agent. Abe called me one night from L.A. around ten o'clock my time.

"We'd like to handle you," he said.

I told him I was flattered and that I would sign if he would represent me.

"I won't be handling you personally," Abe explained, "but I promise you my door will always be open. Any time you need advice or have a question you can walk right into my office."

I thought it over and called back in a few days. "The next time I'm in L.A., can I talk to you?"

I did and Abe ended up handing me over to his protégé, Sam Weisbord. Sam was a real William Morris company man. His secretary at the time was a young man named Mike Zimring. Mike was not yet married and whenever I had to go to L.A., he and I would pal around, go to the movies, grab some dinner. We hit it off from the start, and when he became a runner for the agency, he used to fill me in on all his adventures. He was one of the agency guys who had a beat to cover, spending a few hours a day traveling from studio to studio finding out what was cooking at each one. Mike's beat was "the valley"—Warners, Republic, Disney, Universal. Before long they made Mike an agent. The timing was just right for me.

I was beginning to be shuffled around within William Morris so I called Abe and told him I wanted to deal with just one man there. "Give me to Mike Zimring." Abe did and I couldn't have been more pleased.

One of the great blessings of my career is that my relationship with my agent, Mike Zimring, turned into one of the most cherished friendships of my entire life. When Mike became the head of the literary department at William Morris other agents within the company began calling me, assuming that I was "unattached" once again. Even then the business was more about departmentalization than relationships; everyone expected that I would have to find someone within my "actors" slot. But once again I called Abe and he arranged everything so that I could stay with Mike. I think I was the only actor he handled for many years. Mike remained my agent for over forty years, probably a Hollywood record, but more important, he remains today my dearest friend in the world.

I was still a contract player when Mike first began to represent me and I made plenty of grade B movies during the years when I was also making films like *Waterfront* and *Baby Doll*. World War II movies like *The Halls of Montezuma* and *I'll Take the High Ground,* and even that ultimate in fifties' pop culture, a 3-D movie called *Phantom of the Rue Morgue.* In that one I got to camp it up as an evil mad scientist with an ape as my sidekick.

Yeoman directors like Lewis Milestone and Richard Brooks helmed these pictures. They harbored few grandiose illusions about creating fine art but they knew where to put the camera and get shots that would cut together to make a movie.

Generally, the producers were still running the show. I remember that I had been working for Warners for two years, usually dealing with studio executive Steve Trilling, when the studio leant me out to MGM to make *I'll Take the High Ground.* My friend, Dick Widmark, was playing the lead, so I was looking forward to a good time. MGM welcomed me warmly. Studio head Dore Schary had a trademark bottle of cream sherry waiting for me in my dressing room and he even came down to the set to greet me personally.

He said, "Karl, I want to make you comfortable and I hope you have a good experience on my lot."

I thanked him and added, "You know, I've been working at

Warner Brothers for two years and I've yet to meet Jack Warner."

We shot *I'll Take the High Ground*, a run-of-the-mill war picture, and I went back to Warners a few months later to make *Phantom of the Rue Morgue*. Somewhere around the third or fourth day of shooting, while I was waiting on the soundstage, I heard a booming voice.

"Where's that goddamn Karl Malden?"

"Here I am."

It was Jack Warner. "You wanted to meet me? Here I am."

I think I said, "Well, I'm pleased to meet you." But it didn't matter. He'd said what he had come to say and he was out of there. Jack Warner was there to run the shop, not to make friends. He let his directors deal with pesky chores like actors.

One of Warner's contract directors was Gordon Douglas who directed me in *Bombers B-52*. He had cut his teeth on the Our Gang comedies. A "dees," "dems" and "dose" kind of guy with no high-fallootin' artsy pretensions, he just got the work done.

The real star of the movie was the plane, but the character everyone noticed was the girl. She was Natalie Wood, nineteen years old, full of life, and as beautiful as a girl could be. Wherever Natalie was, the scene was the same—boys, boys, boys! They swarmed around her constantly. But when it came time to work, Natalie was a complete professional.

That same year I filmed *Fear Strikes Out*, which was the story of baseball player Jimmy Piersall. Anthony Perkins played Piersall and, though he didn't know the first thing about the game and had to be taught how to throw a ball from the outfield, he ended up turning in a stunning performance. I played his demanding, domineering father. I didn't worry about playing a real person this time because he was already dead, so I really let myself go.

I kept trying to find some connection to my own situation

with my father. I remember really locking into the scene where I visit Jimmy when he's playing ball for the minor leagues. He proudly tells me his batting average has him in second place. My line was, "That's not first." I delivered it without even looking at him, as though I was ashamed of him. When we were shooting the scene, the moment didn't particularly register for me. But later, when I saw it for the first time on screen, I was suddenly back in Gary. I heard my father speaking from my own mouth. I understood what had motivated Jimmy Piersall's father; like my father, he just wanted his son to do better. No one had the power to affect Jimmy like his father. My father, too, could be warm and gregarious with other people, but could turn to me and say something, without meaning to, that cut through me like a knife.

When Jimmy Piersall saw the picture, he said to me, "Boy, you made my father mean."

I said, "He was mean, wasn't he?"

"Yeah, but not that mean."

I had to wonder where that had come from in me. I hadn't tried to make him the father from hell. I always kept in mind that he thought he was being a good father, trying to do the best for his son. No man wakes up in the morning intending to be mean; no villain (unless extremely poorly written) wants to be evil. You have to play heavies as people reacting to a particular situation in a particular way, people backed into a corner.

While I was filming *Fear Strikes Out* in '57, Dick Widmark came to me with a novel offer. He had optioned a play about the Korean War called *Time Limit* by Henry Denker. Dick and a highly acclaimed film editor, Bill Reynolds, were planning to produce the film version together and they wondered if I would direct it. The play was still running on Broadway so I told him that I would go see it when I returned home to New York.

I was concerned about dealing with the scope of a war picture, but the play intrigued me. I thought it might be something I could direct because, like all good drama, it was really about relationships. Thematically, the play dealt with the code of ethics in the army. It portrayed the North Korean army torturing American prisoners, some of whom were branded traitors when they broke and divulged information. The play asked the question, "What would you do if you were caught in a situation like this?" I took the plunge and signed on as the director.

Since I had been away from home so much, Dick agreed that I could stay in New York and work with the writer, Henry Denker, on trying to open up the play. Meanwhile, Dick and Bill Reynolds remained in Los Angeles working on the story there. Every so often we would compare notes. After a few months we took the best from both versions and created a pretty good script.

Then my work as a director really began. Whereas I was accustomed to breaking down every scene in terms of what my particular character was about, now I had to look at every single scene in terms of what the entire story was about. Instead of focusing on the arc my character would make from the beginning to end, I now had to keep a much broader overview in mind. I can't say that one was necessarily easier or more difficult than the other; they were just very different processes. They say that every actor sees the movie or play he is in strictly from the point of view of his own character. The actor playing a servant in *Hamlet* would have us believe that the play is all about an underpaid footman who had done his best to keep things running smoothly in the castle while his self-absorbed employers took him for granted. That is an actor's prerogative, not a director's. I had to remember that.

We had twenty-four days to shoot *Time Limit*. Its schedule was actually very much like a TV movie long before there were such things as TV movies. Its budget was even smaller than a TV movie. We couldn't afford to hire the most expensive cast, but Dick and I assembled a really good group. Richard Basehart, Carl Benton Reid, and both Rip Torn and Martin Balsam in their first substantial movie roles. And, of course, Dick Widmark would be starring.

I wasn't worried about my actors delivering. I hired a lot of theater actors and knew they could manage the two-, three-, even four-page takes I had in mind. What worried me was the camera, placing the camera for the best effect. That's where I was a novice and needed to protect myself. I wanted to establish a rhythm without too many cuts. Bill Reynolds ended up being on the set every day and his editor's eye was invaluable. He would tell me when I needed to pull in here or get an over-the-shoulder there. He taught me to get those shots when the opportunity presented itself, when I was all set up for them anyway. That way, if I didn't end up needing them in the cutting room—fine; if I did need them for cutaways or to punch up a scene, then I would be glad to have them.

One of the perks about having an actor as my producer was that Dick scheduled two weeks' rehearsal. We spent the first week reading the script around a table, just like a play, then getting it on its feet. The cameraman, Sam Leavitt, joined us for the second week. I appreciated that Leavitt was intent on understanding the style I was after. One lunch break, he and I took a walk around the lot. (We were on the old Goldwyn lot on Formosa Avenue in Hollywood.) I told him that I wanted the look to be simple and straightforward, nothing fancy.

But I had one scene in mind where he could get as artistic as possible. There was a scene in the prison camp where the prisoners of war have to take a vote to decide which one of them is going to kill the one among them who, they have discovered, informed to a guard. I had thought long and hard about how to make this balloting visually compelling. This would be a critical moment not only dramatically, but thematically. To me, this was the core of the film. Who among us watching the film could say how he would behave, whether he, too, would break down under that kind of pressure? I realized the prisoners slept on mats next to a fire, so I decided they would take twigs and char the ends. The twig without the burn mark would signify the odd man out, the one who would have to kill the traitor. I explained to Sam how I wanted them to reveal their twigs one by one, opening their fists like the petals of a flower, to highlight this crucial moment. I guess my directing was not unlike my take on delivering a long speech. Just keep it moving, keep the story driving forward, until you come to a really crucial moment. Then make it count.

As it happened, our first day we were set to shoot the first shot in the picture. There we were at our Korean camp in the San Fernando Valley. (Nowadays, they'd spend ten million extra and travel to Sri Lanka or somewhere, but this was a story about people—the Valley was okay.) The opening shot of the picture was an attempted escape, one of the prisoners making a dash for a barbed wire fence. I told my cameraman that I wanted to try to do that shot in one take from the opposite side of the fence. This would entail his running up to the fence, starting to climb the wire, and our seeing the Koreans taking aim and shooting him. Leavitt promised me we could.

We built a mound of dirt leading up to the fence so that as the boy ran and ran, he rose up to the barbed wire. Behind him, we could see the Koreans raise their rifles and aim, but then as he rose further, he blocked them from the camera's view. We just heard the rapid-fire shooting as we saw him fly against the barbed wire, propelled by the gunshots.

I think it turned out to be the most effective shot in the picture, but it took much longer than I had anticipated. By the third day of shooting I was really sweating. It didn't seem possible but we were two days behind schedule already.

Sam Leavitt tried to put my mind at ease, explaining that we had never rehearsed the opening sequence. He guaranteed me that when we got onto the stage where everything had been blocked exactly, we'd make up the lost time. And bless his heart, he was right.

My relationship with my star and dear friend, Dick Widmark, ran a little less smoothly for a short while. Dick's method of working didn't quite mesh with Rip Torn who was very much an Actor's Studio method actor. Rip would go off into the corner between takes and mull the scene over for a good ten minutes, working himself back into the mood over and over again every single time. That was not at all Dick's let's-get-it-done style.

When it came time to shoot their big scene together—where Dick is interrogating Rip about what happened to him in the POW camp—I hoped I could somehow make them both comfortable. Rip spent a good, long time preparing himself before we began and then, sure enough, he would retreat to his corner after every take. Five minutes, ten minutes would go by. I'd approach him and ask, "What do you say? Let's go." But he wouldn't budge until he was good and ready. I tried to understand; after all, this was his first big part in a motion picture and it was an emotional scene. I wanted him to do what he felt he had to do in order to properly prepare.

Dick didn't see it that way. After this went on for some time, Dick started screaming at me. "What the hell is he doing, Karl?"

Another take. Rip would disappear into the corner again.

"Karl!" Dick was losing it. "Get him over here!"

Of course, Dick was wearing his producer hat, too, and he was terrified that Rip was going to single-handedly put the picture over budget. It was the first time out for both Dick and me in these new capacities. Dick wanted to keep the picture on track; I wanted to get the best performances I could.

Finally, Dick really let loose at me. I helped fuel the fire by matching him shout for shout. Then he disappeared into his trailer. I just sat and waited. When he came back out he walked up to me and said, "You're fired."

"Should I leave right now?" I asked him.

"No," he answered. "Finish the scene."

I did. And I finished the picture, too. By the next day the whole incident was forgotten. Happily, not only did my friendship with Dick Widmark survive, but a few years later we would end up being down-the-street neighbors. Our daughters would grow up together; my family would spend joyful Christmas Eves at his house year after year; and our friendship endures today.

Back then, I was just happy that we were speaking. *Time Limit* ended up coming in two days under schedule and twenty-five thousand under budget. (Our original budget was only half a million to begin with.) I was proud of that accomplishment and of the picture as a whole.

However, I never had the desire to direct again. Not that burning desire that you really need in this business, a desire so strong that it sees you through all the hardship and heartache. I didn't have the stomach for the politics of directing, running interference between the producers sitting in their offices telling you to hurry up and the actors on the set saying they don't have enough time. I felt like a sergeant, trying to placate one group and protect the other.

What's more, I am basically so highly competitive that I think deep down I knew that there would always be a lot of people who would be better directors than I could ever be. I didn't want to be on producers' "B" list of directors. That is not to say that I had any illusions about myself as an actor, especially not by this point. I knew that I was never going to be a leading man and was more than happy to continue carving out a career of character parts. Besides, they were often juicier than the leading roles anyway, at least for me. When it came to being a character actor, I felt I could hold my own with anyone. I hoped I wouldn't have to be second string as an actor; I knew I probably would be as a director.

Besides, the next picture I was offered to direct was a Western with enormous scope. I wrestled with the decision for a few days, but in the end I knew that wasn't for me. That clinched it. I decided I didn't want to spend the rest of my career worrying about lenses.

I also knew I never wanted to direct myself. I admire people who can do that successfully, but I knew that task would never mesh with my single-minded nature. As fate would have it, I ended up having to do exactly that in my next picture, ironically enough, a Western.

The last picture on my Warner's contract was *The Hanging Tree* starring Gary Cooper. I had worked with Marlon, but I had also known him before he was a big star. Working with Coop was another story; I had watched him on the big screen for years, and there is something about a Western star that, to me, makes him especially bigger than life. I was so excited to be working with him that I completely reverted to being the new kid, so awestruck that it took me several days to warm up and figure out what I was doing. And then it came time for me to climb onto a horse.

I went to our director, a lovely and knowledgeable man named Delmer Daves. "Del, I'm a city boy. I've never been on a horse, especially Western style."

He arranged for me to have lessons with a wrangler. Every day for a week, I saddled up and rode through Griffith Park for an hour and a half. After a couple of days of becoming accustomed to the feel of being on a horse, my instructor suddenly tossed me a softball as we were riding and told me to throw it back to him. We would ride and toss the ball back and forth because, he explained, I needed to get used to being able to do other things while riding. Like delivering dialogue, for example. I was so focused on the horse, I hadn't even thought about having to be able to deliver my lines at the same time. Gradually I relaxed and actually started to enjoy the rides.

Our routine included racing back to the stables. My instructor was riding a racehorse that he was trying to break in to be a saddle horse for the movies. Naturally, he always won. After my six whole days of riding, I was feeling pretty cocky and I said to him, "You always win because you've got a racehorse. It's no fair."

The next day we traded horses. We started racing and, all of a sudden, my spur caught that horse and he bucked. I fell flat on my back. I knew something was wrong, but like an idiot, I got back up onto that proverbial horse and raced back to the stable. And lost, I might add.

I had fractured a couple of vertebrae that got jostled through the whole picture, but I had learned a lesson about horses. A lesson Coop echoed: "Don't ever trust a horse."

"What do you mean?" I asked him.

"You never know what'll spook a horse," he said. "A branch, a sound, a crack in the earth."

I took him seriously. That was a real cowboy talking as far as I was concerned.

He was also a great actor. People used to say he really wasn't acting with his distinctive "Yep" and "Nope." But you could tell when you played a scene with him that he knew himself and the camera so well that he knew exactly what he could do better than anyone else. Some people say that movie acting is all in the close-up, in the eyes, and Coop was the epitome of that art. Less was more with Coop, so much more. And that conveyed an honesty about him that was enormously powerful. I felt that I was still learning film technique at that point and I became fiercely aware of my whole body acting up a storm whenever I played a scene with him.

What you saw was what you got with Gary Cooper. But he also had generous soul and an unexpected twinkle in his personality. We were on location in Yakima, Washington, the heart of the fruit belt. Locals were constantly bringing him flats of fruit, which he would share with the whole cast and crew, so that we were eating apricots and cherries all day.

Coop loved to spend Sunday afternoons taking a drive and often invited me along. He drove what appeared to be an ordinary Plymouth. Whenever a big, fancy car, a Cadillac or a Lincoln, would zoom by he would let it pass and get a good half a mile ahead of him. Then he'd take off. He had a souped-up motor in that old boat of a car and he would just smile as he'd leave the Caddy in his dust in a few seconds flat. I thought to myself, that's exactly the way he acts; that's his style. Let everyone put on a big show and pass him by, then . . . boom! . . . he's snuck up on you in his own quiet way and zipped right past.

After a while Coop would stop at a lake, pull a couple of fishing rods and some tackle out of the trunk and the two of us would fish. Neither one of us were great talkers; truth be known, we'd sit there for hours barely saying a word, but it was a great way to pass a Sunday afternoon. I didn't even mind that I never caught a thing. Coop would catch three or four good-sized fish, turn them over to the chef at the hotel when we got back, and we would have fresh fish for dinner.

One night after we were back in L.A., he invited me out for lunch. He wanted to go to a particular restaurant because his daughter had eaten there the night before and complained to him about how exorbitant the prices were. Coop and I ordered a nice lunch and enjoyed our meal, but when the bill came, Coop hailed the maître d'. Without being hostile or rude, Coop told him that he thought the prices were outrageous. The owner scurried over and offered us our meal on the house, but Coop would have none of it. He paid the bill and that was that. On our way out he said to me, "They'll never make it with those prices," but he never made a scene.

That was Coop; quiet, polite, and supremely effective. In the long run, he was right, too. The place closed in less than a year.

We were in the home stretch of shooting when Marty Jurow, our producer and a good friend, called me to meet him at Coop's house on a Saturday. Our director, Del Daves, had been rushed to the hospital with a bleeding ulcer. Doctors' orders were going to keep him there for a month. Marty sprang the news on me: "Karl, you're going to take over."

I said, "Thanks, but no thanks." But they kept at me.

Finally Coop spoke up. He said he wanted me to do it.

"You're the star," I told him. "It's going to be on your shoulders if I screw up."

He said he didn't care.

I answered, "If I say yes, you remember that."

So I took over the directing. It was the hardest two weeks of work I ever had, up all night preparing the script and acting during the day, never quite able to concentrate fully on either one.

Every little problem falls on the director's shoulders. I remember the second day of my directing began with a scene between Coop and Maria Schell. The camera started on Coop who was playing a pioneer doctor. I had him grinding medicine in a mortar and pestle. We pulled back to reveal him dressed in black wearing his cowboy hat. Then Maria entered and they played the scene. Ever the gentleman, Coop took off his hat when she came in. After the first rehearsal of the scene Coop took me aside.

"Karl, I hate this hairpiece." (It was pretty awful).

I sympathized; as an actor I knew you couldn't do your best work if you didn't feel comfortable.

So I suggested, "Keep your hat on."

He said, "But I'm the hero. When I talk to the girl I should take it off."

I had to think fast. "But this hero is all dressed in black anyway. That's usually for the heavy. See, this guy does things differently."

He laughed and kept his hat on whenever he could.

After the picture wrapped, Coop and I had lunch a few times. Once he invited me to the brand-new home he had just built in Beverly Hills. No sooner had I arrived than he walked me out to the back end of the grounds where he was growing his own corn on about an eighth of an acre (long before it was fashionable to grow vegetables in Beverly Hills). We picked a couple of ears, went back to the kitchen, boiled up some water, and had the best damn corn I ever ate.

After lunch he gave me a tour of the house, particularly pointing out the closet in his study. All his pants, shirts, coats, everything were hanging in order. He was so proud of this, like a kid showing off his baseball trophies. I couldn't get over it. Here was this superstar, in the true sense of the word, beaming over his homegrown corn and his neatly organized slacks. That was Coop. I only wish I could have met him sooner as he died just a few years later.

Fortunately, *The Hanging Tree* shot during the summer. That meant Mona and the girls could spend three months in L.A. with me (minus the three weeks I was shooting in Washington). We had gotten into a routine of renting a house in L.A. whenever I was filming there during the summer. We'd board the Twentieth Century Limited in Grand Central Station and make the trek across the country, switching to the Super Chief in Chicago and hopping off the train in Albuquerque just long enough for the girls to buy a beaded sombrero or a woven coin purse from the Indians selling their wares. The girls got to see the country roll by from an observation car instead of from twenty thousand feet up.

Of course, not every picture was shot during the summer. I was back in New York, committed to trying to stay put for a while, determined to be a little pickier and not take the first film that came along. I wanted to stay home with my family. As fate would have it, my best laid plans evaporated with one phone call. Marlon called and said he was doing a picture that had a part in it for me. I said yes without even reading the script. (I think that was the only time I ever did that and, I might add, if my phone were to ring tomorrow and it was Marlon on the other end with the same offer, my answer would be exactly the same.)

A hot young director, Stanley Kubrick, was attached to the project briefly, but before long he dropped out, claiming "creative differences" as I recall. I think he was panicked (under-standably so) about the fact that the script had no ending and we were counting down to the start date. That left us with all the elements in place except a director. The studio, Paramount, informed Marlon he would have to take the reins. He agreed, but asked for a couple of months to work on the ending. Paramount refused, insisting he start immediately. And so we all jumped in headfirst on *One-Eyed Jacks*.

I had seen Marlon direct a scene once at the Actors Studio so I had every confidence in him. He was surrounded by top flight people; everything about the production was first rate—cameraman, costume designer, the entire crew. It was fitting that Marlon end up directing because this picture was his vision. He was producing it as well and he had helped write the script; he brought the bat and ball so we were all ready to play the game according to his rules.

Best of all, no one could rush Marlon. Unlike when I had directed, he didn't care one whit when the front office began breathing down his neck. He had hired a lot of actors from "B" westerns and the ingenue, Pina Pellicer from Mexico, had never even been in a movie before. Marlon had enormous patience with them and was determined to take all the time he needed with his cast, including himself.

I remember the day we were shooting the scene on the beach where he examines his smashed hand, tries to use it and cannot. He wanted the waves to come rushing in and smash against the rocks. The tide had something else in mind that morning; there were no waves at all. Both Marlon's coproducer, Frank Rosenberg, and the assistant director suggested we shoot another scene.

"No," said Marlon. "Find out when the tide is going to turn."

Word came back that we would have to wait until noon—at least. Fine. We waited. Three hours later the waves pounded in against those rocks and Marlon got his shot, one of the most spectacular in the film.

As I have said, one of the great joys in working with Marlon was the constant challenge. By this time I had learned to expect the unexpected with him. The day came for us to shoot the big whipping scene where my character, Dad Longworth, really lets Marlon's character, Rio, know who's boss once and for all. We rehearsed it a couple of times with Marlon urging me on to really crack that whip until I broke a good sweat. Marlon—always an actor first and foremost—finally took the whip from me to show me exactly what he wanted. He started whipping so hard that after a few minutes he let out a scream. He had dislocated his shoulder. We waited for him to get medical attention and then went on with the scene.

Slim Pickens tied Marlon hog-style to the fence and I started to whip him. (From my mark it appeared that the whip was making contact; of course, it never did.) It was hot that day and I was wearing my full sheriff's getup. It wouldn't take long for me to break the sweat Marlon was after. The scene called for me to walk up to him where he was draped over the fence, and say, "Now let's see the kind of stuff you're made of." I delivered the line, then Marlon took one of his patented pauses, looked me in the eye, and spat in my face. He had never done this or even suggested doing this in any of the rehearsals. After the shock, the first thing that went through my mind was that I was not going to be the one to stop the scene. I wasn't going to cry "Uncle!"

I looked back at him and said, "Well, that's a pretty good start," then walked back to my mark and cracked that whip. Marlon told me later that he was gripping those fenceposts for dear life, thinking, "What the hell is Malden going to do now?" He thought I was going to cheat my mark and really let him have a couple of cracks. (The distance had been measured exactly, calculating the twelve-foot bullwhip and my three-foot reach.) But he never yelled "Cut!" As the director he could have, but he just hung on to that fence and waited for the whip to fall.

As a director, Marlon had a flair with actors that even extended to the extras. He must have hired over two hundred extras for the fiesta scene, all professionals. On the second day of shooting that sequence, I noticed him going around from extra to extra, having a private word with each one. He was assigning each extra a category: "You're an 'A.' You're a 'B.' You're a 'C.'" Then he would tell them, "Remember that." As the day progressed, they were all comparing classifications excitedly, but Marlon never referred to the groups again.

The next day we moved on to the scene around the well. As Marlon and I were diagramming the action, I kidded him: "What am I, Marlon? Can I be a 'B?' Will you make me a 'B?'" Finally I asked him what the hell that had been all about.

He said, "I was watching the extras on those first few takes and they weren't giving me anything. Nothing. So I thought they'd give me a little more if they thought I was going to ask them to do something special." He never did ask them, of course, but his instinctual understanding of psychology got results.

On top of all the pressures Marlon had on *One-Eyed Jacks,* or maybe because of them, Marlon's weight was starting to get out of control. He had a magnificent wardrobe designed for himself and looked great at the beginning of the shoot, but before long, he had to order a whole new wardrobe. We were staying at a motel called The Tickled Pink in Monterey, not far from a lovely hotel called the Highlands Inn, which featured four-star food. I remember one night when Marlon had simply had it with his diet. He ordered double everything, then pie a la mode, and washed it all down with a full quart of milk. He just didn't care anymore. The battles he was engaged in with the studio were so intense maybe he needed an outlet, maybe it was food.

Marlon genuinely wanted to say something with this film about human nature—that no individual is all good or all bad. Nothing in matters human is all black or all white; everything is in shades of gray. Everyone has two sides and maybe we only show one side, like a one-eyed Jack, but the other side still exists. Couching this theme in a Western, where the black or white hat traditionally defined the characters, made it all the more fascinating. But Marlon's approach frightened the studio brass who got paid to second-guess the public and had decided the public wouldn't get it.

They made us change two critical scenes, which, I believe, took the guts out of the picture. Originally, my character, Dad, was supposed to be the only character who told the truth in every situation. In the final version I lied to Rio in the scene where he shows up after five years. This made Dad the clear-cut heavy. Because of this studio decision, we boycotted shooting for nearly a month. Marlon felt that strongly about his take on the story. But, ultimately, it became obvious that the studio was not going to budge and, with that, Marlon lost control of the picture.

By the time we shot the ending, which had always been problematic, there was not much of a fight when the studio wanted to make it "happy" (or at least "happier"). The original ending was the stuff of Greek tragedy with my character, Dad, accidentally shooting his own daughter as she rides off with Rio. Rio was to carry her in his arms back into the town square, her lifeless body a symbol of all of their deception. Not anymore. Now Rio rides off through the surf with a parting speech that begins, "You be lookin' for me in the spring. . . ." Although we believed we had made a fine film, this was not going to be the groundbreaking Western we had all hoped to make, the classic it should have been.

From start to finish of shooting, it had been a very long six months (an unusually long shooting schedule for those days).

I think I only saw my family once during those six months when I had a break and flew home for a few days. In some awful way that short visit felt forced, like catching up with distant relatives. Mila was anxious to tell me all about everything that was happening in school, and Carla sat me down in the living room to demonstrate how she had learned to skip and to snap her fingers. The message came through loud and clear: I was missing too much.

For the first time, Mona and I began to seriously discuss moving to L.A. I could no longer deny that was where the work was. It's hard to imagine now, but if signing a motion picture contract tortured me, the concept of actually moving to Hollywood was even more agonizing.

Regardless, when I got back to L.A., I began househunting. First I had to be talked into the wisdom of buying a house, a terrifying idea to me since I had been a renter my entire adult life. Looking for something to buy signified an undeniable commitment to Los Angeles. But who was I kidding? I hadn't worked in New York in over two years. I found a house . . . that everyone hated. I grabbed everyone I knew in L.A. and traipsed them through the house—including Mona's uncle, my dear friend, Aube Tzerko; everyone—and they all hated it. But I tried to look past the red flocked wallpaper and saw potential there. Mona ended up flying out for a weekend and, thank God, she agreed. By the time I wrapped *One-Eyed Jacks* we owned a home, and we made the move in the summer of '59.

A few months after we moved in, we had Marlon over for dinner. He looked around the place and said, "So this is the house that Jack built."

"Yes, it is."

And Mona and I have been living in it ever since. It is the house where our dearest friends gather every December 31 to ring in the new year. It is the house where our daughters grew up and where they both got married. It is the house where our three granddaughters have dropped in for countless after-school tea parties. It is the house where the whole family, now nine of us, sit around that old pine dining room table and wait for Mona to get the giggles. We all make fun of her because, like clockwork, she gets the giggles at the end of every family meal. I think it's because she looks around that old table that took up darn near half our living room in our little New York apartment and can't believe how far we've come and how lucky we are to still have our family around us.

It's home.

Chapter 11

When I moved to California, my career shifted gears. I didn't have to worry quite so much about where the next job would be coming from. For the next ten years, I worked steadily. After each picture I went through what I call my puttering stage where I painted the fence around the backyard, replanted the garden, fixed the rain gutters, that kind of thing. But usually, just when I began to run out of household projects and fret, the phone would ring. I think for the first time I felt at ease.

Of course, I was barely able to enjoy that feeling; something in my upbringing made me suspicious. There had to be something wrong if I wasn't struggling. It was the Serbian way— you're not accomplishing anything unless it's an uphill battle. I had to develop new challenges for myself; now within the work itself instead of focusing on getting the work. For the first time I began to enjoy the luxury of picking and choosing roles a little bit more, and I made a conscious decision—maybe the only thing I deliberately tried to accomplish in terms of shaping my career—to try not to repeat myself. If I had played two detectives in a relatively short period of time, then I'd start turning down detective roles. Too many heavies, then no heavies for a while. I also began to accept certain pictures specifically because I wanted to work with a particular person involved in the project.

Pollyanna marked several firsts for me. It was the first time I worked for Disney, my first picture coming out of my Warner's contract, and the first time that I made a deal for the picture as a whole instead of getting a weekly salary. It was also my first picture as a California resident—the first time I could actually go to work and come home in the evening to my own home; it was a treat for me to be working on a part right there at home surrounded by my family.

The audience was to be introduced to my character, the Reverend Snow, through his first sermon, several pages of chandelier-rattling fire and brimstone designed to put the fear of God into a church full of New England parishioners. It was that speech I couldn't wait to sink my teeth into when I first read the script. I decided to pattern the delivery after a Serbian priest I had known in Gary, and, keeping him in mind, I spent a couple of months working on the speech every morning up in my little study, often waking up the girls by shouting at the top of my lungs. By the time I was ready to shoot the speech, Mila and Carla were letter perfect on it as well. To this day Mila remembers it better than I do.

The girls were also delighted when I invited my young costar, Hayley Mills, over for the afternoon one Sunday. She came with her mother and younger brother and all the kids had a wonderful time teaching each other British and American versions of hide-and-seek. Hayley was about to become a star, but she was totally unaffected, a little girl just like my daughters, dashing through the yard trying to get "home" before she was tagged. I think that quality came across on screen and helped to make her so appealing. Like Natalie Wood, Hayley was a young actress whose performance never veered into the precious or self-conscious. You believed her one hundred percent; she was never condescending toward her own childhood, a trap so many young actors fall into.

She also had the good graces to be nervous. If I remember correctly, Hayley's first day of shooting was in a scene with me. Pollyanna's curmudgeonly aunt who runs the town has sent her to deliver a message to me, a mandate really, regarding what Bible passages I should use in that Sunday's sermon. Pollyanna and I, the town reverend, sit on a log and she tells me all about the "happy texts" from the Bible. Hayley was completely prepared but very tense. We rehearsed the scene a couple of times and I was trying to warm things up so much that I could feel the scene turning to mush. I was trying to figure out what to do when we broke for a few minutes. I looked at her adorable little face and said, "You know, Hayley, yours is a lot smaller, of course, but your nose is just like mine." She burst out laughing. Whenever I felt her tensing up, I'd just point back and forth between her nose and my own. We were friends from then on.

Working on the Disney lot at that time was good, old-fashioned fun, more like being on a college campus than a movie studio, with Goofy Drive replacing frat row. Walt was very much a presence, the concerned and interested dean. He knew everyone who worked for him by name, first and last, and ran that studio with a personal touch. The day after I shot my long sermon, Walt made a point of seeking me out to tell me he had just seen the rushes and how happy he was with them. He even sent me a sixteen-millimeter print of the speech. He made working at the studio that bore his name a total pleasure.

I went from working with one of the youngest stars on the scene to working with a star who had already had a legendary career. When Delmer Daves offered me a picture called *Parrish*, I was not overwhelmed by the script, a rather ordinary soap opera built around the world of tobacco farming. However, I couldn't resist the opportunity to work with Claudette Colbert. I was even supposed to be her love interest, which, I would soon learn, meant spending more time at the tailor shop creating a magnificent wardrobe than in front of the cameras.

What was fascinating to me about making this film was having the chance to watch two different schools of acting in action. Claudette was the consummate pro. One or two rehearsals and she was ready for a take. What was at that time the younger generation—Troy Donahue, Connie Stevens—had a completely different style. They were often unprepared and relied on blocking time to learn their lines. I understood their difficulty, though; they had been thrust into leads too fast. Through little or no fault of their own, these kids weren't up to the task.

Claudette, on the other hand, had worked her way up gradually. She was here on this picture some thirty-five years and fifty-plus films after starting out. The comparison between Claudette and our younger costars, studio manufactured commodities, made me grateful for the twenty years of struggling under my belt.

I didn't need a specific reason—no juicy speech or a particular costar—to say "yes" to my next picture. *How the West Was Won* promised to be a mammoth film with a great cast and a series of great directors, each assigned a different episode about the history of the West. Henry Hathaway—Screaming Henry, as I called him—directed the segment I was in. I once asked Henry why he always screamed at everyone. His answer was that he didn't know how to direct actors; he couldn't talk to them in acting terms, so he just tried for tension on the set in hopes that some of that electricity would show on the screen. Whatever works.

It hardly mattered in *How the West Was Won*. It was a picture of gargantuan scope, as much about spectacular vistas, stampeding buffalos, and warring Indians as it was about the people making the trek across the country. I was the head of one of those families, married to Agnes Moorehead and the father of two daughters, Carroll Baker and Debbie Reynolds. There was no getting around it; that was me, always the father. It amused me that during the course of our segment, Carroll Baker's character fell in love with Jimmy Stewart's character since Jimmy was a good five years older than I. Jimmy and I used to kid each other about it.

Once I said, "Hey, Jimmy, how about trading hairpieces so I can be the hero and you can be the father?"

He said, "You give me the five hundred bucks I spent on this rug and you got a deal."

We shot my segment for three weeks in Paducah, Kentucky. It was rough physically; we had to get up at five in the morning for makeup, including, in my case, a big full beard, and drive to a location two hours away. Then we shot in the midsummer heat in our heavy wardrobe. We'd been there a week or so when

Carroll Baker woke up one morning violently ill. They called in a local doctor who diagnosed her as having appendicitis. Her husband refused to let them operate and demanded the company fly in Carroll's personal physician. When that doctor arrived he disagreed with the diagnosis, claiming she just had the flu. Sure enough, within a few days she was good as new and back to work.

In the meantime Jimmy Stewart and I had chatted with Carroll's "big city" doctor about how hard it can be to find good medical care on location. He did some research and found the name of a good local doctor in case anyone should get sick again.

A couple of days later I woke up in the middle of the night with severe abdominal pain. I managed—barely—to crawl to the bathroom where I spent the rest of that interminable night rolled into a fetal position on the tile floor, just waiting for morning. I'm not sure I had ever been in so much pain.

I called in sick and Henry Hathaway said, "You just have the flu."

"No," I insisted, "I've had the flu. This is no flu."

Henry called the same doctor he had first called for Carroll. This time the poor guy was terrified to look at me, let alone examine me. He called in a nurse to take my blood for testing, but then he was afraid to read the results. By now I was writhing in pain. I demanded they take me to the hospital and somehow when I got there, I remembered the name of the local doctor that Carroll's doctor had recommended.

"Get me Dr. Fowler."

Fowler checked me out and said I needed to get into the operating room at once or else my appendix was going to burst.

Meanwhile, Screaming Henry is shouting, "Don't operate! That's what they said about Carroll. It's just the flu!"

Luckily, they got me into the operating room and got my appendix out just in time. It had, in fact, already burst and apparently a little stone just happened to have lodged in the hole preventing more widespread peritonitis. I spent the next few days in Intensive Care receiving wonderful medical attention and an earful of promises from Henry that when I returned to the set they'd take good care of me. He promised I'd have a cot right there at the ready at all times. He was saying any and everything to get me back to work, but Dr. Fowler told me it was up to me; I should be the one who called the shots about when I went back.

He said, "When you feel like you're ready to have a good steak, let me know." That took about eight days. On the ninth day, I notified the production brass that I was ready to go to back to work.

My first day back it was a hundred degrees in the shade. I was dressed in ten pounds of clothes, and we were shooting the scene where my family is preparing to head down the river. It was supposed to be the night before our departure and I had to sing, loudly and enthusiastically, urging everyone at the campsite to join in. It was a long day's work and there was no cot and no time to use it had there been one. I had had just enough time to phone Mona before I went into surgery—literally as they were wheeling me in—and she had flown out immediately. When she saw the working conditions, she nearly burst into tears. I tried to assure her I was fine, trying to convince myself as well.

We shot that scene for three days, then flew home. Mona breathed a little easier, thinking the shoot at the studio would calm down.

Hardly. Our first day back we went right into the giant tank at MGM. We were on a raft on hydraulics so that it could buck and lurch with the waves. Above it all were two five-hundred-gallon release tanks, one on each side. The plan was to really get the waves pitching, then drop the water. We had to find something, some part of the raft, to brace ourselves against and something else to hold onto in order not to tumble into the water. We may have been in a tank, but we really were shooting the rapids. Of course, my whole midsection was still all taped up, but I held on and rode it out, praying my stitches wouldn't pop. At least the sequence looked great, and the flu never seemed so bad ever again.

Doing *Birdman of Alcatraz* after *How the West Was Won* sounded pretty good. The warden's office, a jail hallway, a prison cell. Nice and tame; I could handle that. The warden was an interesting character with a subtle conflict. He respected what the Birdman was doing, but was bound by his duties as warden to show him no special privileges.

Birdman was all Burt Lancaster. He produced it, helped direct it, and wrote a lot of it, as well as played the lead. The picture was a great vehicle for Burt and he did a wonderful job with the part, but I felt that he didn't help the film in any other way.

He would stay up all night with the writer working on the scene for the next day, then hand the rest of the actors the new pages in the morning. Twice I was embarrassed in front of the crew by not knowing my lines, an especially humiliating situation since Burt knew not only his own, but mine as well, having written them all the night before. The third time this happened I took the pages Burt handed me and said, "Let's go into my trailer until I learn this." He balked, but I had decided I just wouldn't work until I felt as comfortable with the new version as I had with the old. It took me about an hour and then we shot the scene, and Burt never did that to me again.

My contract on *Birdman* called for billing with Burt above the title (in other words, before the title of the film came on screen). But when the picture came out, there was Burt's name alone before the title. I confronted him about it and he assured me there had been a mistake. However, it was too late to do anything about it. I realize that billing doesn't seem like a very important issue, but I had worked long and hard to achieve "name above the title" status because, to me, that had always signified a certain degree of success. I guess it was a symbol from my early New York days. When I first arrived in New York, an actor's name above the title on a Broadway marquee meant more than that he was a star. His name meant an automatic stamp of approval; to a great deal of the theater-going public, it meant this play was going to be worth the price of a ticket. This "mistake" on *Birdman* ate at me more than if I hadn't been paid.

William Morris stepped in and tried to settle our dispute. After some haggling they agreed that the production company would pay for me to have a P.R. man for two years, something I had never had any interest in. I would rather have had the billing, but I gave in. I'm afraid the P.R. firm had their work cut out for them since my life didn't lend itself to publicity very well. I was the worst kind of client—I didn't do anything worthy of keeping my name in front of the public and I didn't do anything necessary to keep away from the public. (Of course, this was in the days when people cared about keeping certain kinds of information private instead of actually using it as fodder for great publicity.) Basically, I was home with my family; I wasn't out making the Hollywood party rounds every night.

I've never figured out how people keep that up when they're working in the movies. In fact, that was one of the strong points of working in films instead of plays. As I went from film to film, I realized that the lifestyle of a movie actor really did suit my particular body clock better than the theater. (During the run of *Streetcar*, I was always so eager to get to bed after the show that I would take off my coat on the ride up in the elevator, start to unbutton my shirt as I walked down the hall, and be half-undressed by the time I stepped into the apartment. One night, Mona threw me a surprise birthday party, but the guests got the surprise when the guest of honor arrived half-dressed.)

Late nights were tough, but early calls were never a problem for me. To this day, most mornings I have to force myself to stay in bed until the sun comes up. And if I was stimulated, I could keep going all day, even though I have trouble making it past eight-thirty in the evening when I'm not working.

On *Gypsy* we had long days and a very long shoot, but it was a joy from start to finish. We shot entirely in the studio, no locations, and I was working with two of the most professional women in the business—Rosalind Russell and, now several years after *Bombers B-52* and all grown up, Natalie Wood. Though they were of two different generations, they were two of the most dedicated actresses I have ever worked with.

Gypsy was one of the very few films I really sought out a part in. One of the biggest mistakes I made in my career was never knocking on the doors of producers and directors just to get to know them, to say I'd love to work with them some day. Since I wasn't on the party circuit where a lot of business gets done, I should have made it a point to make myself known to the people I genuinely wanted to work with, but I never did. However, when I heard that Warners was turning the Broadway musical *Gypsy* into a movie, I dropped in on good ol' Abe Lastfogel again. I told him I just knew that I could play the part of Herbie and that I had always wanted a chance to sing and dance. A few days later Abe called to tell me I had an appointment with the director, old-timer Mervyn LeRoy.

Mervyn opened the meeting. "Abe tells me you want to be in this picture. Can you sing?"

"I've done some singing." (I didn't tell him it had mostly been in the Karageorge Choir.)

We talked a little more, then Mervyn said, "The part's yours." Everything in this business should be so simple.

Roz Russell had already begun working on the part of Mama Rose. Within a few weeks she called to invite me to her home in Beverly Hills to rehearse the musical numbers. I spent a few afternoons there with Roz and a piano player, practicing. There was no such thing as too much preparation as far as Roz was concerned. I remember a conversation I had with her when she said that she believed part of the actor's responsibility was to keep the director stimulated. "He has to be there every day, every shot," she said, "and if he's not feeling up to par one day, it's the actor's job to help him, to stimulate him and make him want to work." You just don't get more professional than that.

Nothing phased Roz Russell. At the end of one of her big numbers, "Some People"—a long song with a lot of business— she was supposed to put on her hat, pick up her old-fashioned hat pin, practically a foot long, stick the pin through the hat and storm out of the house. She did it once, twice; then on the third take she put on the hat, picked up that enormous hat pin, and stabbed herself right in the skull with it. But she didn't miss a beat; she yanked that thing out of her head, maneuvered it back through the hat, and marched out of the house, singing the whole while. When the take was over and she removed her hat, blood was dripping down her head from a deep gash. No matter; she was the embodiment of the-show-must-go-on attitude.

I wasn't used to playing the love interest and initially I was a little concerned about that aspect of the part. However, after I rehearsed together with Roz a few times and I discovered how much I admired her iron work ethic, I grabbed onto that professional admiration to help Herbie fall in love with Rose.

All that rehearsing with Roz helped me to relax enough so that I thoroughly enjoyed the musical numbers when the time came. Of course, I had been rehearsing the numbers with a second-string Rose and Louise at home. As soon as the routines were choreographed, I taught them to Mila and Carla. Every night after dinner, the girls filled in for Roz and Natalie and we'd run through "Together Wherever We Go." I must admit, the three of us got to be pretty good.

It seemed like Mervyn LeRoy—a lovely, gentle man—spent as much time on the phone as behind the camera. When he left the phone, we would rehearse the scene until everyone was comfortable, then he would take his seat in his director's chair and say inevitably, "Now give me a nice, warm scene." That was the extent of his direction. Toward the end of the shoot, I couldn't resist kidding him. When he would finally get off the phone, I'd call him over and say, "Mervyn, we're ready to give you your nice, warm scene now." Despite Mervyn's limited direction, he did create a nice, warm set and shooting *Gypsy* turned out to be so much pure fun I was sorry when Mervyn uttered his only other bit of direction, "That's a wrap!"

Another wonderful, if very different sort of company was assembled for a film called *All Fall Down*. Unlike a lot of the films I took during the sixties, I accepted *All Fall Down* for all the right reasons—a great part in a great script by William Inge; a great director, John Frankenheimer; and a great cast, notably Angela Lansbury, Warren Beatty, Eva Marie Saint, and young Brandon de Wilde. All these elements came together to make a wonderful little movie that told the story of what would today be termed a "dysfunctional" family; a family plagued by alcoholism, sibling worship and sibling rivalry, misplaced lust, dark secrets.

This was a case, however, of studio politics squelching a film. Between the time MGM first committed to the project and the time the film was released, there had been a shake-up in the upper echelon of the studio management. I don't know if it was just studio politics that forced them to decide not to give the picture a break, or if the powers that be were really afraid of this look at the underbelly of a seemingly typical American family, but the film was released with very little publicity and closed soon after.

I must admit that the main reason I wanted to be in a picture called *Come Fly With Me* had nothing to do with the script (a fluffy romantic comedy about three stewardesses and the men in their lives); or the director (Henry Levin, a decent craftsman who was absolutely lost with actors); or even the cast. It was the location. Europe. I had never been. The shoot coincided with my daughters' summer vacation so we could make it a family holiday. What could be better?

Mona and I decided to do it up right. We packed an old-fashioned steamer trunk and sailed on the Queen Mary from New York to London, an adventure that set the tone for a magnificent first trip to Europe. I shot in London, Paris, and Vienna while Mona and the girls spent their days sightseeing. To round out the perfect picture, whenever Mona and I wanted to go out for dinner or see a play in the evening, we had a built-in babysitter, one of the young actresses in the movie named Dolores Hart.

Dolores was a beautiful actress, then in her midtwenties, who was playing one of the stewardesses. She adored spending time with my daughters and quickly became like a member of our family. She was happy to babysit with them and took particular delight in scaring them half to death with ghost stories, which she would read to them by candlelight in her darkened London flat.

When the picture was over and we all returned to L.A., Dolores remained close to my family, especially to the girls. She continued to babysit on occasion and often would pick Mila up from school on half-day Fridays to take her out to lunch and to go shopping. The girls were so excited when Dolores became engaged and asked them to be her bridesmaids. Dolores had a luminous quality about her that cast a magic over everything she did; the idea of being in her wedding was like a fairytale come true.

Mila and Carla had already had a couple of fittings on their dresses when Dolores appeared at our door one day with the news that she was calling off the wedding. A few days later she came over with what amounted to all her worldly possessions—jewelry, purses, knick-knacks—and told the girls to take whatever they wanted. She said she was moving away and that, I will never forget her exact words, it was "an affair of the heart."

We all assumed this meant she was leaving her fiancé for someone else. She was an exquisite young woman and for most young men, to meet her was to fall in love with her. However, a few months later we received a letter from her informing us that she had joined a convent in New England. And there she has stayed these thirty years. It is a particularly rigorous order, a working farm, I believe, and she now presides over it as Mother Dolores.

We still correspond on occasion. When I became president of the Motion Picture Academy I sent her an Academy sweatshirt. She sent me back a snapshot of her wearing the Oscar sweatshirt over her habit; I keep the picture pinned to my bulletin board to this day. Dolores had had a difficult childhood and I think she was looking for some kind of connection to people; she was hungry for a family and we were all so pleased that she chose ours even if it ended up being for such a short time.

❦

I was always gratified when a director called me back to work for him again. When Henry Levin asked me to do *Murderer's Row,* it sounded like fun. It was the next of the silly Matt Helm series (part of the sixties' spy craze) starring Dean Martin as the supercool secret agent surrounded by a bevy of beautiful girls in bikinis. This particular Matt Helm outing, *Murderer's Row,* featured a dozen gorgeous girls, one for each month of the year.

I thought it would be a kick to work with Dean and it was. His whole style was built around making fun of himself and the situation with that easygoing charm of his. He knew what he could do and he did it well. And he always did it the first time. Dean was definitely a one-take actor. One day after we had done a scene together he asked me, "Do you like doing just one take?"

I said, "It doesn't bother me. Two, three, that's okay, too. I don't care."

Dean jumped in, "Don't say that to anyone."

He wanted to keep it his way—one take and print it.

When I read the script for *Murderer's Row* I thought I had a brilliant idea of how to approach this character, an idea that was in keeping with the tongue-in-cheek attitude of the picture. This guy was supposed to be an international con man, so I thought wouldn't it be great if he had an international mish-mash of an accent—a little Swedish, a bit of Russian, a tad of French, a touch of Irish, a Scottish clip? I thought I'd just inter-mingle all these dialects, and that's exactly what I did. All through the shoot, no one said anything—not Henry Levin, the director; not Dean; no one. I thought it was going along great. But when I finally saw the picture I realized my stroke of bril-liance was the worst damn idea I ever had in my life. A little of this and a little of that had made one big mess. Instead of com-ing across like an international con man, I had made an inter-national ass of myself.

Whereas Henry Levin had been something of a nondirector, John Ford knew what he wanted. And if you gave him a fight on the way to getting it, he was all the happier. I worked with the legendary, cantankerous Ford on a picture called *Cheyenne Autumn*, and I remember the morning we were set to shoot my two big scenes. I was playing a German cavalry officer whose troops had rebelled against him and kept him prisoner locked in his cabin. Both these scenes took place in the cabin, and Ford came to me that morning and asked if I had any ideas. I suggested that maybe I should be sitting on the edge of the cot when the soldiers entered.

Ford said, "How about standing in front of the fireplace with your hands outstretched on the mantle, feet spread so we can see the fire, and we'll shoot you from the back."

Fine, great, sounded good. It took us all morning to shoot the scene, then we broke for lunch. When we reconvened it was time to shoot the second scene in the cabin. Again, Ford asked me, "How do you think we ought to do this scene?"

"Well, maybe this time I should be on the cot waiting for the soldiers," I suggested.

He came back, "How about at the fireplace, hands outstretched along the mantle, feet spread so we can see the fire, and we'll shoot you from the back."

My brilliant comeback: "That's what we did this morning." As if he didn't know. He was looking for an argument; he just loved to bait his actors.

He looked at me with that patch over his one eye and said, "Does it matter?"

I could tell from the way he said it that there was only one answer. "No, sir, not at all."

So we shot the scene. Hands outstretched on the mantle, feet spread so you could see the fire, from the back. He was right; it wasn't too bad. Ford knew Westerns and the composition of individual pictures, visual images that bespoke the West. Part of his particular gift was that he knew Western lore and was able to put it on the screen. I heard that when he signed on to do a film he would stay in bed for days looking through his vast collection of books on the West, studying pictures and marking ones that he could use, basically recreating real historical tableaus on film.

As gruff as he was, Ford enjoyed the highly civilized daily routine of afternoon tea. I observed this tea-time ritual every afternoon for several weeks before, one day, he said to me in his typical bite-your-head-off manner, "What's the matter? Don't you like tea?"

I said, "Yes, I like tea."

"Well, how come you don't have tea with us?"

"I thought it was a private party."

"It is," he told me, "but I'll invite you if that's what you want." So that's how I became a member of the tea break.

That was John Ford's M.O. even in social situations. Put the onus on you, make you feel like he was doing you a favor. But he was the boss and his crustiness was part of his charm. I never felt that I was really a John Ford actor—an actor who didn't need words—but I was glad to have a John Ford film under my belt.

Throughout my career I had also hoped to count a Spencer Tracy film among my own. I was more than looking forward to working with Tracy when I was hired to be in *The Cincinnati Kid*. I was ecstatic. As fate would have it, Tracy had to drop out of the picture due to ill health and I ended up working with another legend, Edward G. Robinson.

Preparing for the part of Shooter, the card dealer, in *The Cincinnati Kid* was a real treat for me. I had always been a magic fan, a would-be magician, so I couldn't wait to get my hands on a deck of cards and learn how a professional dealer would handle them. I hooked up with a professional card man, Jay Ose, a one-time con man who was one of the most talented close-up magicians I have ever seen. He taught me everything I needed to know—dealing seconds, dealing from the bottom, all the tricks. I couldn't wait to take my seat around that table on the set and start dealing.

All around that table sat a really solid, first-rate cast, actors who were really sure of themselves—Eddie G., Joan Blondell, Ann-Margret. Everyone around that poker table could steal the scene at any moment. We all knew it and that brought a wonderful electricity to the set. Except for the star of the film, Steve McQueen; for him, that knowledge brought only anxiety.

I had always heard stories about some of the old-time stars refusing to let another actor touch them—to break the aura around them—but I had never encountered that personally until working with Steve. During one scene, I happened to put my hand on his shoulder. He stopped cold and said, "Don't ever touch me."

I must have smiled because he snapped, "Do you have a problem with that?"

I said, "No, but where did you ever pick that up?"

"I just don't like it."

So that was that. We did the scene again and this time I didn't lay a finger on him.

Maybe he didn't want any other actor touching him or maybe it was just me, I don't know. But I did find out that he had something against me when I worked with him a second time in

Nevada Smith. Our director, Henry Hathaway, invited me to dinner one night specifically to ask me exactly what I had done to Steve McQueen. I told him I hadn't done a thing. Henry informed me that Steve had tried his damnedest to veto my being in the picture. It gnawed at me through the whole shoot; what had I ever done to Steve McQueen? I couldn't imagine until one of the guys at William Morris clued me in. Years before when I had been casting *Tea and Sympathy* for Kazan in New York, I guess I had seen Steve for the lead, though I had no memory of him. He didn't get the part and, apparently, he held it against me all that time. I still say he wasn't right for the part.

I wish he had just told me up front when we started working on *The Cincinnati Kid* so that maybe we could have laughed about it and put it behind us. Though Steve was not one to laugh much. He was always a bit of the outsider. I don't know why, but he didn't come along when Eddie G., Ann-Margret, and I went back to New Orleans for the grand opening of the picture.

It was one of those great big, old-fashioned premiers, but New Orleans style. Parade cars, a Dixieland band, huge crowds—the kind of thing I remembered seeing in newsreels as a kid. We were there for three days, and I remember that one night Eddie asked me to go with him to a special place he had heard of for dinner.

We drove about an hour out of town before we turned up a long driveway surrounded by lush greenery that led up to what looked like a grand old colonial estate, columns and all. When we stepped inside, all the restaurant personnel (black men wearing tuxedoes) snapped to attention around Eddie. They led us to the tremendous dining room and sat us—just the two of us—at a table for ten.

Eddie said, "Let me order." And I spent the next few hours eating one of the best meals I have ever eaten in my life. Oysters, shrimp, real Southern fried chicken, the works.

At the end of the meal when Eddie asked for the check, the chef, a very young man, emerged from the kitchen. He wouldn't hear of Eddie paying. Eddie insisted but the young chef simply refused to let Eddie pay.

"My father would kill me if you paid for this meal, Mr. Robinson. You of all people."

Eddie asked, "Who's your father?"

The young man answered; it was an Italian name, and he said he was from Chicago.

Eddie sent his regards to the chef's father, we thanked him profusely, and said good-bye. On the way back in the car I asked Eddie what that was all about.

"It happens all the time," he said. "They think I'm one of the boys. I know who the father is. He set the kid up in the restaurant business."

I got the picture. I had just eaten a four-star New Orleans meal courtesy of the Chicago mob . . . and of course, courtesy of the fact that everyone, including the mob, loved Eddie G. Robinson.

I remained dear friends with magician Jay Ose after *The Cincinnati Kid* and called on him a few years later when I was making a movie called *Hotel*. When I was offered this picture, they wanted me to play the part of the man who is interested in buying the hotel, the part Kevin McCarthy ended up playing; but after reading the script I had my heart set on Keycase, the hotel thief. The producers thought I was crazy; that part had virtually no lines. But that was precisely what appealed to me; how to make something with no dialogue come to life.

Once I talked them into giving me that part I asked Jay Ose to set me up with some of his cronies who had firsthand knowledge of how a hotel thief would operate. We met at the Magic Castle in Hollywood and over a cup of coffee, they explained to me that the script was all wrong. The script called for Keycase to do a series of jobs during his stay at the hotel, breaking into one room a night. These ex-thieves filled me in; that's not how it's done. Instead, they explained, you move into the hotel, case the place to see which rooms are the most promising, devise a plan, hit all the rooms in one night and get out. That made sense. I brought it up with our director, Richard Quine, and he agreed.

The fun of the character was in showing Keycase enjoying what he did for a living, which, at the same time, made him a nervous wreck. (Not unlike being an actor. Every job was opening night for this poor guy.) I decided his preparation for the big night should be like a ritual. The script called for him to put on rubber gloves, obviously so that he wouldn't leave fingerprints. But I wanted to go all out with the gloves, like a surgeon preparing for an operation—shaking talcum onto my hands first, putting them on finger by finger just so. This was a man who took pride in his work. He was a class act.

The film ended up something of a "B" movie, a precursor to all those sweeping television series featuring multiple story lines and lavish sets. In fact, the studio was renting out our enormous set, portion by portion, to various TV series to use at night after we had wrapped our day's shooting, not really a vote of confidence in the picture from the studio management. Regardless of the film's lukewarm reception, Keycase remains one of my favorite roles.

I fell in love with two other roles around this time, oddly enough both clowns of some sort. One was in a novel called *The Flight of the Dancing Bear* and the other was in a script I read called *The Day the Clown Cried*. *Dancing Bear* revolved around the relationship between a Russian circus performer, a bear trainer, and his bear. Their act amounted to a role reversal between the animal and the human, and the story featured one of the most charming setups I had ever read.

The American Embassy in Russia requests some local entertainment for a gala, so the Commissar sends a dance troupe, some singers, and the nationally famous act of the Dancing Bear and his trainer. When it comes time for the bear to perform, everything in the Embassy is sparkling and glistening, but the dazzling crystal chandeliers and shiny satin fabrics disorient the bear. He gets a little punchy and before you know it, the poor bear is knocking over tables and upsetting everything in the room. The trainer thinks he will be sent to Siberia and that the bear might be put to death, so he takes his beloved dancing bear and flees. What he doesn't know is that the audience found their act all the more hilarious because of the upset and that the bear was the big hit of the evening. The rest of the story consists of the "couple's" picaresque adventures as they escape across the Russian countryside together.

The Day the Clown Cried was a heartbreaking piece about a German clown in World War II. When we meet him he is a cocky, obnoxious braggart. One night he is drunkenly mouthing off about the Nazis and he lands himself in a concentration camp as a political prisoner. Since he is a political prisoner and not a Jew, he thinks he is superior to everyone there. One day, quite by chance, he happens to make some children in the camp laugh when he accidentally falls in the mud. Because he is still a clown, a performer, and can't resist the sound of their laughter, he begins to do a little routine for them, there in the mud, until more and more children have gathered round, all laughing and forgetting their surroundings for a few brief moments. He develops a relationship with the children in the camp, which causes him to evolve from a self-centered loudmouth to a man willing to make the ultimate sacrifice. At the end of the picture, he volunteers to lead the children—who have grown to love and trust him—into the gas chamber, because he knows they will go unafraid if he takes them. It was a redemption story of such power that you could not help but weep over it.

These were both parts that I ached to play and I shopped both projects around town with increasing frustration for a good year apiece, only to learn that I am not a salesman. There is a talent to being able to sell something and I clearly didn't have it. No matter how much passion I had for these two stories, I couldn't get the projects off the ground. Maybe I wasn't willing to stick with them long enough—three, four, five years. Sometimes I think I should have tried harder because both stories have haunted me ever since. Selfishly, I guess I felt each, in its own way, could have been the part of a lifetime.

When I met Frank McCarthy, the producer of *Patton*, I really realized the importance of stick-to-itiveness as a quality in a producer. A former aide to General George Marshal during World War II, Frank himself was a one-star general and being a general is not very different from being a producer. After the war, Frank had become a producer at Twentieth Century Fox, and the Patton story had been his pet project for some thirteen years before he was able to interest the studio. To his credit, he had not given up because he believed in the project.

When I was hired to play General Omar Bradley, it was similar to my *Waterfront* days; here I was playing a person who was still very much alive, someone I had to be accountable to—only this time, instead of a turned-around collar, he wore four stars on his shoulder. The prospect was a little daunting, if exciting. I instituted my usual policy—clear the social calendar entirely and hole up in my little room above the garage, just me and my new constant companion. In this case, the character of General Bradley.

The General graciously agreed to sit down with me for a few hours every day for five days and go over the script page by page to discuss his character as written. The first day I arrived at his home in the Trousdale Estates I said, "General, I don't care to know about the man in the uniform. People will know about that the minute they see the wardrobe. I want to know about the man from Missouri." And that is who I got to know.

He explained to me that when he graduated from high school there was nothing for him to do but what every other boy did in his town—get a job laying railroad ties. He had been a good student and his teachers kept on him, admonishing him that he would be wasting his life if he took that job. However, he couldn't afford to go to college so they suggested he apply to a military college. When he was accepted at both army and navy, he chose West Point. Instantly, I had found something in him I could relate to; we had both had poor upbringings and West Point was his way out, his Goodman Theater.

After a few days, I said to him, "Somewhere in the film I'd like to pick up a piece of straw or a twig or something and start to chew on it." I hoped to suggest the man from Missouri underneath the uniform, the man who was so clearly the "real" Omar Bradley. He laughed and said, "Guys always used to raise Cain with me 'cause I chewed the tip of my pencil. If you want to chew a twig, fine."

We continued to move through the script together until we came to a point where I already had an approach in mind. It involved a confrontation with Patton. I said, "General, you have always been cool, quiet, calm, up to here. I thought this would be one moment where I'd really let go."

"Hm-hmm," he said. He had a sort of high voice. "I understand."

We continued on until about ten or fifteen pages later, he stopped me. "Karl?"

"Yes?"

"You know that place where you wanted to let go?"

"Yes?"

"Is it really necessary?" Bradley asked.

"Well, what would you do?" I asked him.

"I'll tell you. I'd just look him in the eye and quietly, with all the intensity I could muster, tell him exactly what I wanted him to do. And he'd do it."

"Why?" I wondered. "Why would he do it?"

Bradley smiled a little. "Because I've got one more star on my shoulder than he has."

That clinched it. I played the whole part without ever really blowing my top at Patton.

I knew that the character would take on even greater definition when I started working with George C. Scott. (I had worked with George once before in *Hanging Tree*, which was his first picture.) In terms of the film, the character of Bradley stands in relief against Patton. We shot for six months in Spain—Madrid, Pamploma, Almeria, Segovia—and George C. Scott was at the center of every scene. George turned in what I believe was (to this point) the definitive performance of his career, but the demands of the part took their toll on him.

He has made no secret of the fact that he was drinking heavily at the time, but it was always after-hours.

No matter what personal demons George Scott was battling, he showed up and delivered every day of that shoot. Bradley, a man given to mild-mannered understatement, had told me that Patton was a "difficult" man, but that we were lucky he was on our side. When we finished the shoot, I phoned Bradley to tell him I thought it had gone very well and that I hoped he would be pleased. He asked about George Scott as Patton and I told him if there was ever a Third World War, I wanted to fight under George C. Scott. Bradley understood exactly what I meant.

During this entire ten-year period from *Pollyanna* to *Patton*, the year I worked the most I think I filmed four pictures. I began to realize that a good year usually meant two or three pictures and that meant maybe thirty weeks of work. That left far too much downtime for my liking. There is only so much gardening you can do and so many books you can read before you begin to feel like a lump. One afternoon I was waiting for the girls to get home from school when the phone rang. The head of the drama department at Emporia State Teacher's College (where Mona had gone as part of a special program when she was in high school) wondered if I would be interested in lecturing. I told him that I didn't particularly believe in lecturing about acting. To act is to do.

He came right back, "Then come and stay for a while and work with a group."

I took him up on the invitation. Maybe it was because I had never gone to college, but the idea thrilled me. After my visit to Emporia, I couldn't wait to get back to another campus. It took me about six months to devise what I thought would be a really solid program that revolved around the kids' critiquing one another's scene work. I would run a workshop that was all about trying something—anything—getting up there and making a fool of yourself if you had to. Invariably, a few professors would ask if they could observe, "audit" my seminar. My standard response was, "You're welcome to participate, but that means you have to get up there just like the rest of us." Boom—they'd be out the back door in a flash.

After going to a few more schools (New Mexico and Denver), I began to realize that the same scenes kept cropping up in the students' work. Scenes from classics like *Glass Menagerie, Death of a Salesman, Our Town*. No wonder; these plays were gifts to actors.

Since these were all plays from my era in New York, shows that I knew some little interesting tidbit of back story about, I decided to experiment with taking some of these scenes, six of them to be exact, and writing a show around them. From then on, I offered colleges two choices: a regular workshop or a workshop that would culminate in a few performances that would be open to the entire school and surrounding community. Most of them chose the show. Besides raising money for the drama departments, producing the show involved more members of the department because we would need a full crew.

I called the show *The Divine Hypocrites,* taken from the Greek term for actors. Actors were the "hypocrites" of Greek civilization because they played with false faces using false devices in false situations; "divine" because they used all this deception to reveal the truth.

While we grappled with the concept of dramatic truth in the workshop, my experience at colleges forced me to confront a truth about myself. By placing myself in a situation where success depended entirely upon my ability to communicate with people, my students, I had to work through my old fears and insecurities. As my students worked toward uncovering the divine universal truths dwelling in their scenes, I struggled to work through a truth dwelling within me. As I stood before these various groups of kids and worked with them day after day, I had to learn, by necessity, to become more comfortable with being myself and not always another character when I was in front of a group of people.

That turned out to be a lucky thing. I believe that television requires that an actor let more of himself show through than any other medium. As I visited colleges throughout those years, I had no idea that I was going to have to rely on being able to relax a little and be myself a whole lot more than usual when I hit the streets of San Francisco a few years later.

facing page:

**My old buddy from summer stock drops in
on the San Francisco station house.**

Chapter 12

Sometime in the early sixties, Abe Lastfogel, still the godfather of the William Morris Agency, called me into his office for a powwow. He told me that Danny Thomas was producing a television series about a cop on the beat and that the part was mine if I wanted it. I tossed and turned that night, weighing the offer. Once again, the lure of a regular job was pretty strong. But, finally, I went back to Abe and told him I didn't think I wanted to do a series right then.

With great confidence he said to me, "It'll make you rich."

"Don't make me rich. Make me happy."

"What will make you happy?" he asked.

"Some good parts in films," I told him.

And I got some good parts for the next ten years, roughly from *Pollyanna* to *Patton*. Every so often during that period of time, Mike Zimring and I would discuss whether or not the time was right for me to do television. I felt that I had started at the bottom in the theater and worked my way up for twenty years, then started at the bottom with bit parts in films and worked my way up for another twenty years. I didn't feel like starting at the bottom again. To me that meant refusing to make a pilot, the sample show that is used to sell a series. I was finally comfortable in my career and I couldn't stomach having to get out there and sell myself again after all these years. Mike understood. In fact, there were a couple of times when the money was so tempting that I began to waver in my decision, but Mike talked me out of it. Not many agents would do that, but Mike was always looking out for me far more than for his ten percent.

On two occasions a television producer named Quinn Martin inquired about whether or not I'd be interested in a series and, both times, Mike and I explained my position to him. When Quinn called a third time, he said, "Don't say anything until I finish. Just listen."

So I listened.

He explained that he was going to do a detective series for ABC. Twenty-six weeks guaranteed. No pilot.

I was really listening now.

Quinn asked me to read the book on which the series was to

be based. It was called *The Streets of San Francisco*. I read the book that night. It would make a typical Quinn Martin show. A murder in the first five minutes, a chase somewhere in the second half hour, and we solve it all by minute fifty-seven. I thought this was what I had tried to avoid. But a whole year's work sounded pretty good. It felt like the right time to take the plunge. Besides, I was sure it would only be one year, though in the back of my mind I was going through the same upheaval I had when I had made the transition from theater to film.

Shortly after I signed on to do the series, Quinn invited me to his office one day, saying, "I have a young man here I'd like you to meet. I think he'd be good for your partner."

I walked into the office and, the minute I laid eyes on this kid, I said, "Good enough for me."

Quinn looked at me, surprised.

"I'll tell you why. I see that cleft in his chin." I turned to the young man. "You're a Douglas, aren't you?"

He started to laugh. "Yes, I am. I'm Michael."

We made small talk and when we parted company that day I told him to send my love to his father, my old Tamarack Playhouse pal, that great ballroom dancer, Izzy Demsky.

The next time I saw Michael was just a few days before we started shooting the show. He said to me, "My dad said to listen to Karl. If anyone can teach you, he can." That was one of the great compliments of my life.

Michael and I were playing partners and, like real police force partners, we came to rely on each other very quickly. We watched each other's backs. Early in the first season, our director had set up a driving shot that called for us to head down California Street, make a left in front of the Fairmont Hotel, and head down one of those famous San Francisco hills. *Streets* was one of the first shows to be filmed on location and I had mentioned to Quinn Martin that I thought we should take advantage of that, that there should be three stars of the show— Michael and me and San Francisco. There was no argument from anyone. Our directors naturally wanted to feature the city's magnificence. For this particular shot, the camera was mounted on a huge crane to take the whole panorama in. Michael was behind the wheel. He happens to be a wonderful driver, but he wasn't familiar with the terrain yet. We made that turn in front of the Fairmont at fifty-five or sixty miles an hour and suddenly we were airborne. My eyes popped. I looked over at Michael; he wasn't smiling. He looked at me and I looked at him for what seemed like a good long time, long enough for me to say, "What the hell's going on here? This isn't supposed to be for real!" When we finally landed, half of the bottom of the car was torn out.

The stuntwork aside, that first year of *Streets* was brutal. Quinn Martin had made a deal with Warner Bros. to use its Burbank studios as a home base for the show. The plan was to piggyback two episodes one onto the other. We would shoot the first show's interiors on the Warner's lot, then travel to San Francisco to shoot the exteriors for that show and the second show, then back to L.A. for the second show's—along with the third show's—interiors, and so on. The plan made sense on paper; it sounded practical, sort of like episode leapfrog, but in reality it made for a messy, exhausting year for everyone involved in the show. All I remember of that year was running for red-eye flights. It felt like being in the middle of a whirlwind where all we cared about was getting one show in the can and going on to the next. I had no concentration, no focus. People ask me if I predicted Michael's enormous success, but honestly, I could barely observe him that year. The scripts were coming in late;

the crew suffered from battle fatigue; we actors were always confused. The work was shoddy, plain and simple.

By the end of that year I said, "Count me out if the network picks it up. I can't live like this." It had become more important that we make it to the airport—whether LAX or San Francisco—for the midnight flight than that we nail the scene properly. Not for me.

They came back with, "So you want to live in San Francisco full time?" I'm sure they expected me to say no, but I surprised them. I said that would be fine if it meant a calmer schedule. Quinn told me that San Francisco would still qualify as a location, which contractually would mean we would still be working six days a week, but I agreed with that. It was a location, albeit a permanent one. I didn't care about the long days and long weeks. I knew that staying in one place would work better for me and for the L.A.-based members of the crew who were also doing all that traveling.

However, we still had the problem of the time frame for the scripts. I knew I couldn't do decent work unless I got my script at least three days before that show began shooting, but I worried that the move, which would also put more distance between us and the writers, would mean even later scripts. I asked Quinn to start the writers on the new season while we were on hiatus, but that meant we needed an early pick-up from the network. I told him to use me as his big problem. "Tell them I won't come back unless we live in San Francisco full time and unless I get the scripts three days ahead."

Their response? Too expensive to move everyone up there. Quinn mediated. Would I be willing to cut the schedule to twenty-three instead of twenty-six shows per season? I agreed if "they," the network, would be willing to guarantee that they would notify us whether or not the show had been picked up for the following year at least two weeks before we went on hiatus at the end of every shooting season. They agreed, so we all packed our bags for San Francisco for eight months out of the year.

Now that everything was ironed out, the men in charge at William Morris started making noises about renegotiating my contract. I didn't understand what they meant. I had signed a five-year contract with standard raises built in every year. Just because the show was a hit, I couldn't justify asking for a better deal. They started in with the "That's the way it's done. Everybody does it." A great way to get me not to do something. Again, Mike Zimring became my ally against the men he worked with within the Morris office. Ultimately, I went back to work on the second season with my original contract. Who knows if I made the right choice but my word and my signature were worth more to me than the extra money. And I made a grateful friend of my producer, Quinn Martin, who was gracious enough to thank me countless times during the rest of our run.

By the end of the second year, all of us working on the show had developed a smooth-running routine. We found a rhythm that worked and stuck with it. And, by then, Michael and I were having fun with each other. My goal became to turn out a solid, reliably entertaining version of what this was—a good, old-fashioned cop show. I had no illusions about creating great art. In fact, I remember that early on Michael, like a lot of young actors, was inclined to take long pauses to make his points.

I took him aside and said, "Look, when you do shit, do it fast. We're doing shit. Don't take all that time. Let's try to be ahead of the audience." He caught on fast and we developed an energy, a momentum that, I hope, kept our audience involved. When we had to go to a door, we ran to the door. That kind of thing.

But we never ran with our guns drawn. At least I didn't, not

just for the sake of having them drawn anyway. This was an issue I felt very strongly about and one about which Michael and
I disagreed. Philosophically, Michael was equally anti-gun;
however, he thought we'd look like fools if we were running
around without our guns at the ready. I decided that I was going to pull my gun at the last possible second in any situation
regardless of whether that was totally realistic. So, in many
scenes I would walk into the office, take my gun out of the hol-
ster and put it away in a drawer. I didn't want the gun to seem
like an extension of the character, an appendage like it is on so
many cop shows. I never kidded myself; I knew that was the extent to which the show was socially redeemable. Beyond that, it
was Mike Stone and Steve Keller keeping the streets of San
Francisco safe, with the help of quite a roster of guest stars.

Our show played host to a remarkable variety of actors. The
opening two-hour episode featured two wonderful actors, Ed-
mond O'Brien and Eileen Heckart. Close to the end of our last
season, an episode revolved around the character of a body-
builder with an uncontrollable temper played by an unknown
named Arnold Schwarzenegger. In between, we showcased
some faces that were relatively unknown at the time, people like
Peter Strauss, Joe Don Baker, Sam Elliot, Tom Selleck, Don
Johnson, and Nick Nolte. But some of my favorite times were
when we had on the old-timers like Lew Ayres and, from my
early days in New York, Luther Adler, not to mention my dear
friend Sam Jaffe.

When Luther reported for work, he appeared on our set with
a big paper sack full of bright red tomatoes. "They're from my
farm," he said. "I held them on my lap all the way across the
country for you." I was delighted to have the tomatoes, but
mostly I was thrilled to host Luther himself, the star of *Golden
Boy*, the first play I did in New York. I felt like I had come full

circle, particularly since Sam Jaffe was a guest on the same episode—Sam who had taken me by the hand at one of my lowest moments and gotten me that part in *Uncle Harry*. I was so honored to have Sam on the show that I took the honey wagon and gave him my trailer for the week. Of course that was nothing compared to what he had done for me thirty years earlier.

I wonder if the young man who directed that episode remembers the third or fourth day of shooting as well as I do. The story dealt with these two old friends who were trying to get one of their grandsons out of trouble. In order to do so they had to trace the boy's footsteps to find a shoebox of cash he had stowed somewhere. They try to uncover it everywhere, finally deciding they might as well check down in a manhole. The two of them, Sam and Luther, were to get down on their knees, push the manhole cover to the side, and Sam was to reach way down inside and pull out the box. This was a show in itself. They had rehearsed this bit once when our young director asked Sam to stay down longer before emerging with the box. Sam put the box back, did the bit, bent down into the manhole for a little longer and came back up with the box.

"No, Sam. I wanted you to stay down longer. This time, count to eight."

"Fine," said Sam in his quiet, unflappable way.

And he did it again.

This time, the director told him, "I wanted you to count to eight, remember?"

Sam smiled at him. "I can count. I can count fast. I can count slow. I can count in Yiddish. I can count in Spanish. I can count in German. I can count anyway you like. How do you want me to count?" And, one by one, he demonstrated all the various ways he could count.

By this time Luther and I were like little kids whose buddy is needling the teacher. Luther was laughing like mad and I was trying to hold it together, but we couldn't even look at each other because we knew we'd really break into hysterics.

The poor director just looked at Sam and answered, "Just stay down a little longer."

Sam and Luther did the scene again—without any further direction. And they were perfect. Sam stayed down, came up, did everything just right. I think they managed the rest of the week without any further "direction." I almost felt sorry for this young guy who was trying to teach Sam Jaffe about timing. He didn't know what hit him when he came up against Sam and Luther with their hundred years of experience between them.

While some of our directors—both young and not so young— were really just directing traffic, several of them were enormously talented and brought a unique style to their episodes. For example, I vividly remember the episode directed by a young John Badham, which foreshadowed his successful film career. Of course, I remember it from the actor's point of view.

For me, the trick of doing a series became finding some little acting challenge in every episode, something fun to keep the weekly routine from becoming a grind. Once I realized that I was going to be doing twenty-plus of these shows a year for at least five years, I knew I'd go crazy if I didn't find a way to keep it stimulating. Doing a series could degenerate into the same old thing every week or I could use it like a lab to try out different things, things that probably no one else would notice, but would keep my juices flowing.

Badham's episode centered around my being shot and captured by a Chinatown gang. I spent the entire episode in the back room of a warehouse, wounded. I enjoyed coming up with a way to show that I was losing more and more blood and getting weaker and weaker as the show progressed without resorting to splattering widening circles of blood on my shirt. I started out sitting on a box, fairly upright. Every time they cut back to me I was more crumpled until I was finally completely off the box in a heap on the floor. No big deal, but little challenges like that kept the series fun.

I also remember rehearsing one particular scene in that episode. The young gang member guarding me was brandishing his gun, poking me with it, flailing around with it. You see this kind of thing on TV all the time, but it bothered me. I realized that he, the actor, was behaving a certain way because he knew what was going to happen. He knew I, Mike Stone, wasn't going to grab the gun from him; the script didn't call for me to do that. In a way, this goes back to my attitude toward guns on TV shows. This kid was being so casual with the gun that it ceased to be a deadly weapon. Suddenly, during one rehearsal, as he was gesturing near me with the gun, I grabbed it from him and turned it on him. He jumped.

I said, "That could happen, you know."

"But you're supposed to be so weak."

"I think if someone had a gun in my face I'd try to find the strength to take it away."

I guess I made my point. He played the scene differently from then on. Much better, I thought.

Sure, the audience knows that Mike Stone is going to live. But, in order for me to take my work seriously, I couldn't play it like Mike Stone knew he was going to live as well. That would be cheating—the audience and the character. And I knew we would only keep our audience from week to week if they weren't cheated. Whenever Mike was in a situation like that, I had to keep thinking, "I hope this crackpot doesn't pull the trigger," regardless of what the dialogue was. Mike was never supposed to be a superhero; superheroes don't interest me.

The series also became a forum for me to play different types of characters that I had always wanted to play. Our writers, John Wilder and Bill Yates, could always send Mike Stone undercover so, for example, when I told them I thought it would be fun to play a clown, our next murder was in the circus and Mike was slapping on the greasepaint (no rubber nose necessary). We hired a real circus as background and the clowns taught me some of their shtick. We also had my good friend, Michael Strong, on the show to play another clown, so that was a memorable show for me. (That was one of the perks of having a series. I got to invite my friends to guest star whenever I could.)

Before coming into people's homes on a weekly basis, I don't think it was possible to fully understand what an impact television has. When I was in the theater, I could walk down the street and no one knew me. Then I started to do films and, after a while, I would walk down the street and someone would stop me and say, "Excuse me, are you from St. Louis?" or "Do you work in the bank in Boise?" More times than not I'd say, "Yes, I do," and they would be satisfied and continue on. Then I started spending one hour on Thursday nights with people all across the country. Suddenly, people not only recognized me, they thought they knew me.

One morning I stepped out of the Huntington Hotel, my San Francisco home away from home, at seven A.M. to be picked up to go to work. Suddenly someone grabbed me, pointing, and shouted, "He went that way!"

I looked down the street to see a young man clutching a woman's purse that he had obviously pinched on the cable car clanking down the hill. I looked back at the man who had grabbed me. He was now studying me, waiting for me to give chase. Luckily for me, my car pulled up at that moment. I said,

"I'm sorry, I'll be late for work," and ducked inside the car, leaving the poor eyewitness wondering what had happened to the Mike Stone he relied on. Whatever had become of San Francisco's finest?

It has almost become a cliché for actors to talk about the double-edged sword of losing their anonymity. But, like most clichés, it is painfully true. By the fourth and fifth year of *Streets* I really felt myself losing access to one of an actor's most valuable tools: the ability to observe people being themselves as if you were a fly on the wall. As an actor, you try to build a great storehouse of observations, a reserve of detailed information about people—the way one person crossed the street, the way another twirled his spaghetti—to call upon when you're creating a character. By the last year of *Streets* those days were over.

Honestly, the last year of the series ground down to the point where I was just going through the motions. Michael Douglas left the show to produce the movie *One Flew Over the Cuckoo's Nest* and pursue what would become a truly brilliant career. I understood his decision completely; you had to respect his enormous ambition. He had the guts to make things happen and it was his time, but I missed him terribly. Our four years together were a total pleasure distinguished by mutual respect. Because his dad and I had started out together, I always felt that there was an almost familial connection between Michael and me as well. To be candid, I'm not sure I was sufficiently motivated to go through the whole process of getting acquainted with someone else's style all over again.

Michael's replacement, Richard Hatch, was a charming, good-looking young man, but I didn't really see him putting in the effort. After a few weeks I said to him, "You know, if you work hard and we rehearse together you can be a big star."

He said, "I am a star."

"Oh really?" I asked him. "How's that?"

He explained to me that he had been on a soap opera out of New York for a couple of years and had received more fan mail than anyone else on the show. I just nodded and walked away. But in the back of mind I thought, "I've got problems." I'm not proud of it, but I never really put myself out for him again. In my heart I felt that was the end of the show because even though it was a run-of-the-mill cop show, what people responded to was the relationship between Michael and me. We were lucky; our chemistry worked. It was clear to me there was going to be zero chemistry with Hatch.

By that point I couldn't reinvent a character who could better relate to "the new kid." I had begun to play myself more than I ever had in anything else. You have to out of self-defense on a weekly series. There just isn't enough time to answer all the questions an actor normally strives to answer when he's working on a part. "How would this character do this?" "Why would he do that?" When you're working on a TV series, you just do it. In that sense, the audience is getting to know the real you week after week.

The actual term for the audience's ability to recognize and relate to you is called an actor's "TV-Q." American Express was banking on my "TV-Q" when, after my first year on *Streets*, they contacted me about doing commercials for their travelers' checks. I had never done a commercial before and was dead set against it. Mike Zimring talked me into entertaining the offer when he pointed out that Sir Laurence Olivier was, at that time, advertising for Polaroid. His point was well-taken; I couldn't ignore company like that.

When I began to consider doing the commercial, I went to the bank and bought some travelers' checks just to see what it was like. It was easy enough, painless actually. I also remembered that once, when I was making a film called *Billion Dollar Brain* in London several years earlier, my hotel room had been burglarized. The thief had indeed taken every penny of cash but had not touched the travelers' checks. Maybe I was just talking myself into it, but this appeared to be a product and a service I could stand behind. What's more, the people at American Express agreed to my one stipulation—they would wait to shoot until my hiatus. (My one-track mind wouldn't even let me consider doing a commercial while the series was in progress.)

I broke down and shot my first commercial for American Express in one day. I admit it; I assumed this was going to be one of those take-the-money-and-run situations. It didn't turn out that way. Little did I know that for the rest of my life, everywhere I went people would say to me, "Did you leave home without them?" or that every time I pulled out a credit card in a restaurant to pay for a meal, I'd hear, "That better be American Express." I don't mind, though; it means I did my job. The travelers' check division began to show great rises in their sales and they kept me on . . . and on. Ironically, I had finally found the secure job I had always been looking for. I ended up right up there with Mrs. Olson, the Folgers coffee lady, for longevity. Twenty-one years later I was still saying, "Don't leave home without them."

It was 1976. I was working on *The Streets of San Francisco* when my father died. I found it deeply ironic that the project bringing my face into homes all over the world featured the city that had been my father's original destination when he stepped off the boat on Ellis Island those many years before. He had never traveled to San Francisco in all that time. He did not believe it was a place he was meant to be, though once he did say to me, "You see? You are Karl Malden to many people. But to me you are a Sekulovich. And a Sekulovich was meant to be in San Francisco. It was you." True enough.

It certainly was not Pa. When he lay dying, he was still in Gary, Indiana, the place where he had ended up quite by chance . . . or by design. "Sudbina"—fate.

I knew that my father's health was deteriorating. His illness had become too much for my mother to manage so my brothers and I decided the time had come to put him in a home. Across the country, in the Huntington Hotel, I woke up at two o'clock one morning with my heart pounding. "I'm going home."

I went to work that day and told my long-time stand-in—ex-baseball umpire, Art Passarella—that I had had a terrible dream. "I'm going home," I told him, "no matter what."

I called Quinn Martin and explained. He gave me a hard time—that was his job—but I had never taken a day off. I explained that I just needed one day, a Monday, since, luckily, I was already scheduled to have that Saturday off. When Quinn realized there was no arguing with me, he acquiesced.

Strange bits of memories of my father flashed through my mind as I flew to Chicago. I remembered the time I had invited him to Los Angeles for the fiftieth wedding anniversary of dear family friends, the Nikchevichs. He refused to come, repeatedly and adamantly.

"No. No. I can't come," he insisted.

"But Pa, you have to," I persuaded. "They went to Gary for your fiftieth. They're like family."

He kept finding excuses. "It costs too much."

"I'll send you the tickets. Ma wants to come."

He'd come back with another excuse. "It's too far. It takes so long."

"Only four hours, Pa. Not even that."

Finally, the truth came out. He said to me, "Mladen, I cannot hold my water for that long." He could not comprehend that there were bathrooms on the plane.

Finally, I persuaded him and sent the tickets. I arranged with the airlines to take special care of my folks, explaining that this was their first flight. Within a few days they were on the plane. Later, my mother told me how they sat there, waiting to take off. Pa looked out the window and turned to her, "Look at all that snow. We are fools to sit here. We will never take off. We are wasting our time. Planes cannot take off in all this snow."

Ma told him, "Just sit and be quiet."

He sat a little longer, and a little longer after that, and after a while he must have dozed off for a bit without realizing. When he woke up, he looked out the window again.

"See, I told you we could not take off in all this snow."

Ma explained to him, "Those are clouds."

He simply couldn't believe it. "We are going . . . ? Going . . . ?"

He had lived his entire adult life in the United States, but he was still that astonished young boy from Bileca.

I was waiting at the gate when my folks stepped off the plane. There was Pa in his traveling ensemble—hat, good suit, over-coat—clutching a bottle of champagne.

He thrust the bottle toward me proudly. "See this?"

"Sure, Pa. Where'd you get that?"

"You see other people, they got it?"

"No, Pa," I said. "Just you."

"They give me this because I am good passenger."

During his visit I took him to buy a new suit. I remember that it cost a hundred and fifty dollars, which was more than my father could have ever imagined spending on a simple suit of clothes. He stood even more erect and played the part of the visiting dignitary to the hilt when we came home and he modeled it for my mother and Mona.

"You see this suit?" he said, patting the material. "Mladen paid hundred and fifty dollars for this suit. When I die I want to be buried in this suit."

I remembered the visits I made to Gary when my daughters were small. Every single morning Pa would be waiting for his grandchildren with a tablespoonful of honey extended in their direction, admonishing them, "It's the healtiest ting." And they would have to swallow it down just as he did every day of his life.

I thought about how I had always tried to work the Sekulovich name into my films. There was a Sekulovich on the docks in *On the Waterfront*. A Sekulovich was in Omar Bradley's army in *Patton*. A Sekulovich worked in the station house in *Streets*. But the only time my dad ever commented on it was when a Sekulovich occupied one of the cells in *Birdman of Alcatraz*.

Pa said to me, "No Sekulovich was ever in jail."

I remembered a Gary friend telling me how he congratulated Pa after I won the Oscar. "Pete, what do you think? One of us won an Academy Award!"

My dad simply replied, in Serbian, "Mladen won an Academy Award, so it's one of us. If he had gone to jail, he would be Pete's son."

I arrived in Gary on Saturday. My brother, Milo, drove me to the convalescent home where my father was not convalescing; he was dying. The minute I walked in, that unmistakable smell took my breath away—disinfectant and overripe fruit. I could hardly breathe as Milo led me to Pa's room.

I paused in the doorway to try to take it all in. It was a room with four beds. It hadn't been all that long since I had seen him, but Pa looked so tiny lying in that bed that I barely recognized him.

Milo tried to coax him to sip some water, but Pa did not respond. No reaction.

I came in and leaned close to my father. I spoke, in Serbian, "Do you know who this is? I came from California. Tell me that you know who this is. Tell me that you know."

I had been wanting him to answer that question all my life. "Tell me you know who this is, Pa."

I must have been saying that for three or four minutes, begging for him to acknowledge that I was there. Finally, he lifted his head, his eyes still closed.

"You come home, eh?" He spoke in English. His particular English—with an accent so thick he sounded like he had just stepped off the boat. But still, he spoke to me in English.

I leaned in close to him and spoke again, this time half in Serbian, half in English. "Yes, I came home. Don't worry about a thing. I have everything under control. You just relax. You leave everything to me now."

I grabbed his ankle as I spoke to him. The bone nearly pierced my palm.

After about half an hour, Milo suggested we leave. We went to visit my mother and I told her about my conversation with Pa, how he had said, "You come home, eh?"

She looked at me and smiled. "He told me he was going to stay alive until you came home."

The next morning, Sunday, the call came. My father had died.

I had come home. I guess there was a part of my father that wished I had never left. I can only hope that there was also a part of him that was proud that I had.

Orthodox tradition demands that the deceased lie in state for two days before the funeral. I had promised the *Streets* company that I would be back no later than Tuesday afternoon no matter what. In retrospect, weighing Serbian tradition against one episode of a detective series doesn't seem like much of a dilemma. But at the time, in the torment of the moment and having made a solemn promise to my producers, I felt horribly torn.

I went to the priest and explained the situation. He gave me an argument, but finally, like Quinn Martin, acquiesced. My father lay in the funeral home for one day instead of two. I guess that compromise symbolized a lot. My father had succeeded in his job of instilling a strong sense of heritage in me. And I had succeeded in my job of going out into the "new world" and working toward a goal.

After the funeral, we went to the church hall where some two hundred people came for the usual lunch after the services. I cannot begin to count the number of people who came up to me and told me how much my father had made a difference in their lives. How he had made them participate in the church plays. How he had made them sing in the choir. How he had made them speak Serbian. And how they had enjoyed it all because of him, how he had always made it fun.

A few men who had worked with him at his first job in this country, in the carpenter's shop, recalled how, every once in a while, Pa would start to sing while he worked. Some Serbian song, of course. The men would pause in whatever they were doing and listen, and for those few moments, the drudgery of their workday lifted.

About a month later when *Streets* broke its hiatus, Mona and I flew to Gary to visit my mother. While there, we spent an evening with all the family. My Uncle Milovan smiled proudly when we walked into the restaurant and the small band began to play "I Left My Heart in San Francisco." I sat next to this favorite uncle of mine who had roomed with my father when they were young bachelors and had ended up marrying my mother's sister.

He leaned close to me and said, "Mladen, I am going to tell you something. Your father," he went on, "when we were young and we were living together and working in the carpenter's shop, one day we were going home on the streetcar and your father, he said to me, 'How would it be if I went to acting school?'"

I looked at my uncle in amazement. How was it I had never heard this before? Why hadn't my father ever told me himself?

My uncle continued, "I told him he was crazy because he did not speak the language. But, Mladen, Petar, he said, 'Acting doesn't come from the language. It must come from here.' And then, Mladen, your father, he reached up and he touched his heart."

facing page:

With Eli Wallach and Robert Webber,

goofing around on the set of *Nuts*.

Chapter 13

When my father was lying in state, we three sons—Milo, Dan, and I—went up to the casket one by one for a moment of farewell. I went first, then Milo. I watched as Milo stood there a moment, then placed something in Pa's hand. Later, outside the church, I asked him what it had been. Milo told me that when he had gone off to war, Pa had given him something else along with the miniature icon. He had given him a tiny silver cylinder containing a morsel of bread and a shred of lamb's wool to signify his prayer that Milo would always have food to eat and clothing on his back. It was something Pa's mother had given to him when he set out for America. On this day Milo had given it back to him.

Symbols. Pa never expressed his feelings toward us, his sons, with words, but sometimes when it really mattered, I guess he tried with symbols.

I spent the first few years after my father died continuing to work on *Streets*. After the series ended, I moved through a couple of lackluster disaster movies. (I use the term to characterize both the genre and the finished products.)

I took some solace in the fact that I was not alone in these turkeys. Wonderful actors like Michael Caine and Sally Field starred in one, *Beyond the Poseidon Adventure*, while I had the enormous pleasure of working with Natalie Wood for a third time and with Sean Connery on the other, a picture called *Meteor*. It was almost worth doing *Meteor* just for the dinner party that came out of meeting Sean Connery.

About halfway through the shoot Sean asked me if I ever saw Marlon anymore. I told him that we didn't get together often, but talked on the phone occasionally. He said that he had never met him and would love to, so I told him I would see what I could do.

I invited Marlon, telling him that Sean was eager to meet him, and Marlon accepted on the condition that it be just a small gathering. Fine. It was all arranged. Sean and his wife. Dick and Jeannie Widmark. Marlon and his date who, as usual, turned out to be a young Polynesian beauty. He introduced her to us all, explaining that she was here attending Marymount College and that she didn't speak English.

When we sat down to dinner, this young girl sat next to me

while Marlon sat next to Mona. Marlon did a good ten minutes on what a wonderful woman Mona was, even rising to his feet and circling the table as he held court. Sean was getting quite the show and I think he enjoyed it.

Meanwhile, I had a nice, little chat with Marlon's young lady friend who, as it turned out, spoke English fairly well, certainly well enough to participate in the conversation. I never quite figured out why Marlon pretended otherwise; he always had reasons that only he knew. It didn't matter. It was a great evening. When Mona and I bought that old pine table in New York—our first piece of furniture—we never could have guessed that it would have so much star power around it forty years later.

After doing a couple of movies like these that, despite their top-notch casts, really starred a sinking ship and a giant hunk of high-tech papier-mâché, I felt no qualms about returning to television. Just as the line between theater and film had eventually blurred for me, so now had the line between film and television. I was ready to go where the good parts were. (And still am.)

When a three-hour TV movie and subsequent six hours—what they termed a "limited series"—called *Skag* was offered to me, I was ready to go back to the small screen. When I first read the script, Skag was a Polish foundry worker from Pittsburgh trying to hold onto the values he was raised with as the world was changing around him. He was a proud man with an unwavering sense of right and wrong, clinging to his integrity as one son drank too much and a daughter slept around, and, in general, spat in the face of their upbringing.

I immediately wanted to play this man. Although his children were—thankfully—nothing like mine, I identified with his background so strongly that I asked if he could be made Serbian instead of Polish. I said, "Let's put him in the open hearth. Let's have him sing in the Church choir instead of dancing the polka down at the Lodge." Maybe it was because my father had died just a few years before—whatever, I felt the need to take this character whose heart and soul were like mine and make him over so that all the external details of his life matched as well. The timing was uncanny; basically, I was transforming Skag into my dad. Here was a character who led the life I would have led if I'd stayed in Gary.

We worked hard on the three-hour opener and it turned out to be a piece of work I was very proud of. I suggested that the production company go to Saint Steven's, the local Serbian Orthodox cathedral in the Los Angeles suburb of Alhambra, where the priest happened to be a childhood friend of mine from Gary. The church hierarchy requested a copy of the script before agreeing to let us shoot there. Then they granted us permission and, I must add, cheerfully accepted hefty payments for the use of the location, for the choir and the choir director, and for the priest himself who would be featured in a scene. We shot the sequence and Saint Steven's appeared in the film.

However, they must not have read the script very carefully, because when the church powers-that-be saw the finished product, they were outraged. They wrote a letter to a newspaper distributed throughout the Serbian community blasting the movie. How dare we present Serbs in this manner? The letter protested that this "negative" depiction was not "realistic," that it neglected the love of God and country that the immigrants had instilled in their children. I wish I had had the guts to say, "What do you mean? Do you mean to pretend that no Serbian family has the problems that any other normal family might have, that being Serbian provides you with a protective shield against the real world?" But I didn't. I didn't say a thing. I'm chagrined to admit that I just didn't respond.

I took this incident very personally. For the first time in my entire life I was actually ashamed that these were my people, people who had accepted generous payment and then attacked in the most self-serving way. I felt that I had always tried to project them well by living the best life I knew how. Now here they were, telling me that this story was a disgrace when, in fact, it was a good, solid story about people who were flawed human beings first, Serbs second.

I had been working so hard for the past thirty or forty years that I had moved away from the Church. When Mila and Carla were young and I used to drive them to school in the morning, I fell into the habit of occasionally stopping into a church on the way home. I didn't care what the denomination was. I'd just sit in the back and enjoy the solitude, study the stained glass windows, think. I preferred being there in the quiet to going to services. Gradually, I had begun to drop back in on the Serbian church on our Orthodox holidays, not for the religion but for the culture, to touch base with my heritage. But this experience set me back. It reminded me that politics run our church like, in my opinion, most churches, and that politicians, even politicians with turned-around collars, are often in the business of whitewashing reality whenever it serves them. The fact remains that I knew Serbian drunks and that I had known young Serbian girls for whom going to church every single Sunday morning did not protect them from getting pregnant on Saturday night.

I must admit that I still harbor a great deal of bitterness about this incident. As I have gone through life, whenever I met a fellow Serb I felt an automatic comradery, something like what I imagine belonging to a fraternity must be like. There was a certain bond, a shared history. I cannot count the number of times a young person has virtually appeared on my doorstep, his only introduction being his Serbian heritage. I have tried not to let this episode color my reaction to these people, often young actors looking for advice, but I must admit I did take the incident as a personal betrayal.

Fortunately, shooting a film in Yugoslavia reminded me that the hierarchy of the Church and the people of the country can have two completely different characters. Making *Twilight Time* restored my faith in the Yugoslavian people.

Over the years I had become friendly with an L.A. restaurateur named Dan Tana who is—what else?—a Serb. Dan still lived part-time on the magnificent little island of Hvar off the coast of Yugoslavia. Like so many people in L.A., Dan harbored a secret desire to be a movie producer and we often discussed the sorry state of the films coming out of Yugoslavia. He assured me they had the equipment and the personnel; they just kept choosing poor scripts. I told him to start hunting for a story we could both believe in and we would see what we could do.

Dan found a little piece called *Twilight Time*, a simple story about an aging vintner and his grandchildren. He raised three million dollars—half from private sources, half from MGM— and off we went.

We shot about an hour from Trieste in the tiny village of Bouzet where our company took over the only hotel. The crew had to double and triple up because the hotel only had about sixty rooms. This was post-Tito Yugoslavia, still communist, of course—a Yugoslavia where no one spoke against the government and where the entire country was paying for the debts acquired under Tito. Every day on our way to work we would pass plentiful vegetable gardens full of gorgeous tomatoes, cucumbers, everything; but every night at dinner we ate soup and little else, nothing green, nothing fresh. Everything the farmers grew was earmarked for export to pay back what Tito had borrowed.

The makeup of the village where we were working mirrored the village in the story. Old people and children. Almost everyone in between had left the country to earn a living elsewhere. Just as cousins of mine were doing, they sent money home from Germany and other places—money and promises to send for the rest of the family. In our story, no sooner do this old man's children leave their own young children in his care than he realizes he is dying.

This old man was supposed to have been a wonderful dancer in his youth and the one aspect of the part that concerned me a bit was the dancing. Back in L.A., I had hired Marge Champion to work with me. She choreographed a lovely number and showed me how it could be made to work in any type of location where we might end up. I'm sure the villagers thought I was crazy when they saw me out there, after we had wrapped the day's shooting, rehearsing my dance all alone in the town square.

I enjoyed working with the little boy and girl who played my grandchildren. I was never a believer in the old adage about avoiding working with dogs and children. On the contrary, I usually find working with kids a delight. The trick is to let them do whatever they feel like doing and play off of that; you're doomed if you try to manipulate a child into doing something specific you have in mind. I look forward to letting them stimulate me because I think, often, they instinctively come up with something more creative than I could have dreamt of. Besides, I always figured I had nothing to worry about because I had worked with the biggest child of all—Marlon Brando (and I mean that in the kindest sense).

I know that no one saw *Twilight Time*, but filming in this little Yugoslavian village proved to be one of those rare and special experiences that only come a handful of times during a career.

If you really want to know where you come from, you can't just visit for a day or even a week. For me, you really need to work there. After two months of living with these people, these peasants—of eating every meal with them and working with them—I knew who they were and where my folks had come from. These were people who had nothing, but whatever they did have was yours if you needed it.

They were also people who enjoyed a good time. When you don't have much, the slightest bit of good tiding provides you with double the joy. The big event in this village was when the government truck would swing into town with a sixteen-millimeter print of some old movie and they would project it in the Church or the schoolhouse. But they didn't need entertainment from the outside. The blessing of the wine was reason enough for great exuberance.

It came as no surprise that these were people with a fierce work ethic as well. I remember an old woman in particular—she must have been about ninety—who would appear near where we were working every afternoon around four o'clock. She would make her way over to a pile of cherry wood, pick up an old axe, and start splitting wood. After a couple of weeks of observing this I asked some of the crew, all young and fit, why they didn't help her.

They said, "That's what she does."

I didn't quite understand what they meant.

"That's what she lives for," they told me.

After a few more days of watching her I couldn't help myself. I approached her and asked if I could help.

"If you wish," she said, "go ahead."

I picked up this old-fashioned axe that weighed a ton and started chopping. I have never chopped harder wood in all my life. It just wouldn't split. Obviously she had the knack. Finally, I had managed to split about five pieces when she said, "That's enough. That's all I need for today."

I asked her, "What do you do with this wood?"

She picked up the wood and led me to a tiny shed. She pulled open the rickety door and the smell of smoked meat wafted out. She was smoking prosciutto. That was her special job in this little village and she knew how to do it better than anyone, right down to her own trick for splitting this incredibly hard wood. No doubt about it; these people were possessed of a remarkable and unyielding tenacity.

That aspect of this old man I knew how to play. In that respect I was playing my father. In any situation that arose in the story, I just asked myself, "What would Pa do? How would he react?" I was finally playing this man who was everything I had always tried to get away from. The experience filled me with a strange sense of déjà vu, a nostalgia for a time and place that were not really a part of my own past, but of my father's.

Twilight Time was released in 1982 for about a week and a half. I divided the next five years between a couple of features and TV movies, including the miniseries *Fatal Vision* based on the Joe McGinniss book about the Jeffrey McDonald case. I think *Fatal Vision* marked the first time I actually received mail criticizing me just for playing a part; people felt that strongly that Freddy Kassab, the stepfather and grandfather of the victims, was wrong in accusing his son-in-law, McDonald, of the hideous murders. But before accepting the role, I asked the screenwriter, John Gay, if he had invented any part of the story to make it more dramatic. He assured me that he had not invented a thing, that all the facts were traceable to court transcripts and the McGinniss book.

This time I did not want to meet Kassab before shooting the picture. For some two years he had believed in his son-in-law's innocence, and his change of heart was a slow, excruciating process. I was concerned that if I met him, his current belief in McDonald's guilt would influence the way I played the earlier portion of the script. I was, however, happy to meet him after we finished shooting. He confirmed my suspicion; all he talked about was McDonald's guilt and how, as long as he, Freddy Kassab, was alive, his son-in-law would stay behind bars.

I was delighted to win an Emmy for this part, but equally pleased that Kassab thanked me for how I had portrayed him.

I segued from the much ballyhooed *Fatal Vision* to a small film sponsored by American Playhouse and PBS. Then I got a call from my old Group Theater buddy, Marty Ritt. It was back again to a high-powered, star-studded, all out Hollywood production—the feature film *Nuts*. Marty sent me the script for the part of Barbra Streisand's stepfather. (The stepfather had molested her as a child, which was the catalyst for her becoming a prostitute.) I read the script and told Marty I'd love to do it.

With great chagrin, Marty called back a few days later. "Karl," he said, "Barbra says she doesn't know you. She wants to meet you."

There was a point, several years earlier, when I probably would have bristled. I thought I was past having to tap dance for parts, that I had accumulated a body of work that, hopefully, spoke for itself. But I was finally over that; it didn't bother me this time. I said to Marty, "Let's meet her." So we set up a date.

I drove to Barbra's spectacular home in Bel Air. Her gift for interior decorating was obvious at every turn; if there was one beautiful Tiffany lamp in the room we were in, there must have been eight Tiffany lamps. The house reflected Barbra in every way—great taste, great charm, great glamour. Marty and I sat for about five minutes in this lovely room before Barbra entered. She almost had a birdlike quality about her; her moves had a sharpness to them, a purposefulness. (I am a huge fan of hers and, at first, it was difficult to imagine that incredible voice of hers coming out of so petite a woman.) I wondered if secretly she and I were both sitting there thinking, "We've got the only two noses in Hollywood that have never been touched by a plastic surgeon."

We started talking about the script and the play from which it had been adapted and I told her I thought the father was a wonderful part. No problem. That was basically it. After a little more chitchat I said good-bye and Marty stayed behind.

A few days later Marty called with that same tone in his voice. "Karl, I'm embarrassed to tell you this, but she wants you to read."

"Why?" I asked him.

"I don't know."

I thought it over for a minute. I couldn't even remember the last part I had read for, but I sure could remember all those parts I had read for that I never got. Finally I said, "What the hell have I got to lose? Marty, let's go in and read."

A couple of days later the three of us were back in the same exquisite room. Same Tiffany lamps. Barbra sat on the same sofa. Marty sat in the same chair and so did I. I had my script in hand and I noticed that Barbra's assistant held her script. I thought, what the hell, and turned to Barbra, "What's the matter, Barbra, don't you read?"

"Yes, I do," she said. "But what I'd like to do is just hear you. If I'm reading I can't concentrate."

So I read with the secretary.

When we finished, Barbra asked if perhaps I would like to play a different part, the head of the psychiatric hospital. I thought, "I've had it. Whether or not I get this part, I don't care anymore." So I said to her, "No, Barbra, my heart is set on the father."

"But you'd be so good as the doctor."

"No, thank you."

"All right," she said. "Let me think it over."

Once again I said good-bye. Once again Marty stayed behind. A few days later he called again. "Okay, you're playing the father."

The shoot was like old home week for me. I was with old friends—Marty Ritt, Eli Wallach, Maureen Stapleton—all of us who had been striving to forge some kind of career when we were young together in New York. We all understood each other. Throughout this shoot, we were each other's biggest fans and advisers. It was great fun to watch one another take our solo turn on the witness stand in this courtroom drama.

When, for example, Eli was on the stand and Marty would call, "Cut!," Eli would look over to me. I would smile and nod, sometimes hold up one finger for one more take. And then when I was on the stand Eli would do the same thing. It had nothing to do with usurping Barbra's power or Marty's; it was just wanting the other person to be as good as we knew that person was capable of being. We had seen the best we all had to offer so many times before.

At one point when I was on the witness stand, I gave Maureen and Eli a good laugh. Richard Dreyfuss as the defense attorney was interrogating me. He was really good in the part; he absolutely captured that certain cockiness that lawyers have. After a couple of run-throughs of the scene, he began to move closer and closer to me. This was the scene where my character finally blows up, delivering a speech directed to Barbra's character. Every time we did the scene I told him I thought he shouldn't come so close to me because in the state that my character was in, I would lash out at him if he got that close. That energy had to be directed entirely at Barbra, not at him. I told him if he kept coming too close, I felt like this guy I was playing would kill him. Richard agreed. But somehow the scene kept moving him to edge closer and closer. Finally, he came so close that I grabbed hold of him by his arms and lifted him right off the ground. Still in the scene, I started to shake him. It was exactly what I was afraid would happen. When I pulled myself together and put him down, he backed away.

Richard said, "Now I know what you mean." He looked over his shoulder at the gallery; they all laughed. I think Richard laughed, too. He understood that we were both just two actors who got carried away, literally. I know that he never again came closer than six inches.

Nuts was Barbra's picture from start to finish. She wanted the film, like everything else she does, to be perfect. I respected that about her enormously; however, she wanted that so desperately that it was sometimes destructive for the morale of the company and, I think, even for herself. She had hired professionals but somehow could not step aside and let them do their jobs. Her concentration was spread so thin that I believe she let her own part suffer. I may be projecting my own single-mindedness onto someone who is more able to concentrate on many things at once, but I know that the atmosphere on that set did not permit Marty Ritt to do his best work.

At one point Barbra came up to me and said that she had specifically hired Marty because he was supposed to be good with women. What had happened, she wondered.

I said, "Barbra, let him direct." But it is just not in her makeup to turn over the reins. She must have realized this herself because she has directed herself ever since.

Though Marty was suffering through this shoot, he and I often enjoyed having lunch together just like old times. We reminisced about the old days in the Group and, inevitably, Kazan's name came up. Marty had been blacklisted and had never forgiven Kazan for his stance during that era. They had not spoken for those thirty years.

I remembered how, all those years ago, Marty and I used to meet at a deli in New York for breakfast and I would say, "I understand your point of view, but how can you completely forget what Kazan did for you?"

Marty would acknowledge that Kazan had given him his start as a director, but would say, "I can't forget. I can't look him in the face and tell him I forgive him. I just can't."

Here we were in 1987 still having the same discussion. I would say, "If he suffers, that's in his own soul." And Marty would stick to his guns. As much as I would have enjoyed seeing these two old friends reconcile, I admired Marty's position. It would end up that he maintained it until he died a few years later. To be honest, I cannot imagine caring about a cause that much. Maybe that is something lacking in me, but to this day I just cannot care about abstractions with the passion that I have for friendships or work.

And family.

About five years later my brother, Milo, died. I was working on a TV movie that was shooting in, of all places, Topeka, Kansas—one of Mona's hometowns. It plagues me to this day that I wasn't with Milo when he died, though I had been able to see him a few weeks before.

Milo's death hit me much harder than my father's and played havoc with me for at least a year afterward. I honestly had not realized how much he meant to me. When we were kids, my father called him "Slow Motion," but he wasn't slow; he just had his own pace. Milo was someone who would always do whatever you asked without any of the usual, "Do it yourself." Even when we were kids. He never complained, he never hated anyone or anything. He was someone who wanted to live his life as an honest man and worked hard to do just that.

My youngest brother, Dan, had left Gary long ago, ending up teaching in Southern California. Milo was the brother who stayed home, whose ambitions never extended beyond the boundaries of Gary. After Milo had retired from his managerial job at Sears Roebuck, where he had worked his entire life, I invited him to come and live in a weekend house Mona and I had recently bought in Santa Barbara. He had always loved to fish and I remember saying to him, "You'll have the whole Pacific Ocean."

In his typical way—quiet and gentle—Milo said, "Lake Michigan is big enough for me."

Over the years I would go back to Gary to visit and my old friends would treat me like a big shot just because my face was on a screen. But I would look at my brother Milo and think that here was a life that was a complete success. Milo worked hard, he was a loving father and husband, and he honestly never said a bad word about anyone. Even now, five years after his death, my brother continues to inspire me. He had a truly good soul. As long as he had his family around him, all he ever needed beyond that was contained in that little silver cylinder our father had given to him. Food on the table and clothing on his back.

facing page:
Mona and me, on our fiftieth
anniversary.

Chapter 14

Despite my apolitical nature, when I was asked to serve on the board of the Screen Actors Guild I was curious enough to accept. I was interested in how things actually got done, in how what went on around that conference table impacted the working actor, if at all. So for six years before doing *The Streets of San Francisco* I served on that board. It happened to be the period of time when the big guild issue was the length of the actor's work day. We succeeded in creating a contract that mandated an eight-hour work day (nine including lunch), but somehow over the years, that day has stretched longer and longer once again.

I resigned from the board when the series took me to San Francisco and I could no longer make the meetings. Then, several years after the series was over, I was elected to the Board of Governors of the Academy of Motion Picture Arts and Sciences. I always enjoyed the meetings and was honored to represent my branch. I think everyone there felt the same way and I was continually impressed by the dedication each and every individual brought to the sessions. These were all experts in their own particular fields, three members per each of the thirteen branches, each with a different viewpoint and often a different bias, but all there for one reason—to further the state of motion-picture making and smooth the way for filmmakers to do the best work possible.

In my fifth year on the board, about a week before Academy elections, I got a call from a board member named Charlie Powell who represented the public relations branch. He very much wanted to be president and asked if I would nominate him. I told him, "Charlie, I know you from the meetings. I know that you are a hard-working member, but other than that, I really don't know you. I don't know enough to talk about what you have done." He assured me that wouldn't matter; if I nominated him, he would have someone else second the nomination and that person could talk about his accomplishments. Fine—I agreed to nominate him.

A few days later my phone rang again. This time it was director Norman Jewison calling from Canada. He told me that there was a group on the board who was hoping I would run for president. My answer? Ridiculous! I told him there were many members far more capable than I of running the meetings. I thanked Norman, but laughed it off.

Another call came. This time it was producer-director Gil Cates with the same request. "It's about time an actor was president again," he said. It had been at least twenty-five years since Gregory Peck had served as president of the Academy. Again, I told Gil thanks, but no thanks.

A third call. Richard Zanuck this time. "Please, Karl, consider running." I explained to him as I had to Norman and Gil that I had promised someone else I would nominate him. Richard said that didn't matter. I could go ahead and nominate whomever I wanted, but that wasn't going to stop them from nominating me. "Let the chips fall where they may," he said. It honestly had never crossed my mind to run for this office; I felt like I was back at Emerson School and it was senior class election time all over again.

I called Powell and told him what was up, explaining that under these circumstances I thought it would do him more harm than good if I nominated him. He graciously understood and used the exact same phrase, "Let the chips fall where they may."

At that next Monday night meeting, both Charlie and I were nominated. The voting took place and no one was more surprised than I with how the chips fell. I won . . . even though I had voted for the other guy.

At that same meeting, Bruce Davis was promoted from assistant director to executive director of the Academy. When we saw each other the next day I said to him, "We're both freshmen." We shook hands and went to work. Bruce showed me to the president's office, a good-sized room on the seventh floor of the Academy building on Wilshire Boulevard in Beverly Hills. The room held a big round table with chairs all around it, and cabinets containing books, memorabilia, and awards. I turned a chair to face a small table up against a wall and used that as my desk.

I asked Bruce if it would be all right to hold weekly meetings of the administration to discuss what needed to be accomplished that week. Bruce said no one had ever done that before, but he thought it was a fine idea. So every Monday morning I would stop at a little bakery on the way in, pick up some Danish, and we'd all convene around eight-thirty. I was thankful that the staff took me up on my offer. They didn't need these meetings; I did, to give me some direction and assurance.

I took over the presidency of the Academy in August. The first thing everyone told me was to start working on the Oscar show immediately even though the show was some seven months away. All the ex-presidents put the fear of God into me, claiming that the Oscar show was the albatross that came with the job and that finding someone to produce the show was the most difficult task that lay ahead. Fortunately for me the exact opposite proved to be true. Bruce Davis told me that Gil Cates had mentioned that he had an idea for that year's show. He suggested I call Gil and find out what it was. I met Gil over breakfast at the Beverly Wilshire coffee shop. (Now I was president—breakfast meetings and everything!) Gil explained that since movies go all over the world, why shouldn't Oscar? With the help of six or seven satellites we could do an international broadcast. I loved the idea, but already I was thinking like an administrator. Wouldn't that cost an awful lot? Gil said he'd find out.

The cost ended up being less than we had anticipated . . . and I had my producer. Gil ended up producing the show for me all three years of my presidency. The morning after each broadcast he always said, "Never again," but he always came back after a good night's sleep, ready, willing, and able.

Within my first week "in office" I began to receive calls and letters from agents pleading a case. They were launching a big campaign to be admitted as voting members of the Academy, rather than just nonvoting associate members as they had traditionally been. I talked to some past presidents and they all told me they had received the same calls and letters. The usual M.O. had been to bring the issue before the board where the agents were always voted down. Agent membership always had been a touchy subject, extremely divisive, and several people advised me to simply ignore the problem. But it seemed to me that it was silly to waste time and energy on the same issue over and over again. I organized a committee of all the past presidents—Fay Kanin, Gregory Peck, Daniel Taradash, Richard Kahn, Walter Mirisch, and Gene Allen—with the goal of creating a definitive policy that would decide this question once and for all.

This presidents' committee met once a month for a good three hours, often longer. Early on we realized that the agent issue necessitated a close look at the Academy by-laws, which had been written some sixty years ago. When we examined them we discovered that they were largely obsolete. We were dealing with an entirely different industry now, so the task at hand broadened to include totally revamping the by-laws wherever necessary. Our committee began to make recommendations to the board as to how to update the by-laws and, gradually, the changes were voted on and implemented.

That still left the agent question. Most everyone believed that it had been a mistake to admit P.R. people many years before and that admitting agents as voting members would repeat and, in fact, compound that mistake. Even so, we invited several representatives from different agencies to come and present their case.

They all spoke eloquently about how the business had changed, how the advent of packaging pictures had drastically altered and elevated agents' positions in the industry. Committee members wondered aloud how we could deny that agents would simply vote for their clients right down the line. In my opinion, none of the agents ever answered this concern satisfactorily. I felt that over the past few decades, more and more focus has been on the deal; often, once the "package" is assembled and the astronomical salaries set, the actual film becomes secondary. The business end of this industry has been suffocating the artistic end and I felt that this should remain The Academy of Arts and Sciences, not become The Academy of Arts, Sciences, and Business.

It finally came time to vote. Just before the vote was to be taken, one member of our committee announced that should the agents be admitted, he would personally resign from the Academy. Needless to say, all hell broke loose. Other members said they couldn't possibly vote with such a threat hanging over them, but this particular person held firm. That was how strongly he felt about the issue. Ultimately, we decided to make a unanimous recommendation to the board that the agents' status within the Academy remain the same and that the by-laws reflect that. The board concurred wholeheartedly.

That issue resolved, we set our sights on more mundane matters. At one of the board meetings someone made the offhand remark that the seats in the Academy theater were falling apart. He had been to one of the Sunday afternoon screenings the day before and had squirmed in his seat all through the movie to avoid being jabbed by a wayward spring. We decided that we would replace the seats in the theater.

At the next meeting someone from the scenic designer's branch mentioned that we might as well change the carpet while the seats were ripped out. Then someone else mentioned that we'd have to replace the curtain so it would all match. I think it stayed that way for a couple of meetings. Then someone said, "You know, the theater hasn't been painted in a helluva long time. While the place is empty, that would be the time to paint."

Within a few weeks, we had decided to completely remodel the entire theater. Of course, as in any remodeling situation, all surprises are for the worst. We discovered that building codes had been changed since the theater was first constructed and that current fire regulations were not being met. The acoustical equipment was atrocious. The back of the theater was nothing but a brick wall without the proper scaffolding on which to hang sound equipment. The little holes in the perforated sound-board had actually been painted right over. What's more—one good shake, and the whole place would crumble.

The project ended up taking a year and a half and costing six million dollars, but—thank God—in the end, we created a magnificent, state-of-the-art movie theater.

The Academy had long been searching for a new site for its extensive library. Part of it was, at that time, crammed into the fourth floor of the Academy office building; vast portions of it were located in warehouses in various locations around town. When someone—a researcher, student, film historian—needed something, weeks would often go by before it could be located. There was always talk of a new space—other warehouses, a site in Pasadena, a building here, a building there—but nothing ever panned out.

A few years before I became president, Bruce Davis and Linda Maher, the Academy librarian, had found a site for the library. At the corner of Olympic and La Cienega Boulevards sat the old Beverly Hills Waterworks. Once a spectacular edifice, now covered in graffiti and a makeshift shelter to the homeless, the building was about to be torn down by the city of Beverly Hills. Preservationists were insisting this was an historic landmark, but they were losing the battle. It was an ideal opportunity for the Academy to step in. We could salvage the building and have our new library.

The floors were tilted so that water could run down into the troughs and, like the theater, the entire structure needed to be earthquake-proofed, but the good news was that the tanks in the basement were ideally tempered for storing film. They just had to be transformed into vaults. Once that was accomplished, the tanks would be a film preservationist's dream come true.

The by-laws of Beverly Hills prohibited selling the building, so the Academy leased it for fifty-five years with an option for another fifty-five. We paid for it in cash. My predecessor, Richard Kahn, had shoveled the first scoop of earth in a groundbreaking ceremony, but nothing much had been done since. No wonder. It was going to cost seven million dollars.

We were about halfway through remodeling the theater when I remembered about the library. I asked Bruce, "Have they been collecting money for the library?"

"No," he said. "Call Bob Rehme."

So I called Bob Rehme, a talented producer who was serving as the head of the Academy Foundation (the fundraising arm of the Academy). Bob said, "No one has asked me to do anything."

I told him, "I'm asking you now."

"If I'm going to go out there, Karl, you're going to go with me."

"Fine."

So we started raising money for the library.

The very idea of fundraising—the most heinous of all tasks—embarrassed me terribly, but I understood the necessity. The Board of Governors didn't want to have to rely on the Academy membership from year to year to keep the library running and thereby possibly jeopardize other projects and Academy functions. Our job became to raise money for a foundation that would take care of the library in perpetuity.

When I had first been elected president, I felt largely ill-equipped for the job. I didn't know the first thing about parliamentary procedure and I'm not great at hand-shaking. But I figured I could play the part. For the first time in my life, I dressed up and drove down Sunset Boulevard to Beverly Hills five days a week to spend a good four or five hours "at the office." I even had a secretary (Cheryl Behnke, who helped me look good when I wasn't sure what I was doing).

The library fundraising campaign made this picture complete. Now I was having business lunches every day where, over salad and iced tea, I was tossing around figures that made my head swim. The first organizations we contacted were the studios. We asked each for a quarter of a million to be donated over a period of five years and, happily, not one refused. Sigh of relief.

Then we started in with individuals. Bob Hope was the first to come through. We were overwhelmed by his generosity when he donated one million dollars. In his honor we named the lobby of the library The Bob Hope Lobby.

Then we went to the Cecil B. DeMille Foundation. Bob Rehme was busy with a picture so John Pavlick, a professional fundraising consultant whom we had hired, joined me to meet with DeMille's daughter and her husband who presided over the Foundation that bears her father's name. We ordered lunch and engaged in a little small talk. Then she asked, "How much are you asking for?"

Pavlick and I looked at each other, swallowed hard, and said, "One hundred thousand?"

Without missing a beat, she said, "I think that could be arranged."

Pavlick and I left the restaurant absolutely glowing.

Two days later she called. "We've decided . . . " she began. My heart sank. I thought, "This is it. This is the way this whole thing is going to go."

"We've decided," she went on, "to give you one million if you will call the main library the DeMille Library."

I practically ordered the plaque as soon as I hung up the phone.

We were on a roll. I have always loved a challenge, to be working toward a goal, and now that I began to look at this project in those terms, I couldn't wait to sit down at the lunch table and deliver my pitch. Much to my amazement, I even began to think like a fundraiser. Bob Rehme and I were flying to New York when I turned to him and said, "Why are we just staying with movie industry people? What about other corporations?" When we landed at JFK we made an appointment with the head of a company where I had a little "in"—American Express.

The American Express honchos explained that they don't normally participate in that kind of thing, but would consider doing so in this situation since, by then, I had been affiliated with them for some fifteen years. They called the next day with a three hundred thousand dollar contribution. And also with the question that was their due. "What do we get for that?" I asked if I could select something for them and they agreed. I decided on the American Express Conference Room. They were gracious enough to request that the plaque read: "The Karl Malden Conference Room Courtesy of American Express." Boy, did my stock go up with the Academy.

With the theater gutted and the library project in full swing, I lay awake nights thinking that I was going to go down in history as the president who bankrupted the Academy of Motion Picture Arts and Sciences. Luckily that didn't happen.

After three years of lunches and phone calls, Bob Rehme and I had raised twelve million dollars and built the Academy a library. A place where future generations can come and see what we did, how we did it, and why we did it that way, all under one roof.

Building the Academy Library will always be one of the highlights of my career for me. When we opened the library, the Academy threw a party there on three consecutive evenings so that all the Academy members could tour the building. As I have said, I am not one for the "meet and greet," but I was absolutely thrilled—more than that, I was proud—to stand at the door alongside Bruce Davis and welcome every single person to the new library. For a kid who didn't know how to read—was never read to and certainly never set foot in a library—the Academy Library was as much a personal accomplishment as a professional one, maybe more.

Between remodeling the theater, building the library, and putting on the Oscar shows, I devoted my three years as president to nothing but the Academy. For the first time in my life that meant putting acting on the back burner. I had the time to look back because, for once, I wasn't so focused on the next part. I began to realize that this career of mine had afforded me an awful lot of opportunity, more than I could ever have imagined. What's more, it had taught me an awful lot, too. It had taught me all kinds of skills—sublime and ridiculous—from riding a horse to dealing cards like a pro, from rolling the perfect cigar to pulling off the perfect circus trick. It had taken me to places all around the world, from small towns in the South to the capitals of Europe, from college towns across America to a tiny Yugoslavian village like the one my father had come from. And, most of all, it offered me the greatest gift any actor can have: the chance to rub up against all different kinds of people. I've been hunting with Mississippi rednecks; I've walked the beat with San Francisco cops; and I've been presented to the Queen of England.

But like all actors, I was always in the process of learning about human nature along the way. What makes every individual unique and, at the same time, what is human in everyone.

Looking back on my career I realized that, ultimately, what it really gave me was the thing I always felt I was lacking; that thing that other people had that always intimidated me and often kept me from extending myself to them. It had given me an education. My career had been giving me that all these years and only when I stopped to catch my breath did I realize it. It was, of course, a different kind of education, not a classic one, but an absolutely magnificent one nonetheless. In many ways it was, to my mind, the best kind of education because it was based on experience. For those periods of time when I was working on different projects, I was there, participating completely in a different reality. What more wonderful way to learn?

And I am still learning. The second year I was president of the Academy, the Post Master General of the United States called and asked if they could use the Academy theater to present the new Movie Classics series of stamps. We were happy to host the afternoon and when it was over, the Post Master thanked me and invited me to serve on the Citizens' Stamp Committee.

"Sure," I said. "When do I start?"

Now, once every three months I fly to Washington, D.C. along with representatives from all different fields: the graphic arts, advertising, academia, sports. We discuss what upcoming stamps should be, who should be on them, what they should look like. So even at my age, I'm still learning about how things are done and about people in different walks of life. I know I'm there representing the theater and films, industries centered in

New York and Los Angeles, but I hope that I'm also there representing milkmen and steelworkers from Gary, Indiana.

❧

So there I was. March, 1990. Backstage in the dark at the Dorothy Chandler Pavilion, swallowing hard. My heart was pounding, just like it had over fifty years before when I stepped onto the stage in *Golden Boy*. Though I had rehearsed my speech a thousand times, I was still worried about flubbing. But this time, on this night—finally—I was no longer afraid that I didn't belong there.

I had always felt a freedom and a sense of assuredness when I was on stage that I never felt as a human being. But that night I felt as comfortable in my own skin as I had in Mitch's in *Streetcar* or Herbie's in *Gypsy*. Maybe I was playing the ultimate part, the part of the president of the Academy, but even so, maybe, too, I finally believed that fifty years in the business had actually earned me that part.

It had originally fallen to me to bring America into my immigrant home. Little did I know when I left that home how much of the world I would see and how many different kinds of people I would meet. But my father had done his job well. No matter how big my world got, I kept my Serbian heritage alive within me.

Though I fought it as a child growing up, I am glad that my heritage stayed with me. I cherish it to this day. I still enjoy listening to the music of the Orthodox Church. I still enjoy speaking the language whenever I have the chance. And I am glad that, without even realizing it, I instilled the same love of that heritage in my own children and even my grandchildren. That Serbian strain must be made of sturdy stuff. If too much time goes by without our throwing a Serbian picnic, my daughters and granddaughters all start complaining. So Mona and I invite all the clan and throw a real Serbian party. Complete with the food I grew up eating and the "tambouritza" music that filled the house I grew up in. It warms my heart to watch all my girls—my daughters and their daughters—dance the Serbian "kolos" around the pool in the backyard as the "tambouritza" play the songs I grew up singing.

It's a sight that reminds me of how lucky I am to have my family. Never one to diminish the role of fate, "sudbina," I know in my heart that luck had very little to do with it. My wife, Mona, had everything to do with it. She has always been and continues to be my luck. If I have been fortunate enough to build a life of which I can be proud, then Mona is the foundation on which that life was built.

People ask me how I have managed to stay married for fifty-eight years. The answer is easy. I married the right girl. We must have done something right. In a town where divorce is so prevalent, not only have we stayed married—happily—but we must have set a pretty good example as well. Both our daughters are following in our footsteps. Mila and her husband, Tom, have been married for twenty-eight years; and Carla and Laurence have been married for fourteen. I know they'll all catch up with us some day. We are the closest family I know, ridiculously close almost. My grandchildren come with an entourage of parents, grandparents, uncles, aunts, and cousins to nearly every single school program, soccer game or recital. I have no illusions about being the perfect father. I know that I missed a lot when Mila and Carla were growing up. Actors are migrant workers; we go where the work is. I am so thankful to have the chance to be there for my grandchildren, Alison, Emily, and Cami. I absolutely adore them.

Oscar, Emmy, Academy Library. Those are all prizes that I won because I took a gamble or two. Doc Gnesin asked me to gamble on myself when I arrived at the Goodman Theater. Little did I know that was just the first of many. I was too young for this part, too old for that one, all wrong for another, but I took the gambles. And, out of those gambles, I fashioned a career. I often went from flop to flop on Broadway, but I also got to originate characters created by Maxwell Anderson, Arthur Miller, and Tennessee Williams. I have been in my share of turkey movies and in far more than my share of landmark films. I am grateful for the prizes, more grateful for the work, but I am old enough now to believe that my marriage and my family are by far my greatest accomplishments.

In a profession that is all illusion, it doesn't leave much room for the actor to have any illusions about himself. An actor must have a very hard-boiled look at himself and continually assess his talents and his shortcomings. An actor can never permit himself the luxury of saying, "I know how to do this now. I've done this before." Just like the writer facing the blank page, the actor starts fresh every single time. It is an arduous, painful, and often demoralizing process. We suffer through those feelings to get to the moment when it all clicks. But in the meantime we feed on the hope that that moment exists somewhere out there.

Some time in the late thirties when I first arrived in New York I was looking through an arts magazine someone had left lying around. I don't remember where, maybe backstage at the Belasco. I don't remember what the magazine was, but it's a good guess to assume it was Russian. At that time, the last word on theater was always coming out of Russia, usually from Stanislavski. And I don't remember the exact words. But I do remember reading something that stuck with me all these years. I have rephrased it, but the idea was this.

"I believe that life created artistically on the stage is superior entertainment. And that superior entertainment is educational. Therefore, an actor spreads culture. His profession has dignity. If he respects his profession then he makes others respect it. He has a right to be proud of it."

I know I am.

Index